THE STORY OF LATINO PROTESTANTS
IN THE UNITED STATES

The Story of Latino Protestants in the United States

Juan Francisco Martínez

WILLIAM B. EERDMANS PUBLISHING COMPANY
GRAND RAPIDS, MICHIGAN

Wm. B. Eerdmans Publishing Co.
2140 Oak Industrial Drive NE, Grand Rapids, Michigan 49505
www.eerdmans.com

26 25 24 23 22 21 20 19 18 17   1 2 3 4 5 6 7 8 9 10

ISBN 978-0-8028-7318-7

Library of Congress Cataloging-in-Publication Data

Names: Martínez, Juan Francisco, 1957– author.
Title: The story of Latino protestants in the United States / Juan Francisco Martínez.
Description: Grand Rapids, Michigan : William B. Eerdmans Publishing Company, [2018] |
    Includes bibliographical references and index.
Identifiers: LCCN 2017029704 | ISBN 9780802873187 (pbk. : alk. paper)
Subjects: LCSH: Hispanic American Protestants—Religion.
Classification: LCC BR563.H57 M3625 2018 | DDC 280/.408968073—dc23
    LC record available at https://lccn.loc.gov/2017029704

This book could not record the testimonies of all those who have been a part of the Latino Protestant story. So I dedicate it to the generations of Latina and Latino Protestants who faithfully and anonymously lived out their Christian commitment. Thank you for your lives, for your witness, and for the opportunity of telling a part of our common story.

Contents

Foreword

I have repeatedly said, and I am becoming increasingly convinced, that history is always written not so much from the past of which it speaks as from the present which the historian experiences and the future for which the historian hopes or fears. I have also said that quite often history is not just about the past but also about claiming the past for a particular present. It is in these two ways that good history is creative. As I read this book, I see both of these dimensions of creative history reaffirmed.

It is clear to me that this book is written from the perspective of the early twenty-first century and with a view to the hopes and challenges of coming decades. While the book is obviously sustained by well-researched data from the past, such data are organized and analyzed in ways that clearly reflect the present day with its challenges, hopes, and fears. There are numerous indications of this.

In the first place, this book is written from a pan-Latino perspective that would have been difficult a few decades ago. Earlier histories of Latino Protestantism tend to be regional, dealing for instance with Mexican American or Puerto Rican Protestantism. Even in those cases in which the scope is wider, various Latino populations are usually discussed in separate chapters or sections, relatively independent from one another. However, this reflects a situation that was typical of the twentieth century but is rapidly changing in the twenty-first. In the twentieth century, it was fairly easy to distinguish Latino subgroups on the basis of their country of origin or their ancestral connections. (I did edit one such book about Hispanic Methodism!) These distinctions were reinforced by the possibility of describing each subgroup within the context of a geographical area—Mexican Americans in the Southwest, Puerto Ricans in the Northeast, Cuban Americans in Florida. This is no longer possible. Already in the late twentieth century there were signs that such distinctions were becoming much more complex. The censuses of the late twentieth century increasingly showed that when Cuban Americans moved out of Florida they tended to settle in places with other significant Latino populations. The same was true of Puerto Ricans who moved away from the Northeast as well as for all other subgroups. Today, Puerto Ricans can be found in large numbers not only in the Northeast but also in the Midwest, in California, and in Florida. Cubans are numerous in the Northeast, the Midwest, and elsewhere. There are thousands of Guatemalans in Alaska and vast numbers of Central Americans in California, Texas, Florida, and elsewhere.

This means that a new Latino reality is emerging in the United States—which by now is one of the largest Spanish-speaking countries in the Western Hemisphere. Mexican Americans meet more Puerto Ricans, Cubans, and Colombians in the United States than Mexicans ever meet in their homeland. Colombians in Florida mingle with Nicaraguans and Cubans in ways that are still unthinkable in Bogotá or in Managua. Traditional foods are shared. Regional colloquialisms become widespread. Feelings of fear and anger stemming from the evident xenophobia in contemporary political discourse are shared by most. Intermarriage across the lines forming the various subgroups is common. Even issues of identity—issues having to do with the degree to which one still belongs to another country and culture and the degree to which one is or wishes to be assimilated into the dominant culture of the US—while different from subgroup to subgroup and from region to region, are still parallel across the board. In short, what is happening in the Latino community in the US in the early twenty-first century is that a new people is being born.

As is always the case, the birth of this new people is both exhilarating and painful. Latinos in the US are and will remain as varied as any other people or nationality. There are differences of perspective and opinion. There are disagreements across the political spectrum. As this book amply shows, religious and denominational commitments vary both in content and in intensity. But still, even amid those many differences—and in a way also because of them—a new people is being born. Even the matter of whether to call ourselves Latinos and Latinas, Hispanics, or some other name is a sign that something new is emerging that is still seeking for a way to understand and to name itself. (Every name we might give ourselves is the result of conquest, colonialism, or racism. And then there is the issue of gender and inclusivity, to which we must find our own solutions, for the ones that are usually employed in English do not quite work in Spanish. But that is a matter for another essay.)

The book now before us is a clear sign of this reality. It is not a history of Mexican American Protestantism, or of Protestantism among Dominican Americans, but rather of Protestantism within this emerging people still searching for a name. It is not even a collection or a juxtaposition of these various stories, but rather the single telling of a complex and multiform reality. This is one of the reasons why it is a book that could not have been written a few decades ago and that is also a sign, not just of the past behind us, but of the future ahead.

Second, the assertion that history is written not just from the past, but also from the present, is borne out by the manner in which this book deals with denominational differences. They certainly are there, and there are times when one must speak of Latino Methodism, Presbyterianism, or Pentecostalism. Indeed, many of the sources that this book employs are former histories written from a clearly denominational standpoint. But the fact is that such histories do not reflect the present—or even the past—reality of Protestant Latino experience. For most Latino Protestants, denominational affiliation has always been a secondary matter. This comes in part from the experience of Latin America, where long-standing pressure and even persecution from Roman Catholics led Protestants to think of themselves as one, even though belonging to different denominations. Over against Roman Catholics, Protestants of various denominations call themselves "evangélicos." It has also been reinforced by the experience in the United States, where within most denominations Latinos and Latinas are marginalized. This is clearly true even of those "mainline" denominations that have developed strong programs of Latino ministries, and more so in those other denominations that only pay lip-service to the new demographic configuration of the country. People in Latino congregations seldom feel connected to the judicatories to which their congregations belong, and often find more in common and even more support among Latino congregations of a different denomination. This means that, similarly to the manner in which they must navigate the issue of cultural identity, many Latinas and Latinos have to navigate a tension between their own culture—however this may be defined—and the denomination to which they belong. This is illustrated in the present by the many instances of Latino ecumenical and interdenominational movements, organizations, and programs. Usually created without the official participation—and sometimes even without the knowledge—of denominational structures, these movements, organizations, and programs provide for many Latinos and Latinas opportunities for participatory and collaborative action and reflection that their own denominations do not provide. But it is also illustrated in the past by interdenominational dreams and goals such as the attempt long ago to create a single Protestant Latino denomination in Texas.

In this respect, too, this book clearly reflects the situation emerging in the early decades of the twenty-first century. It would have been quite simple to employ the various denominational stories already in existence in such a way as to produce several parallel narratives. To some, such a procedure might even seem more complete, for many of us, as we look for the references to our own denominational history, will be able to think of other organizations, people, and events that could be mentioned in this book. But such completeness would have been only superficial and even fictitious, for the full experience of Protestant Latinos and Latinas in past centuries would have been truncated or twisted in order to make it fit denominational paradigms.

Third, this book is an example of history that takes the present seriously as a lens into the past. Thus, it clearly takes into account the tension Latinas and Latinos experience today between a welcoming nation that acknowledges the work and contributions of immigrants and one where hatred of any who are different has become an acceptable commonplace and even a political asset. One often finds in the Latino community a painful ambivalence toward the US that is parallel to the ambivalence with which many in the US community see them. When we look at the mood of the nation today, we see people torn between their hatred for Latinos and other immigrants, on the one hand, and the degree to which the nation's economy and social structure need those very immigrants, on the other. Similarly, quite often today in the Latino community one finds a painful tension between gratitude for this nation and all the good it has done and symbolized, and anger at the manner in which the very principles that made the country admirable are trampled by xenophobia and political expedience.

On this point, too, this book uses the present as a lens through which to look at the past and to see in it elements that would otherwise remain hidden. The story that emerges as one looks at the past through this lens is one in which the tensions that have recently come to the surface were always present. These tensions existed not only in society at large but also within the churches. On the one hand, there was an admirable commitment on the part of many churches and denominations to welcome the Latino population, to evangelize it, and to plant churches in its midst. On the other hand, there was always the fear—often unspoken—that an excessive Latino presence would change the ethos, worship, and polity of existing churches and congregations. Therefore, Latinos and Latinas were welcomed, but only up to a point. This is a reality that by their very nature denominational histories tend to leave out, but of which one hears echoes throughout this book.

In the very first paragraph of this foreword, I said that creative history not only looks at the past through the lens of the present and the future but also claims that past for a particular present. Thus, it is possible to read the epistles of Paul, at least in part, as arguing that the Hebrew Scriptures and history belong to those who have experienced Jesus as the Messiah. Later, Augustine and Pelagius argued over who could claim Paul; Protestants and Roman Catholics vied for the possession of Augustine; Calvinists and Arminians argued for the possession of Calvin; and so on.

On this point also I find the issues raised in this book particularly exciting. As one reads this story, one sees repeatedly that present-day Latino and Latina Protestants can claim to be genuine heirs of much of the best of both the nation and the churches within it. The author himself is a fifth-generation Protestant in the US—which is much more than many nativists can claim today. And the story itself, usually seen as a series of actions of various churches and missionary agencies for the benefit of the Latino community, now seems to be much more a story of self-reliance and self-propagation. Evangelization was not only the work of missionaries from another culture but also the work of many *abuelas* and *bisabuelas*, of underpaid and often unsupported pastors, and of congregations whose very own denominations did not consider "viable." Thus, just as Paul claimed the Hebrew tradition for this group of apparent newcomers who later came to be called "Christians," we now claim for ourselves not just a little piece or a corner of the joint history of the church, but all of it, for in this new people with a new citizenship that is attained by the power of the Spirit and the waters of baptism, we are all newcomers, and not one of us is a naturally born citizen.

JUSTO L. GONZÁLEZ

Preface

When my great-great-grandmother Rafaela García became a Protestant believer in south Texas around 1900, she became part of the small group of Latina Protestants in the United States. This group of people was doubly marginalized in the country. They were "Mexicans," so they were marginalized in US society, but they were also Protestants, so they were marginalized in the predominantly Latino Catholic communities in which they lived as well. Though the first Latino Protestants converted in the 1850s and there were Latina Protestant congregations in the Southwest from that time, this group of believers would be largely invisible well into the twentieth century. The popular US press would not "discover" them until the latter part of that century when one of several waves of new Latin American immigrants brought increasing growth to Latino Protestant churches. This growth was so significant that government agencies, both major political parties, economic interests, and the mass media all began to recognize that this group of people could have an important influence on the national landscape.

The story of Latino Protestantism cannot be told without understanding the unique connection between the United States and Latin America. Several authors have demonstrated the almost direct relationship between US interventions in Latin America and migration north. But the migratory patterns began when the United States conquered the Southwest from Mexico (1848) and later took over Puerto Rico from Spain (1898). Since those initial events, one can trace a fairly straight line between US interventions in Latin America, changing immigration laws in the United States, and the ebb and flow of migrants from Latin America. The first Latinos became US citizens when the United States "migrated" the border south, and Latinos have been migrating north whenever the United States gets involved in Latin America.[1]

There is also a clear link between US expansionism and Protestant mission work in Latin America and among the Mexicans of the Southwest. Protestant missionaries first went into what is now the US Southwest as Americans were beginning to migrate west into the region during the Mexican period. The mission work would expand once the United States took the Southwest from Mexico. In a sense, if not for US expansionism, there might not be a history of Latino Protestantism to tell.

Latina Protestants have been a very small part of US Protestantism until recently. But Latino Protestant ministry has always been in the background, a small part of the mission efforts of many denominations. Most major US denominations had begun some work among the "Mexicans of the Southwest" by the first part of the twentieth century. During the early years that work was often linked to mission work in Mexico (or Latin America in general) because all "Mexicans" were perceived as foreigners, including those born in the United States. The groups that had worked in northern New Mexico, such as the northern Presbyterians and northern Methodists, might distinguish between the "Mexicans" and the "Spanish Americans," whose roots in the Southwest dated to the late 1500s, but most denominations merely referred to all the Spanish-speaking people of the Southwest as "Mexicans." During the early years of Protestant mission work, the "Mexicans" in the United States often served as bridge people to work in Mexico, and converts from Mexico also became missionaries to US Latinos.

The religious links between the United States and Latin America became more complex as Protestantism developed in that region, particularly in the second part of the twentieth century. As Pentecostal and, later, neo-Pentecostal churches began growing in the region, more Latin American immigrants were already Protestant when they moved to the United States, and they often brought their churches with them. Though most of those churches began as ethnically based congregations, some of them slowly began to have an impact in the United States at large. The immigrants who joined existing churches often brought their spiritual fervor into their new church homes.

Today, the picture continues to develop and expand. Because of the in-

---

1. See, for example, Juan Gonzalez, *Harvest of Empire: A History of Latinos in America* (New York: Viking Penguin, 2000); Felipe Fernández-Amesto, *Our America: A Hispanic History of the United States* (New York: Norton, 2014); David G. Gutiérrez, ed., *The Columbia History of Latinos in the United States since 1960* (New York: Columbia University Press, 2004).

creasing growth of the Latino population, Latino Protestantism is likely to be an increasingly important part of the Protestant picture in the United States. Some of these Latina Protestants will be new migrants, but many will be US-born Latinas. So the history of Latino Protestantism is linked to the history of US expansionism, is the story of Protestant missionary work among US Latinos, and is also closely tied to the history of how Protestantism developed its own Pentecostal flavor in Latin America and then migrated north.

This book will look at Latino Protestantism as a clearly identifiable group, which means that it will study Latino Protestant churches, denominations, and organizations. It will mention, but will not chart, Latino presence in non-Latino Protestant churches, though this is a phenomenon with a long history and growing importance among Latina Protestants. Latina presence will continue to increase in "non-Latino" Protestant churches, but its impact is beyond the scope of this book.

Also, although the takeover of Puerto Rico in 1898 is an important marker in US Latino Protestant history, the island has a unique relationship with this country, connected to it but not fully a part of it. Because of that complex relationship, for the purposes of this book, Puerto Rico will be treated as separate from the fifty states, even though some denominations include the island as part of their US structures. This means that Protestant mission work and development on the island are not included in this book, except as that work impacts US Latino Protestantism, mostly through migration and denominational links.

The popular media and most US Protestants "discovered" Latino Protestants during the latter part of the twentieth and first part of the twenty-first century. Chapter 1 describes Latina Protestants today with an emphasis on the diversity of the Latino community, focusing on national backgrounds, cultural adaptation and structural assimilation, linguistic issues, and ethnic identity maintenance. It describes the connections of Latino Protestantism to Latin American Protestantism. It also briefly describes the growing influence of Latino Protestantism in the United States and elsewhere.

The second chapter provides a broader historical context to Latino Protestantism and includes a section on a Latina Protestant historiography. It provides the theoretical framework for chapters 3–8 and explains the basic structure for these chapters. Some may find it a bit technical and may be tempted to skip it. Nonetheless, it explains the assumptions behind the book and why the history is told the way it is.

Chapter 3 describes Protestant missionary efforts among Latinos in the nineteenth-century Southwest, from 1848 to 1900, in light of US expansionism into the region and the Caribbean. The chapter focuses on the Southwest, where almost all Protestant missionary work among Latinos was done during this period. But it also briefly touches on Puerto Rico and the eastern seaboard, particularly as the nineteenth century comes to an end.

The first part of the twentieth century saw the first significant expansion of Latino Protestant churches. The events that had the most impact on the Latino community and on Latina Protestantism during this period (1901–1940) were the Azusa Street Revival, the Mexican Revolution, World War I, and the Great Depression. Chapter 4 describes how most Protestant denominations started Latino ministries throughout the United States. It also describes the beginning of the first Latino-based denominations and how racism, deportations, and the tensions between Latino and Anglo Protestants played a role in the development of Latino Protestantism.

Chapter 5 begins as US immigration policies changed, once again, with the beginning of World War II. During the war the Bracero Program brought thousands of Mexican workers into the country. The end of the war brought the large first wave of Puerto Rican migrants to the Northeast. The Bracero Program would end with the 1965 immigration law. At the same time, the Cuban Revolution (1959) and the US invasion of Santo Domingo (1963) brought a new flow of immigrants, many of whom were from a different social class than the majority of existing Latino communities. Protestant churches responded to each of these migratory flows with new types of ministry outreach. Latino Protestants also started new churches and movements. During this period evangelical and Pentecostal churches began to overtake the historic denominations that had dominated Latino ministries up to this point. The civil rights movement influenced some historic denominations to change their ministry focus from starting Latino churches to addressing the social concerns of the community. Ecumenical relations and the changing understanding of mission among many historic denominations also changed how they related to mostly Catholic Latinas.

The 1965 immigration law and the East-West tensions created new migratory flows from Latin America (1965–1985). Chapter 6 describes how changing laws, a changing world order, and US interventions in Central America created new migratory patterns, new diversities in the Latina community, and new ministry challenges among US Latinos. Though the majority of Latinas have always been US-born, these new immigrants motivated renewed ministry interest in Protestant churches. While mainline denominations were concerned with issues like the sanctuary movement and the protection of refugees, Latino evangelicals and Pentecostals started new churches among the various immigrant groups. Also, the growth of Protestantism, particularly Pentecostalism, in Latin America meant that more of the new immigrants were already Protestant. Some of them brought their own churches and movements with them, and others arrived in the United States and started new movements. But the majority came to the country and joined existing Latina churches. Because of the differences between Protestantism in the United States and in Latin America, as Latino Protestantism grew in the United States, it began to look much different than the US Protestant population at large.

The 1986 amnesty law legalized several million people, including many Latino Protestants. Their legalized presence provided stability for a growing number of Latino Protestant churches. It also gave those who qualified the opportunity to petition for their families to come to the States. But the increasing militarization of the US-Mexico border by the Clinton administration in the 1990s changed the patterns of temporary migration and began to create a new generation of undocumented people from Latin America.

Chapter 7 describes the period (1986–2000) in which Latina Protestants were finally "discovered" within the popular imagination of the United States. The community continued to grow rapidly and to expand into new parts of the United States. Growing churches and movements gave Latino Protestants new prominence, but also more diversity because of the different streams of Latino Protestant growth. Acculturation patterns created a new generation of Latino Protestants that were not a part of Latino churches. Even as the vast majority of Latino Protestants spoke of the importance of belonging to ministries that worshiped in Spanish, a growing number attended churches that worshiped in English. Many of these latter churches were theologically and liturgically similar to the Spanish-language Latino Protestant churches.

Latino Protestantism experienced extensive growth during this period. Chapter 7 outlines the sources of that growth, which include conversion experiences, Protestant immigration from Latin America, and Latino Protestants in non-Latino churches. This chapter also includes a brief list of the major denominations, movements, and organizations developed by Latina Protestants during this period.

Chapter 8 describes how Protestantism has developed a unique identity in Latin America and among US Protestant Latinos and how we arrived at where we are today (2001–present). The increasing size of the Latina community has generated a number of major studies of Latino reality and, specifically, of the religious changes happening among Latinos. The chapter addresses why common US categories of Protestants (mainline, evangelical, Pentecostal) are often inadequate to describe Latino Protestants. It describes some of the ways Latino Protestants have attempted to describe themselves. It also describes the role of the principal Latino Protestant denominations in the growth of the community.

The last chapter outlines the principal challenges facing Latino Protestants in the United States. It looks at the pressures of cultural adaptation and assimilation, Latino Protestants' relationships with Latin American Protestants, their place in US Protestantism, and scenarios of what Latino Protestants might look like in the future. Chapter 9 also describes how Latinas are prepared for ministry and lays out important characteristics needed by future Latino Protestant leaders.

Because of the growing size of the Latino Protestant community over the years, the earlier chapters will include more specific information about what each denomination did, while most chapters will include only representative examples of what was happening during the period discussed in the chapter. Clifton Holland has identified over 150 denominations in the United States with some type of Latino-focused ministry.[2] This does not include the large number of independent churches and movements. Any attempt to specifically describe the work of all these organizations would change the nature of this book from a history to a compendium of denominational stories. Therefore, the book will mostly reference the largest (at least two hundred churches) and the oldest denominations that have ministry in the Latina community. It will also mention denominations that changed the focus of Latino Protestant ministry in some significant way. Each chapter will also include short biographies of Latina leaders who embodied the principal issues faced by Latino Protestants during the period being addressed in the chapter.

This book completes the cycle of books, chapters in books, and journal articles that I have written over the years on Latino Protestantism. It began with *Sea La Luz*, on the origins of US Latino Protestantism, and continued with *Walk with the People*, on ministry in the Latino/a community, and *Los Protestantes*, a broad overview of Latino Protestantism. It also included two edited collections, *Iglesias peregrinas en busca de identidad* and *Vivir y servir en el exilio*,[3] and numerous chapters in books and journal articles.

2. Clifton L. Holland, "Appendix II: A Statistical Overview of the Hispanic Protestant Church in the USA, 1921–2013," in *The Hispanic Evangelical Church in the United States: History, Ministry, and Challenges*, ed. Samuel Pagan (Sacramento: NHCLC, 2016), 495–517.

3. Juan Francisco Martínez, *Sea La Luz: The Making of Mexican Protestantism in the American Southwest, 1829–1900* (Denton: University of North Texas, 2006); Juan Francisco

Writing a book about Latinos begs the question of why I use the term "Latino" as opposed to "Hispanic." Most writers treat these as synonymous terms, as do I. And both terms have major problems. Both come from the efforts of imperialistic projects, be they Hispanic (Spain) or Latino (France). And the term "Hispanic," as used in the United States, is clearly a social construction that is not necessarily accepted by US Latinos.[4] But because it is useful to this book to have a shorthand term for this population, I chose the term "Latino/a," recognizing that others will choose "Hispanic" or even reject both terms.

Using the term "Latino" also raises the question of gender, since Spanish is a clearly gendered language. I am committed to inclusive language, something that looks different in English than in Spanish. "Latino" is masculine in Spanish, while "Latina" is feminine. Because almost every time I use the term "Latino" or "Latina" I am referring to the whole of the community, and am not being gender specific, I have decided to use the two terms interchangeably throughout the book. So readers should recognize that I use both "Latina" and "Latino" to refer to all members of the community, unless I specify otherwise.

This book was born in my own history. On my mother's side I am a fifth-generation Latino Protestant, a rare bird indeed. I am grateful to my ancestors Rafaela (great-great-grandmother), Anita (great-grandmother), Juanita (grandmother), and Bertha (mother) for the rich heritage of faith they gave me. In many ways, this book is a chance to tell their story and the history of the community of which they were, or are, a part.

The text itself comes out of years of research and writing, beginning with my doctoral studies. It also reflects my life, ministry, and academic work. A key strand of my life's ministry, writing, and research has been Latino Protestantism. This means that many people have been a part of this project. My

---

Martínez, *Caminando entre el pueblo: Ministerio latino en los Estados Unidos/Walk with the People: Latino Ministry in the United States* (Nashville: Abingdon, 2008); Juan Francisco Martínez, *Los Protestantes: An Introduction to Latino Protestantism in the United States* (Santa Barbara, CA: ABC-CLIO, 2011); Juan F. Martínez Guerra and Luis Scott, eds., *Iglesias peregrinas en busca de identidad: Cuadros del protestantismo latino en los Estados Unidos* (Buenos Aires: Kairos Ediciones, 2004); Jorge E. Maldonado and Juan F. Martínez, eds., *Vivir y servir en el exilio: Lecturas teológicas de la experiencia latina en los Estados Unidos* (Buenos Aires: Kairos Ediciones, 2008).

4. See Paul Taylor et al., "When Labels Don't Fit: Hispanics and Their Views of Identity," Pew Research Center, April 4, 2012, http://www.pewhispanic.org/2012/04/04/when-labels-dont -fit-hispanics-and-their-views-of-identity/.

ancestors, particularly my grandmothers and my parents, were my forebears in the faith whose story I am telling. But I also have to thank Drs. Paul Pierson, James Bradley, Dan Shaw, and Charles Van Engen at Fuller Theological Seminary for their support. I am also clearly indebted to Dr. Justo González, who was my mentor even before he knew me or had read any of my work. This book also became a reality because of the support of Michael Thomson from Eerdmans, and the many conversations I had with him.

This book and all the research and writing on Latino Protestantism were strongly supported by Olga, my wife of over thirty years. She was a strong cheerleader, and she encouraged me throughout my professional life. And though she passed away from cancer before I signed the contract for this book, I have to recognize that her energy and commitment were also a key part of this project. Since I signed the book contract, I have started a new chapter in my life, and so I also thank Ruth, my new wife, for her support and encouragement.

And so I am thankful to God, to family, to mentors, and to the Latino Protestant communities that have nurtured my faith, provided me opportunities to serve and to grow, and trusted me to be a part of the ministerial preparation for their pastors and to tell their story.

JUAN FRANCISCO MARTÍNEZ

Abbreviations

AETH	Asociación para la Educación Teológica Hispana
AG	Assemblies of God
AHET	Asociación Hispana para la Educación Teológica
AIC	Asamblea de Iglesias Cristianas
AMEN	Alianza Ministerial Evangélica National
APHILA	Academia para la Historia de la Iglesia Latinoamericana
ARIS	American Religious Identification Survey
ATH	Asociación Teológica Hispana
ATS	Association of Theological Schools
BGCT	Baptist General Convention of Texas
CARA	Center for Applied Research in the Apostolate
CEHILA	Comisión para el Estudio de La Historia de las Iglesias en América Latina y el Caribe
CIA	Central Intelligence Agency
CLADIC	Concilio Latinoamericano de Iglesias Cristianas
CLANY	Concilio Latinoamericano de la Iglesia de Dios Pentecostal de Nueva York
CLUE	Clergy and Laity United for Economic Justice
COGIC	Church of God in Christ
CSO	Community Service Organization
GSS	General Social Surveys
HABBM	Hispanic Association for Bilingual-Bicultural Ministries
HBCT	Hispanic Baptist Convention of Texas
HCAPL	Hispanic Churches in American Public Life

HMC	Home Missions Council
HSP	Hispanic Summer Program
HTI(C)	Hispanic Theological Initiative (Consortium)
LABI	Latin American Bible Institute
LCMS	Lutheran Church–Missouri Synod
LPAC	Latino Pastoral Action Center
MAP	Mexican American Program
MARCHA	Metodistas Representando la Causa de los Hispanos Americanos
MB	Mennonite Brethren
MEC	Methodist Episcopal Church
MECS	Methodist Episcopal Church, South
MI	Iglesia de Dios Pentecostal, Movimiento Internacional
NAE	National Association of Evangelicals
NAFTA	North American Free Trade Agreement
NaLEC	National Latino Evangelical Coalition
NCC	National Council of Churches
NHCLC	National Hispanic Christian Leadership Conference
PARAL	Program for the Analysis of Religion among Latinos
PCUS	Presbyterian Church, US
PCUSA	Presbyterian Church (USA)
PROLADES	Programa Latinoamericano de Estudios Sociorreligiosos
SBC	Southern Baptist Convention
SDA	Seventh-Day Adventist Church
UFW	United Farm Workers
UMC	United Methodist Church
UPC	United Pentecostal Church

Chapter 1

Latino Protestantism Today

One of the signs that Latino Protestants had "arrived" was the cover of *Time* magazine on April 15, 2013. "The Latino Reformation" issue highlighted the work of the National Hispanic Christian Leadership Conference (NHCLC), the most well known of the national Protestant organizations, and its leader, Sammy Rodríguez. It also focused on the largest Latino Protestant church in the United States, New Life Covenant Church in Chicago, and its pastor, Wilfredo de Jesús. *Time* had earlier described Luis Cortés, of Esperanza USA, as one of the most influential evangelical leaders.[1] Voices that had not been accounted for in the national media were finding their way into the national consciousness.

The 2013 article mentions that Southern Baptists hope to have seven thousand Latino churches in the United States by 2020. In it Richard Land, former president of the denomination, tells Baptist pastors that they ignore the Latino reformation at their peril: "Because if you left [Washington, DC] and drove all the way to L.A., there wouldn't be one town you'd pass that doesn't have a Baptist church with an *Iglesia Bautista* attached to it. They came here to work, we're evangelistic, we shared the Gospel with them, they became Baptist."[2]

Interestingly, this increasing recognition of the growth of Latino Protestantism also highlights the complexities of the Latino Protestant community. In the first place, the very existence of a Latino Protestantism makes it clear that not all Hispanics are Catholics, still the default assumption for many,

---

1. David Van Biema et al., "The 25 Most Influential Evangelicals in America," *Time*, February 7, 2005.
2. Elizabeth Dias, "¡Evangélicos!," *Time*, April 15, 2013.

and it also points to the fact that a growing number of Latinas are converting to Protestantism. But by highlighting Sammy Rodríguez, Wilfredo de Jesús, and Luis Cortés, *Time* brings out another complexity of the community. All three leaders are of Puerto Rican descent, though Puerto Ricans make up less than 10 percent of the Latino community. Even though almost two-thirds of all US Latinas are of Mexican descent, the most well-known national Protestant leaders today do not come out of that community. This indirectly points to a third complexity, the status of Puerto Ricans. They are US citizens by birth but are usually seen as immigrants when they migrate to the mainland. This (indirectly) places the focus on the fact (fourth complexity) that, even though Latinas are seen as immigrants, the majority of them are born in the United States.

Latinas in the United States Today

Even a quick peek under the umbrella of the term "Latino" or "Hispanic" begs the question whether there is "really" such a thing, or if this is merely a social construction that made sense to the US Census Bureau but does not adequately define or describe the diversity of those under the US Census category of Hispanic. At the time of writing, the US Census Bureau is attempting to come up with a new and more effective way to count those identified as Hispanic for the 2020 census.

To understand those called Latino Protestants, one needs a sense of who Latinos are. Latinas come from varying national backgrounds, have become part of the United States in different ways, have different levels of Spanish-language ability, relate to the dominant culture in different ways, and maintain a distinct ethnic identity at different levels. Latinos constitute 17 percent of the US population with about 55 million people. Of all Latinas, 55 percent live in California, Texas, and Florida.[3] Almost two-thirds (63 percent) have ancestral links to Mexico. Claiming at least 1 million people are Puerto Rico (9.2 percent), Cuba (3.5 percent), El Salvador (3.3 percent), the Dominican Republic (2.8 percent), Guatemala (2.1 percent), and Colombia (1.8 percent). The rest claim as their native country another nation of the Spanish-speaking world, including Spain. The category "other" claims

---

3. Jens Manuel Krogstad and Mark Hugo Lopez, "Hispanic Population Reaches Record 55 Million, but Growth Has Cooled," Pew Research Center, June 25, 2015, http://www.pewresearch .org/fact-tank/2015/06/25/u-s-hispanic-population-growth-surge-cools/.

6.8 percent, and often includes those who trace their lineage to before the US takeover of the Southwest but do not find an appropriate category on the census form to specifically identify themselves, so they often choose "other."[4]

The common narrative in the United States is that all Latinas are immigrants or descendants of immigrants to this country. But many of the "other" Hispanics trace their lineage in the Southwest to the sixteenth, seventeenth, or eighteenth centuries. Their ancestors settled in the region, and later generations became US citizens when the Treaty of Guadalupe Hidalgo (1848), ending the Mexican-American War, granted them US citizenship. Puerto Ricans find themselves in a similar situation, since they became part of the United States when the island became a US colony after the end of the Spanish-American War (1898). So, when Puerto Ricans move from the island to the mainland, they are not "immigrating" if that means crossing a national border, since they are merely moving from one US territory to another. But they are referred to as immigrants, because they are coming to the mainland, even though they were US citizens before they arrived. It is also often overlooked that the majority of Latinas has always been US-born, even during the periods of significant migration from Latin America.

Most of the rest of the Latino population does have immigrant roots, though their histories often look very different from each other. Cubans were accepted as exiles after the Cuban Revolution (1959), and to this day any Cuban who arrives on US soil is almost automatically granted legal status, even if he or she enters the country illegally. Dominicans also first arrived in the United States in significant numbers after the US occupation of Santo Domingo (1963) and the US decision to deal with the ensuing political crisis via immigration. Because of this unique link, most Dominicans enter the United States legally through family reunification.[5]

The border regions between the United States and Mexico also represent unique situations, particularly in Texas. Many of the ancestors of the people from that region lived on both sides of the river before the US takeover (and do so to this day), and so the moving of the border separated families, who continued to connect across the border. Many border people moved back

4. Sharon R. Ennis, Merarys Rios-Vargas, and Nora G. Albert, "The Hispanic Population: 2010," 2010 Census Brief, United States Census Bureau, May 2011, http://www.census.gov/prod/cen2010/briefs/c2010br-04.pdf.

5. Chiamaka Nwosu and Jeanne Batalova, "Immigrants from the Dominican Republic in the United States," Migration Policy Institute, July 18, 2014, http://www.migrationpolicy.org/article/foreign-born-dominican-republic-united-states.

and forth throughout the nineteenth and twentieth centuries, until changing laws on the border made that movement more difficult.

The other significant Latino populations come from Central America and are directly linked to the violence of the civil wars of the 1970s and 1980s in which countries in this region became proxies in the East-West conflict. The massive killings of civilians (over 250,000 in Guatemala, 200,000 in El Salvador, and countless others elsewhere in the region) caused many to seek sanctuary in the United States.

In spite of the significant migration, almost 65 percent of Latinos are US-born.[6] This percentage will continue to grow as the number of US-born Latina children continues to outpace the number of new immigrants. New migration will continue to feed the Latina community and keep it tied to Latin America. But most of the continual growth in the community will come from US-born children.

National backgrounds and migration stories tell one part of the story. But Spanish-language usage, cultural adaptation, and ethnic identity maintenance all point to other important factors in understanding Latino Protestants, and the Latina population at large. These help us understand who Latinos are today and how they participate in dominant society and in Protestant institutions.

Most Latinos have a strong emotional attachment to the Spanish language, but this does not necessarily translate into its usage in everyday life. When asked, 95 percent of Latina adults state that it is important that future generations of Latinos learn to speak Spanish.[7] But Spanish-language usage and fluency drop by generation. In second-generation Latinos, 82 percent say they can converse in Spanish (71 percent say they can read it). By the third generation, 47 percent say they can speak Spanish fluently and 41 percent say they can read it;[8] overall, 90 percent of Latinas can speak English to some degree, and 78 percent can speak Spanish fluently.[9] There

6. Jens Manuel Krogstad and Mark Hugo Lopez, "Hispanic Nativity Shift," Pew Research Center, April 29, 2014, http://www.pewhispanic.org/2014/04/29/hispanic-nativity-shift/.

7. Mark Hugo Lopez and Ana Gonzalez-Barrera, "What Is the Future of Spanish in the United States?," Pew Research Center, September 5, 2013, http://www.pewresearch.org/fact-tank/2013/09/05/what-is-the-future-of-spanish-in-the-united-states/.

8. "Between Two Worlds: How Young Latinos Come of Age in America," Pew Research Center, December 11, 2009, updated July 1, 2013, http://www.pewhispanic.org/2009/12/11/between-two-worlds-how-young-latinos-come-of-age-in-america/.

9. "Hispanic and Latino Americans," Wikipedia, last modified March 25, 2017, https://en.wikipedia.org/wiki/Hispanic_and_Latino_Americans.

are also over two million non-Hispanics who speak Spanish at home.[10] This means that the number of Spanish speakers in the United States continues to grow, though not at the same pace as the Latino population. The size of the Spanish-speaking population makes the United States one of the largest Spanish-speaking countries in the world.[11]

Use of Spanish also tends to be linked to ethnic identity maintenance.[12] Those who use Spanish regularly tend to have a stronger sense of a Latino identity, though it is not a guarantee of that identity. Losing Spanish is a potential marker of assimilation into majority culture, though there are many English-dominant Latinas who have a strong sense of Latino ethnic identity.

In practical terms, most Latinas are bilingual, and this affects how people live their lives. It creates tensions in the marketplace, as English and Spanish media compete to demonstrate which can best "reach" the Latino community. It also speaks into religious commitments. For some Latinas, worship should be in the "heart" language, so they tend to worship in Spanish, even if their English is stronger. For others, worship and ministry should be polished and well organized, which tends to draw them to some English-language churches, particularly those with a multicultural focus. Others opt for various types of bilingual models that seek to include multiple generations worshiping together.

Related to the issue of language is a person's ethnic self-identity. Even though Hispanic has been used as a legal definition of the community for over forty years, most Latinos continue to use their national background as their primary ethnic identity marker. A majority of Latinos (51 percent) use their family's country of origin as their principal identifier, and only 24 percent prefer a pan-ethnic label, like Hispanic or Latino, as their primary identifier. Sixty-nine percent see themselves as part of different cultures, and only 29 percent state that Latinos have a common culture.

This sense of identity also affects how Latinas see themselves within

10. Camille Ryan, "Language Use in the United States: 2011," United States Census Bureau, American Community Survey Reports, August 2013, http://www.census.gov/prod/2013pubs /acs-22.pdf.

11. According to the Instituto Cervantes study, it is the second-largest Spanish-speaking country in the world, behind only Mexico. "El español: Una lengua viva: Informe 2016," Instituto Cervantes, 2016, http://cvc.cervantes.es/lengua/espanol_lengua_viva/pdf/espanol_lengua _viva_2016.pdf.

12. See my description of ethnic identity maintenance among Latinas in *Los Protestantes: An Introduction to Latino Protestantism in the United States* (Santa Barbara, CA: ABC-CLIO, 2011), 20–24.

larger US society. Latinos are evenly divided as to whether they see themselves as "typical" Americans. The vast majority is happy to be in the United States, and most immigrants would migrate again if given the opportunity. But a plurality (39 percent) feels that the strength of family ties is better in their country of origin than in the United States.[13]

The issues of Latina identity and cultural assimilation are important when thinking about Latino Protestantism for several reasons. On the one hand, a common assumption historically has been that Latinos became Protestants in the United States as a means of cultural adaptation. In this understanding, seen directly or indirectly in many studies of Latino religious identity, becoming a Protestant is a sign of assimilation into majority culture.[14]

But if this were the case, Latina Protestants would demonstrate more signs of cultural assimilation than their Roman Catholic counterparts, such as a primary identification as Americans, the loss of Spanish, and intermarriage with non-Latinos. Various studies have demonstrated the opposite, particularly among Latina Pentecostals, the largest group of Latino Protestants. According to these studies, popular Pentecostalism provides support for ethnic identity maintenance and does not necessarily draw converts toward assimilation into dominant culture.[15]

According to the 2014 Pew study, 22 percent of the Latino population is Protestant. About two-thirds of this population would identify as Pentecostal or charismatic. (About 52 percent of Latina Catholics also self-identify as Pentecostal or charismatic.)[16] The percentage of the Latino population that is Protestant continues to grow, though not as fast as in many places in Latin America. For example, Guatemala, Puerto Rico, El Salvador, Costa Rica, Honduras, the Dominican Republic, and Brazil all have a higher Protestant population than does the United States. This means that immigrants from these places have a higher probability of being Protestant before they

13. Paul Taylor et al., "When Labels Don't Fit: Hispanics and Their Views of Identity," Pew Research Center, April 4, 2012, http://www.pewhispanic.org/2012/04/04/when-labels-dont-fit -hispanics-and-their-views-of-identity/.

14. See Larry L. Hunt, "The Spirit of Hispanic Protestantism in the United States: National Survey Comparisons of Catholics and Non-Catholics," *Social Science Quarterly* 79, no. 4 (December 1998): 828–45.

15. See studies in Martínez, *Los Protestantes*, 59ff.; Hunt, "The Spirit of Hispanic Protestantism in the United States."

16. "The Shifting Religious Identity of Latinos in the United States," Pew Research Center, May 7, 2014, http://www.pewforum.org/2014/05/07/the-shifting-religious-identity-of-latinos -in-the-united-states/.

come to the United States, making migration one of the sources for growth among Latino Protestants. Mexico, on the other hand, is one of the most Catholic countries in the world, and certainly the most Catholic country in the Americas; only 9 percent of the population identifies as Protestant, and most migration from Mexico has come from the most Catholic sections of the country.[17]

If one assumes that these numbers tend to carry over into the various national background communities among Latinas in the United States, then Puerto Ricans and Central Americans will be overrepresented among Latino Protestants, as a percentage of the total Latina population. This may help explain, in part, why Puerto Ricans are "overrepresented" in Latino Protestant leadership, even though they represent only 9 percent of the Latina population.

If one assumes a Latina population of 55 million, then about 12 million Latinos identify as Protestants.[18] The majority of them are connected to US Protestant denominations, though many are part of Latino- and Latin American–based denominations and movements. Because many Latinas live a transnational existence, and faith, they are clearly linked to US Protestantism, but also to Protestantism in Latin America. Many Latina churches in the United States have strong links to sister congregations in Latin America. Often these links are not denominational, but are relational and network based. People and churches connect to the churches "back home," whether or not they have a similar theological tradition. These links are maintained through regular visits and exchanges, financial support and new migrants.

Excursus: The Question of the Latino Nones

The aforementioned Pew study states that Latinos are moving away from the Roman Catholic Church in one of two directions, either toward evangelical Protestantism or away from identification with a specific faith tradition. The implicit assumption is that all Latino nones are similar to their counterparts in majority culture. Though there is truth in that assessment, it also does not

---

17. Agustina Ordoqui, "América Latina, cada vez menos católica y más protestante," *Infobae*, November 23, 2014, http://www.infobae.com/2014/11/23/1610174-america-latina-cada-vez-menos-catolica-y-mas-protestante/.

18. A later chapter will address the complexities of using such a simplistic formula for counting Latino Protestants. But for current purposes, this number is sufficient.

tell the whole story. The Latina nones represent various realities that are not necessarily the same as majority-culture experience.

For example, movement from Catholicism to Protestantism is not always a clean or one-way process. Many Latinas are in an in-between state. They may not have a clearly identifiable church identity but may in fact be moving between the two groups. Also, a lack of church identity does not necessarily mean lack of commitment to the church with which they do not formally identify (for example, some expressions of popular Catholicism). As a result, one sees higher church participation, a more regular prayer life, and a more positive sense of the role of religion among Latinas who identify as unaffiliated than among the unaffiliated within society at large.[19]

Latin American Protestantism
and Its Impact on US Latino Protestants

When telling the US Latino Protestant story, the tendency is to focus on Protestant mission work in the United States. It is impossible to tell the story, particularly of the earlier years, without looking at evangelization and the converts of those missionary efforts. But the story would be sorely incomplete without including the impact of the growth of Latin American Protestantism, independently of US Protestant missionary efforts, on US Latina Protestant communities.

The history of Latin American Protestantism is far beyond the scope of this book. But the dynamic north-south, south-north links have created a transnational Protestant identity that is both linked to US Protestantism and looks beyond it for part of its growth and inspiration.

In the early years, most Latina Protestant converts were the direct result of US Protestant missionary efforts and most Latino churches were directly linked to US Protestant denominations. The vast majority of immigrants from Latin America were Catholics, and the few Protestant immigrants tended to join existing US-based churches. There were a few Latino-based churches and denominations, but they were treated like an exception when describing Latina Protestantism. These groups were usually on the margins of society and often were not even counted in discussions about Latino Protestants.

This began to change with the growth of Pentecostal churches, particularly in the second half of the twentieth century. But the explosive growth

---

19. "The Shifting Religious Identity of Latinos in the United States."

came because of the Pentecostal and neo-Pentecostal churches, particularly in Puerto Rico and Central America, that started in the 1970s. This growth produced new, large churches and megachurches. As people who had become converts in these movements migrated to the United States, some of them brought their churches and leaders with them. Also, US denominations began importing an increasing number of pastors from Latin America, as the number of new immigrants into new parts of the United States seemed to overwhelm many churches and denominations. Many Latino churches, including those within US denominations, have network links into Latin America, and many are doing mission work there. Some of that mission work is more linked to personal relationships than to denominational commitments. The ministries that are part of personal networks are often more enthusiastically supported by Latino Protestant churches.

Ideas and ministry models are also regularly exchanged across the Americas. From Latin America, leaders regularly preach and teach in the United States, creating a constant exchange both north and south. From the United States, a growing number of Latinos are developing ministries in the south. Many Latino Protestant churches have transnational people who live part of their lives "here" and part "there," which adds to this exchange. They become an important link in the global communications networks that keep Latino Protestants connected to Latin America.

Latino Protestant churches grow in three ways: through converts, through Latin American immigrants, and through biological growth. These three represent very different experiences and framings of Protestantism, as will be seen throughout this book. The Latin American connection is maintained through the constant movement of peoples, whose role is often unseen in descriptions of the development of Latina Protestantism.

Latina Protestants in the Larger US Protestant World

The Mexicans living in what is now the Southwest became the focus of some Protestant missionaries in the 1830s while the Southwest was still a part of Mexico. And the first converts became parts of churches that were linked to existing US Protestant denominations. That has been the norm throughout the history of Latina Protestantism, although, as previously stated, a growing number of Latino Protestants are part of Latino- or Latin American–based churches and denominations.

US Protestants have had a conflictive relationship with Latino Protestants from the days of the first converts. For most of the nineteenth and twentieth centuries Latina Protestants tended to be invisible, even in the denominations of which they were a part. At best, they had a marginal role in the structures and often did not have leadership positions even in the "Latino" sections of their denominations.

One of the reasons is that Latino Protestant churches have often been seen as transitional structures. As early as the late 1890s the question arose whether the "second" generation would stay in Latino churches or would join Anglo congregations. This issue has continued to play a role in conversations about Latino Protestant ministry. Are Latino churches structures with a long-term future, or "holding tanks" for Latinas while they adapt to majority culture and "get ready" to be a part of existing English-language congregations?

This has created tensions within Protestant denominations and between majority culture and Latino leaders. Latino pastors want to keep their young people, and some US Protestant leaders assume that the "second" generation will leave for majority culture or intentionally intercultural churches. One sees both tendencies, but also realizes that because of new migration and intermarriage back into the immigrant generation, there is an eternal "second" generation. So the question of the place of Latino Protestants in the larger US Protestant world continues. Do Latina leaders participate representing clearly identifiable Latino congregations, or as part of the larger Protestant world (or both)? Will one model be considered normative, or will there be multiple ways of being a Latino Protestant within existing denominational structures? Which type of Latina leader do the denominations want as they look toward the future?

So Latino participation in Protestant denominations lags behind the population size, as it does in US political, socioeconomic, and other realms. Some denominations are barely "discovering" Latinas, while others are struggling with challenges of incorporating Latino leaders into their national structures. Meanwhile, a growing number of Latinos are joining non-Latino churches, particularly intentionally intercultural congregations. In some of those churches they become "invisible" because no one sees them as a community that needs to be represented in leadership structures. So, even as Protestant denominations recognize that Latinos will be an increasingly important part of their future, they are still struggling to understand what that future will look like.

Latino Protestants as Missionaries to the World

Historically, natives in Latin America and Latinos in the United States have been the objects of Protestant mission efforts. But as these communities develop, they also become mission-sending congregations. The first focus of Latino Protestant mission work is Latin America. A growing number of churches with north-south links are providing financial support to ministries in Latin America. These links are usually mutual, with money flowing south and ministry resources flowing north.

Latin American Protestants have begun sending missionaries around the world, particularly into areas where "traditional" missionaries from the first world are not welcome. Some of these efforts are linked to Latino churches in the United States. A growing number of Latino Protestant churches are finding it easier to link to missionary efforts in Latin America than to efforts of their own denominations in the United States. Others are working through US mission agencies willing to incorporate into their concept of mission work models that make more sense to Latinas.

So, even as it is difficult to define a Latino, and many Latinas are not sure that the category clearly fits them, it is also a complicated task to clearly define a Latino Protestant. There are places where the borders and boundaries seem clear. But in a growing number of spaces it is not clear who fits, who does not fit, or even if this is the correct question. Who wants to fit under the category, and how clear do the lines need to be to tell the story of the community?

There would seem to be a clear answer—the story is about the people who are at the intersection of Protestant and Latina. Yet, for all the reasons already stated, it is not always clear who belongs in the narrative, particularly as one moves further away from that intersection. So this history of Latino Protestants begins at the "clear" intersection and gradually moves out toward the "fuzzy" edges.

Chapter 2

Framing the Latino Protestant Story

One of the many tasks of a historian is to choose the frames within which to tell the story so that it holds together a cohesive and compelling narrative. The frames that seem most useful for understanding Latino Protestantism today are (1) the historical and often conflictive relationship between the United States and Latin America; (2) the migratory patterns that have developed because of that relationship, as seen through migration theory; (3) the changing religious context, both in the United States and in Latin America, using tools of the sociology of religion to understand their impact; and (4) sociocultural analysis of the Latina experience in the United States. As a Christian believer, I also place those frames within a theological understanding that God has been at work in the midst of this story.

Throughout the years there have been several studies of Latino Protestantism. Most of them were either specific denominational studies or broad descriptions of the community for the purpose of encouraging denominations and churches to do mission work among them. Books like *Our Mexicans* (1904) by Robert Craig[1] and *The Northern Mexican* (1930) by Robert McLean[2] represent early efforts to describe the situation from a Protestant perspective and to broadly mention all the known Protestant mission work among "Mexicans" at the time, though these types of studies were usually born within one denominational family and often left out denominations that were outside of their "normal" range of mission experience. (Interestingly, *The Northern Mexican* includes all Latinas under

---

1. Robert M. Craig, *Our Mexicans* (New York: Board of Home Missions of the Presbyterian Church, USA, 1904).
2. Robert N. McLean, *The Northern Mexican* (New York: Home Missions Council, 1930).

the category of northern Mexicans, a problem it acknowledges but does not correct.)

In the twentieth century several denominationally specific studies were published, most after 1960. The Presbyterians published the most material, though there were also several Methodist projects and a few from other denominations. Most of the works were chronological narratives, often written to promote or celebrate the missionary efforts. A few, like *The Northern Mexican*, included some analysis. But only in the latter part of the twentieth century were formal histories published.

The 1980s and 1990s saw an increase in denominational publications as well as the first efforts toward a history that would include all Latina Protestantism. *Republican Protestantism in Aztlán*[3] was written by a non-Protestant Latino and studies the clash between Mexican Catholics and American Protestants, Christians from two very different religious and value systems. *Hidden Stories Unveiling the History of the Latino Church*[4] represented an effort to develop an Academy for the Study of Latino Church History (APHILA by its initials in Spanish), though this effort was short-lived. A decade later, the US chapter of CEHILA (Comisión para el Estudio de La Historia de las Iglesias en América Latina y el Caribe)[5] published *Iglesias peregrinas en busca de identidad: Cuadros del protestantismo latino en los Estados Unidos.*[6] This was the Protestant companion to the earlier Roman Catholic volume on Latino Catholics in the United States, *Fronteras: A History of the Latin American Church in the USA Since 1513.*[7] The number of denominational or regional studies has increased as Latino Protestantism has continued to grow. Some of these studies have analyzed Latina religious tendencies more broadly, while a recent volume has brought together articles on the history, ministry, and

3. E. C. Orozco, *Republican Protestantism in Aztlán: The Encounter between Mexicanism and Anglo-Saxon Secular Humanism in the United States Southwest* (Glendale, CA: Petereins Press, 1980).

4. Daniel R. Rodríguez-Díaz and David Cortés-Fuentes, *Hidden Stories: Unveiling the History of the Latino Church* (Decatur, GA: AETH, 1994).

5. CEHILA is a network of researchers that has worked since the 1970s to study Latin American and Caribbean Christianity from the bottom up. Its most well-known publication is the multivolume *Historia general de la iglesia en América latina* by Enrique Dussel and Comisión de Estudios de Historia de la Iglesia en Latinoamérica (Salamanca, Spain: Sígueme, 1983).

6. Juan F. Martínez Guerra and Luis Scott, eds., *Iglesias peregrinas en busca de identidad: Cuadros del protestantismo latino en los Estados Unidos* (Buenos Aires: Kairos Ediciones, 2004).

7. Moisés Sandoval, ed., *Fronteras: A History of the Latin American Church in the USA Since 1513* (San Antonio: Mexican American Cultural Center, 1983).

challenges of Hispanic Protestantism under the title *The Hispanic Evangelical Church in the United States*.[8] This collection includes some of the latest data on Latina Protestants collected by Clifton Holland.

The United States and Latin America—a Short Historical Review

The links between the United States and Latin America begin during the period of European colonial expansion when England and Spain (and other European powers) were exploring and claiming territory in the Americas, displacing, destroying, or conquering native populations.[9] Both established permanent communities in North America, with Spain establishing Saint Augustine (Florida) and Santa Fe (New Mexico) before the first permanent English colony of Jamestown. The tensions and competition continued throughout the colonial period. Each European nation used its power to disrupt the control of the other and to protect its claims from other European powers. The tensions between England and Spain are particularly important as they provide the background for later, continuing tensions between the nations born out of their colonial projects in the Americas.

Christian faith was an important part of the colonial process for both the Spanish and the English settlers. Both told the story of their expansion into the Americas in religious terms. They saw colonial expansion as part of God's will for them and understood the lands they were conquering as gifts from God. To some extent, people from both countries also saw the ones they were conquering as people they should evangelize.

But there was also a clear sense of religious competition between Protestant England and Catholic Spain. Their various wars, battles, and skirmishes often had a religious undertone. Many in each country saw their encounter with the other as a chance to demonstrate that their expression of faith was more correct. Their expansions were often interpreted as proof of the superiority of their particular religious expression. This tendency would continue beyond the colonial period. For example, in the nineteenth century, many

8. Samuel Pagán and the National Hispanic Christian Leadership Conference, *The Hispanic Evangelical Church in the United States: History, Ministry, and Challenges* (Elk Grove, CA: NHCLC, 2016).

9. The reading of the relationship between the United States and Latin America given in this section follows the perspective presented by authors like Juan Gonzalez, *Harvest of Empire: A History of Latinos in America* (New York: Viking Penguin, 2000), and Felipe Fernández-Amesto, *Our America: A Hispanic History of the United States* (New York: Norton, 2014).

Protestants in the United States would describe the takeover of the Southwest from Mexico as one more victory of English Protestantism over Spanish Catholicism.[10]

The newly established United States of America saw itself as an expansion-oriented country, with many Christians giving a theological explanation to the expansion (i.e., North America was Canaan that would be taken over by the new Israel). "Nations have been driven out before us, greater and mightier than we, that we might enter in, and take the land for an inheritance, as it is this day."[11] Soon after becoming independent from England, the United States began its territorial expansion. The European powers that had held sway in the region, including Great Britain, France, and Spain, ceded their claims to lands that were then gradually incorporated into what is now the United States. People from the eastern seaboard started migrating westward, displacing the native peoples from their historic lands.

While the young country was expanding by taking control of more territory, it was also expanding its political and economic control. The Monroe Doctrine (1823) told European powers to stay out of the Americas. But in practice it gave a political justification for US hegemony throughout the Americas.

Within a few years of US independence from Great Britain, Latin American countries started to gain their independence from Spain and Portugal. Because the newly independent Mexico feared that the United States would try to expand into its territory, it tried to colonize its northern regions with Catholics from several European countries, since it did not have enough people to send to those areas. This plan was unsuccessful, and actually served to speed up the US expansionist project. Many of the colonists invited into Mexico would be at the head of the rebellion that established the Republic of Texas in 1836, with US support. This republic would be accepted as a state in the Union in 1845, against the explicit objections of Mexico, setting up the confrontation that resulted in the Mexican-American War (1846–1848). The Treaty of Guadalupe Hidalgo (1848) that ended that war ceded half of Mexico's territory, what is now known as the Southwest, to the United States. The takeover of the Southwest marked the beginning of a permanent link between the United States and Mexico.

10. See, for example, Hollis Read, *The Hand of God in History; or, Divine Providence Historically Illustrated in the Extension and Establishment of Christianity*, 2 vols. (Hartford: H. E. Robins, 1858).

11. Richard S. Storrs, *Discourse in Behalf of the American Home Missionary Society* (New York: American Home Missionary Society, 1855), 12.

The next direct territorial expansion into Latin America by the United States came with the Spanish-American War (1898). The defeat of a weakened Spain made the United States a colonial power. It took over the Philippines, Guam, and Puerto Rico. The fourth territory, Cuba, became an independent country as a result of the war, though under direct US tutelage.

These territorial expansions created permanent links between the United States and Latin America that would become the connecting points for later waves of migration north. The largest group of Latinas in the United States today, those of Mexican background, began entering after 1848 in various waves that included push-and-pull factors often linked together, such as the "push" of the Mexican Revolution and the "pull" of US involvement in World War I. Each wave was accompanied by an anti-immigrant backlash, like the massive deportations that occurred when the Great Depression began in 1929. Versions of this pattern were repeated several times throughout the twentieth century. Though there were massive deportations after several immigrant waves, the end result of each cycle was that a larger number of Mexican migrants ended up settling in the United States.

US expansionism also created a second migratory bridge, this one between Puerto Rico and the mainland. Particularly after World War II, many Puerto Ricans who had served in the US military had a chance to see the mainland while on US military bases and were attracted to its possibilities. New employment opportunities also opened up in the Northeast, creating the crucial "pull" factor. From the first waves into the Northeast in the 1940s to the more recent waves into Florida, the mainland has become a land of opportunity and an escape valve when the economic situation on the island has become difficult.

US interventions in Latin America have also created important migratory flows. The United States established a very direct influence on Cuba from the time of the Spanish-American War. It enshrined that influence into the Cuban constitution through the Platt Amendment and through direct military interventions. It directly supported the various leaders and dictators who ruled the island through the first half of the twentieth century. The Cuban Revolution (1959) overthrew that imposition and put US friends and allies on the island in direct danger. In response, the United States allowed Cuban refugees to enter the country in large numbers. Those political exiles created a strong political base that has greatly influenced US politics toward Cuba. The result is that even today almost any Cuban who can make it to US soil receives refugee status.

Direct military intervention in Santo Domingo (1963) created a bridge for citizens of the Dominican Republic to come to the United States. And from the 1950s through the 1980s, at the height of the Cold War, the United States intervened, directly and indirectly, in the civil wars of several Central American countries. People fleeing the massive violence of these wars often ended up in the United States. Though the civil wars have ended, this migratory bridge continues to be an important escape valve, as people, particularly children, flee the violence created by gang members deported by the United States back into these same Central American countries.

Smaller migratory bridges have been established because of US policies in Colombia and Venezuela. As Juan Gonzalez argues in *Harvest of Empire*, there is a direct relationship between US interventions in Latin America and migratory patterns from Latin America into the United States.

Migration from Latin America through the Lenses of Migration Theory

The United States tells its national myth as one of voluntary migration, with a focus on European migration toward this country. That myth is exemplified by the poem "The New Colossus" on the Statue of Liberty. According to this understanding, people leave the old to embark upon the adventure of new opportunities. The journey, in this telling, is always unidirectional and permanent. People come to the land of opportunity and never look back.

Most studies of migrants in this country focus only on how the migrant is adapting to life in the United States. In other words, the only important question for many scholars is how well the immigrant is acculturating and assimilating. If people are not following that pattern, then the concern is to understand why things are not happening as "they are supposed to" and what the implications might be.

Yet the story of migration from Latin America has always been more complex and multidirectional. Significant differences exist among migration patterns from Latin American countries, and the reasons for migrating are often also very different. Also, most migrants from Latin America have initially seen their move as temporary. Those who came as political refugees dreamed of returning. And many that came for economic reasons hoped that the move would help them resolve issues in their home country and help their extended families.

Mexico, the country that has sent the most migrants, has an extensive and historical pattern of back-and-forth migration. Though many people have stayed in the United States and have become part of the fabric of the country over several generations, there has also been a constant flow of temporary migrants that work in the States for various periods of time but eventually, permanently return to Mexico. At the time of writing this book, it was estimated that more Mexicans were leaving the United States to return to Mexico than there were new migrants from Mexico.

This pattern has a cyclical tendency that follows changing economic and political issues on both sides of the border. The first major move north included the push of the Mexican Revolution and the pull of World War I. The Great Depression created the first large return, whether voluntary or by deportation. The second significant wave came with World War II. The Bracero agreements brought many temporary workers. After the war, Operation Wetback in the 1950s deported hundreds of thousands of Mexicans and also saw many continue to come and return on a regular basis. (This was happening while the Bracero Program was expanding.) By the 1960s, communities in parts of northern and central Mexico were sending temporary migrant workers to the States on an annual basis. These workers would regularly return to Mexico, some voluntarily and others after being deported. Many of them were farm workers who would return for the next agricultural season.

The North American Free Trade Agreement (NAFTA, 1994) created another major migratory flow from Mexico. When the treaty was first talked about in the 1980s, President Ronald Reagan spoke of having open borders for people, as in Europe. That never happened. But the treaty created two major movements northward. It facilitated the development of border-based assembly plants (*maquiladoras*) that drew many workers from central Mexico to the Mexican border cities, where there were many opportunities for work. But NAFTA also opened the Mexican market to US goods, including agricultural products like corn, which is subsidized in the United States. Small farmers in Mexico could not compete against the subsidized corn, and many of them ended up migrating to the United States to find gainful employment. One of the ironies of that movement is that people who were corn farmers in Mexico ended up working on the large industrial farms that grew the subsidized corn.

During the same period, the Clinton administration began to militarize the US-Mexico border. The administration added many Border Patrol agents, built the first portion of what is now a very long fence, and put up a lot of electronic surveillance.[12] Making the crossing more difficult and dangerous changed the migratory patterns of many people. Historically, for

12. See Joseph R. Rudolph Jr., "Border Fence," Immigration to the United States, accessed March 29, 2017, http://immigrationtounitedstates.org/381-border-fence.html.

many people, particularly from Mexico, working in the United States was a temporary thing. People would cross the border to work and then return home. But as this process became more difficult, dangerous, and expensive (as illegal border crossing was taken over by people-smuggling mafias), more people who crossed decided to stay in the United States.[13]

The 1990s and the first decade of the twenty-first century saw a significant movement of people north from Latin America. NAFTA, the violence in Central America, and the uncertainty of the economies in those countries and in Puerto Rico became push factors. Early in the Bush administration, President Fox of Mexico and President Bush met to try to develop a comprehensive immigration plan between the two countries. But the events of September 11, 2001, took long-term immigration reform off the table. There were several attempts to pass a comprehensive immigration law during the first decade of the twenty-first century, but all the efforts fell short.

The environment for the undocumented has become more complex, particularly given the anti-immigrant vitriol of the 2016 presidential campaign. Because it was impossible to pass an immigration law, the Obama administration both stepped up deportations and attempted to address the situation through executive orders. This created an increasingly broken immigration system, one that will likely continue into the foreseeable future.

It is beyond the scope of this book to give a detailed explanation of migration theory, which seeks "interdisciplinarity, globality, and postdisciplinarity" in studying migration.[14] Because it seeks to study the migrant as an agent in the process, migration theory recognizes that it can no longer focus on an assimilation model, predicting a single outcome, but must use a series of models and perspectives that predict a range of potential outcomes.[15]

Once one looks at the history of migration between the United States and Latin America through that type of lens, a number of things look different. First of all, migration is a multinational issue that has multinational impacts. In the United States the issue is usually seen only through the lens of its impact on this country. But the relationship between the United States and Latin America is such that migratory patterns from Latin America and migration policy in the United States have an impact on both the United States and Latin America.

13. See Rudolph, "Border Fence."
14. Caroline B. Brettell and James F. Hollifield, *Migration Theory: Talking across Disciplines* (New York: Routledge, 2015), 3.
15. Brettell and Hollifield, *Migration Theory*, 16.

Secondly, it is clear that movement has gone in both directions and that many Latin Americans have originally come to the United States with the intention of returning. Many who come to work in the United States have returned, some because they were deported, but most because their plans were always temporary. Migrants from Latin America may see the United States as a land of opportunity, but not always as a place where they want to live the rest of their lives. For many, it has been a source of extra income that was then invested in Latin America. Migration has been and continues to be a temporary or cyclical pattern for many people from Latin America.

Within this more complex reality, many Latinas have developed transnational identities. As stated earlier, they continue to identify with their historical country of origin, and many travel back and forth between the United States and their home country on a regular basis. Many maintain strong emotional links, even though they are proudly US citizens.

It is clear that transnational identity has an impact on how Latinas live their lives in the United States. Importantly, it also plays a role in Latin American countries. Latinos, particularly immigrants, send large amounts of money to their families in their countries of origin. Remittances play an extremely important role in the economies of several Latin American countries, often providing more financial support for the national economy than does US foreign aid.[16]

Because migration flows in both directions, increasing numbers of people in Latin America have transnational identities; they are linked to the United States but live in Latin America. The people that move back and forth keep strong links alive between south and north.

Migration theory also addresses the impact of changing laws, policies, and attitudes in the host country. Part of the reason for migratory cycles is changing attitudes in the United States depending on the economic situation. The United States has changed its immigration laws and its enforcement practices toward people from Latin America many times. It has sought workers from Latin America and then worked to remove them. The immigration reform acts of 1965 and 1986 both had a positive impact on immigrants from Latin America, though other actions have been adverse toward those from that region. These laws and enforcement policies are a reflection of

16. See Miriam Jordan, "Remittances to Latin America, Caribbean Hit $68.3 Billion in 2015," *Wall Street Journal*, February 16, 2016, http://www.wsj.com/articles/remittances-to-latin -america-caribbean-hit-68-3-billion-in-2015-1455598863, and Peter J. Meyer, "U.S. Foreign Assistance to Latin America and the Caribbean: Recent Trends and FY2016 Appropriations," Congressional Research Service, January 7, 2016, https://fas.org/sgp/crs/row/R44113.pdf.

the constantly changing attitudes in the United States toward immigrants, depending on the economic situation in this country.

Because of the way the Southwest became a part of the United States, the social imaginary of people in the region has always been different. For example, for many of those in the majority culture, the Border Patrol and the Texas Rangers represent a "defense" of the frontier, a vision of civilization expanding westward. But many Latinos perceive these two bodies as legally sanctioned entities of oppression. Even as one group glorifies them, another sees them as the public faces of injustice.[17]

Because of the role that faith plays in the lives of so many Latinas, the narrative of migration cannot be told without accounting for how the migrants themselves understand their experience. While the popular US narrative is often either one of illegality ("they are breaking the law") or of victimhood (migrants suffering under people smugglers, the dangers of the journey, etc.), for many immigrants it is one of faith. Many people tell the story of their journey north in religious terms.[18] From their perspective, making it through the dangers and getting past Border Patrol officials are an act of God. They have been able to arrive in the United States because God has protected them from the dangers of the journey, the human smugglers, and the border officials. These very different readings of the events around migration create a clash of narratives that is seldom acknowledged or addressed in any way.

As Latinas migrate, they bring their faith along with them. Because most are either Catholic or Protestant, they usually do not bring new faiths to the United States. But they do bring different ways of thinking about and living out their faith. They bring their particular religious practices with them, and so influence Latino expressions of faith in the United States. Little by little, Latino expressions are also having an impact on the Christian expressions in both Catholic and Protestant churches in the United States.

But the immigrants also influence how faith is lived out in Latin America, by taking their US-based experiences back to Latin America. Many Latinas support the religious structures of their (ancestral) homelands. Latina Catholics support and change the religious sanctuaries in Mexico and Latin America, even though they may be several generations removed from life in

17. See, for example, Alfredo Mirande, *Gringo Justice* (Notre Dame: University of Notre Dame Press, 1987). On a personal level, this author can also attest to the number of times he has been stopped by *la migra* because he is a Latino male.

18. Jacqueline Maria Hagan, *Migration Miracle: Faith, Hope, and Meaning on the Undocumented Journey* (Cambridge, MA: Harvard University Press, 2008).

their home communities. Latino Protestants not only support their families "back home." They also provide financial support for churches and ministries in their home countries.

But migration, and undocumented migration in particular, raises important theological questions for those in the United States who identify as Christians, who claim to be spiritual sisters and brothers of those who are migrating. How does one understand the relationship between national identity and Christian identity? What does it mean in practice to say that a Christian's primary allegiance is to the kingdom of God and not to any specific national government? How do Christians in the United States deal with changes in immigration laws and changes in the way they are applied and enforced?

Undocumented immigration has also been an important political issue in the United States, though its importance ebbs and flows depending on the national mood. There is a historical pattern in which migrants from Latin America are encouraged to enter the United States when it is economically beneficial, but then they are blamed for all types of problems when it is politically expedient to do so. As mentioned earlier, the 2016 elections and the anti-immigrant attitudes of many in the United States have rendered a quick political solution to the current plight of the undocumented unlikely.

Despite the long history of migration between Latin America and the United States, seldom does one hear US leaders recognize the connections between US policies in Latin America and migration flows from that region. On the one hand, there is no public recognition of how US foreign policy influences migratory patterns. But on the other hand, there is also little understanding of how current migration laws are impacting Latin America, and even less about how future flows might impact both the United States and the rest of the continent. Several actions by the Obama administration impacted significantly both the immigrant community and the countries to which immigrants were being deported. The most obvious one was the massive deportation policy. The Obama administration deported more undocumented aliens than the three previous administrations combined.[19] This has disrupted life for families in the United States and has left many in Latin America without a source of income. Related to this has been the US policy

19. See Ana Gonzalez-Barrera and Jens Manuel Krogstad, "U.S. Deportations of Immigrants Reach Record High in 2013," Pew Research Center, October 2, 2014, http://www.pew research.org/fact-tank/2014/10/02/u-s-deportations-of-immigrants-reach-record-high-in -2013/.

of deporting convicted gang members to their Central American countries of origin. This has created major insecurity and instability in many cities of that region. The weak police and security forces in those countries have been overwhelmed by violence that has developed as these US-exported criminal gangs raise the crime and murder rates in this region.

In response, many Latin Americans began sending their children north to avoid the violence. Unaccompanied minors from Central America have arrived at US border crossings; they take advantage of how US officials interpret laws and policies related to unaccompanied minors fleeing violence at home.

Another direct impact on Latin America has been the policy of deporting people whose families are in the United States. These people are left at a Mexican border crossing with little to no support. They stay in the border area and attempt to return to the States because all their family is there. This creates significant social pressures on Mexican border cities because they cannot absorb the number of people deported and left at the border. Though this "ends" the issue from the perspective of US immigration officials, it creates massive problems for Mexican border cities and ongoing problems for US families who need to find a way to continue to support their deported relatives. One unintended consequence is that this policy creates more links between north and south as people, churches, and other organizations seek ways to continue to support their deported relatives and friends.

Because US immigration policy has never addressed the issue of future flow, there is no coherent understanding of the social implications of migration, and deportation, for Latin America and the Latina community. There is a common understanding in the United States that Latinos will structurally assimilate when migration stops. But there is no realistic scenario in which that happens in the foreseeable future. Historically, the flow has increased and decreased at different times, depending on factors in both the United States and Latin America. But the United States has never attempted to develop a coherent long-term policy to address this reality.

Since the time of the Monroe Doctrine, the perception has always been that Latin America is in the United States's backyard. But it seems to be a backyard that is "tended to" only when it has the potential of creating "problems" for the United States. And the solutions given usually only create other problems and unintended consequences, such as new undocumented migration.

Because US immigration policy does not address the problems mentioned, it is unable to provide a long-term solution to the issue of immigration from Latin America. For US Latinas this creates an environment in which Latina identity reflects the intersection between US immigration policy, policies toward immigrants and the deported in each Latin American country, and the choices made by the migrants themselves. Immigrant Latinos live within the reality of US immigration policy, but they also act as agents who seek to make those policies work for them, who work around those policies when they don't, and who make their own decisions about migration based on their own needs, not only on the basis of US economic or immigration policy. This is a dynamic space that is not easily navigated, but which impacts many aspects of Latino identity.

Religious Context

One cannot understand Latinos without understanding the role religious faith has played throughout the history of Latina identity formation. Faith played an important role in Spain's conquest of and migration to the Americas. Popular expressions of Catholic faith became a crucial part of daily life, particularly in the far reaches of the empire and among the conquered. Because of limited resources, most communities in what later became the Southwest had few priests and churches. Yet people lived out their faith and developed forms of popular Catholicism that sustained their lives, though these forms often clashed with official Catholic doctrine. These popular expressions of faith became normative for many people, in spite of the official teachings of the church.

When Mexico became independent from Spain, the lack of priests became more pronounced, particularly in what is now the Southwest. Many of the priests in the region had come from Spain, and when the area became part of Mexico, they left, or were forced to leave. The Mexican Catholic Church found it difficult to produce parish priests, particularly for parishes located outside of major urban areas. So the people continued to practice and develop their faith with little formal theological formation or formal direction from a priest. The need for priests was profound; at the time of the US takeover of the Southwest, there were fewer than thirty priests in the whole region, many of whom were concentrated in northern New Mexico.[20] So, though the people were formally Catholic, and many practiced their faith, there was little formal support from the church.

20. Juan Francisco Martínez, "Origins and Development of Protestantism among Latinos in the Southwestern United States, 1836–1900" (PhD diss., Fuller Theological Seminary, School of World Mission, 1996), 78–84.

The religious environment became even more complicated for Latinas when the United States took over the region. The Mexican Catholic Church had jurisdiction over the churches of the region, naming priests and developing dioceses with their own bishops. California already had a bishop at the time of the US takeover, and Santa Fe, New Mexico, was close to having a bishop named before the takeover. The takeover created a difficult situation for the Vatican, because it now had to reassign the churches in the region to a new bishop and place them under a new national leadership. Though the situation remained unclear for several months, eventually the churches came under the leadership of the US Catholic Church.

The transfer of ecclesial responsibilities happened at a difficult time for US Catholics. There was a strong anti-Catholic sentiment in a predominantly Protestant country. US Catholics of European background were trying to demonstrate that they could also be good Americans. They were very keen to present a certain image to their fellow citizens, one in which Mexican Catholicism did not easily fit.

One of the first high-profile actions taken by the US Catholic leadership was to ask the Vatican to create a diocese in the new territory of New Mexico, with Santa Fe as the see. The Vatican named a French priest, Jean Baptiste Lamy, as the bishop for the new diocese in 1850. Soon after his arrival, tensions arose between Lamy and Antonio José Martínez, the informal leader of the priests in the region. Martínez had developed a small proto-seminary to prepare young men for the priesthood. He was also the spiritual mentor of the most prominent Catholic lay organization among *neomejicanos*, Los Hermanos de la Fraternidad Piadosa de Nuestro Padre Jesús Nazareno (The Brothers of the Pious Fraternity of Our Father Jesus the Nazarene), commonly known as the *Penitentes*.

Lamy had a very different vision of the future than that envisioned by the *neomejicanos* themselves, and the tensions between Lamy and Martínez became public. The bishop eventually removed most of the *neomejicano* priests from their posts and replaced them with foreigners, many of them from France and Spain. (In 1852 there were seventeen *neomejicano* priests. By 1857 there were two.) Martínez was also removed from his position and ended his life in an unclear relationship with the Catholic Church.

Many US Catholics worked from the perspective that Lamy took the correct actions. After the US takeover, US Catholics often described Mexican Catholicism in terms not much different than those used by US Protestant missionaries. There was a sense among the US Catholic hierarchy that Mexican Catholics and their expressions of the faith represented practices that were backward and prohibited them from participation in US society unless profound changes were made. So a plan of Americanization seemed to make sense for the US Catholic leadership.[21]

The changes instituted by Bishop Lamy created long-term tensions with *neomejicano* Catholics, the single largest ethnic group in the diocese. The *Penitente* movement went underground, and a few of its leaders were drawn to Protestant churches (see next chapter). Throughout the nineteenth and well into the twentieth century, relatively few *neomejicanos* would become priests, and it would be the 1950s before a *neomejicano* was named bishop of Santa Fe. This process was seen as necessary by the US Catholic hierarchy, but it came at a great cost. "It left a wound in the side of the Catholic Church in New Mexico which was long to heal, and the scar can yet be felt. To the Spanish-American minority, however, the wholesale removal of the native clergy had been a tragedy."[22]

The issues raised by these differing visions continue to this day. There is a continuing lag in US Catholicism between the official hierarchy and the faith of the majority of Catholics. Even as US Catholicism continues to lose traditional members, it remains strong due to the growing presence of Latino Catholics. Today, Latinos are the single largest ethnic group in US Catholicism, constituting close to 40 percent of the Catholic population, and a larger percentage of practicing Catholics. But those numbers do not translate into similar percentages in leadership roles. According to the Center for Applied Research in the Apostolate (CARA), 38 percent of US Catholics self-identify as Latinas, though only 3 percent of Catholic priests are Latino.[23]

The Mexicans of the Southwest already had their saints and virgins, including popular ones not recognized by the official church before the US takeover. Most of the early immigrants brought their venerations from Mexico, though some from other parts of Latin America brought other expressions of faith with them. Latina Catholics continue to venerate and support the shrines of these saints and virgins, even though they have lived in the United States for several generations.

21. *Death Comes for the Archbishop* tells this story in novelized form from the perspective of Lamy, as the hero who brought necessary change to New Mexico. Willa Cather, *Death Comes for the Archbishop* (New York: Knopf, 1927).

22. E. K. Francis, "Padre Martinez: A New Mexican Myth," *New Mexico Historical Review* 31 (October 1956): 289.

23. See "Fact Sheet: Hispanic Catholics in the U.S.," CARA at Georgetown University, accessed March 29, 2017, http://cara.georgetown.edu/staff/webpages/Hispanic%20Catholic %20Fact%20Sheet.pdf.

Latina Protestantism in the United States was born in the midst of the clashes between Catholicism and Protestantism, and also in the tensions between US formal Catholicism and popular Mexican Catholicism. But the early converts also lived in the midst of a cultural Catholicism where not every Latino had a vibrant faith. Early Latina Protestants told their spiritual story in terms of a contrast to a cultural Catholicism that had not provided them with a relationship with God or a live faith that gave meaning to their lives. Their experience was that they did not find a personal relationship with God until they became Protestants.

But their place in US society has tended to be complicated because they are a minority in the Latino community. During the nineteenth century, many US Protestants did not want Latino Protestants in their midst (see next chapter). And US Protestants have often reflected the changing and ambivalent perspectives of the general population toward the new immigrants, including Latino Protestants. On the other hand, the most significant historical expressions of US Protestantism have not traditionally drawn many Latinas. Latina Protestantism has grown the most in expressions of Protestantism, particularly Pentecostalism, that have historically been marginalized by other Protestants.

Latino Protestants also express their faith in ways that fit the category of popular religion; these ways do not easily fit within traditional Protestantism. These reflect the unique experiences of being Latina and Protestant. One can only fully understand Latino Protestantism if one understands that it is a faith lived at the intersection of a Protestant understanding of Christian faith and the unique experiences of being Latino in the United States.

Sociocultural Analysis

The US Latino experience includes several key components. On the one hand, history and migration theory help us understand how Latinas became a part of this country and how the links to Latin America continue to be important in understanding what it means to be Latino. This part of the equation is crucial because most Latinos continue to use national background as their principal self-identifier, before seeing themselves as Hispanic or Latina.[24] Country of origin is an important part of self-identification for the majority of Latinos.

---

24. Paul Taylor et al., "When Labels Don't Fit: Hispanics and Their Views of Identity," Pew Research Center, April 4, 2012, http://www.pewhispanic.org/2012/04/04/when-labels-dont-fit-hispanics-and-their-views-of-identity/.

But another important part of the equation is the US experience. How do Latinas create culture and identity as an ethnic minority group in the United States? What are some of the ways they develop polycentric identities that retain their allegiance to Latin America and also claim themselves as part of the United States? What role do migration, acculturation, and structural assimilation play in the dynamics of that process? How does using the Spanish language impact identity formation and ethnic identity maintenance?

As I illustrate in other works, Latina identity exists on a continuum between migration from Latin America and full structural assimilation in which people of Latino descent no longer see any lived connection between their daily lives and their ethnic background.[25] Most Latinos are not immigrants, and most have not structurally assimilated into majority culture. Most inhabit the space between these two bookends. It is in this broad space that Latinos develop polycentric identities, navigating between their "Latinoness," often in private spheres, and their participation in majority culture, usually in the public square. But there are also increasing public spaces in which Latinas can express this polycentric identity.

For understanding the history of Latina Protestantism, this issue has several very important implications. While Latina Protestants are mostly people that are part of Protestant congregations that have a clear Latino self-identity, Latino Protestant churches also serve the community as one other place for ethnic identity maintenance and development. Yet it is impossible to talk about this issue without recognizing that a growing number of Latina Protestants maintain a Latino identity but are not part of Latino churches.

Toward a Historiography of Latina Protestant Religious Identities

To date, there has been one major attempt to develop a historiography of Latina religious experience in the United States.[26] Hjamil Martínez-Vazquez argues that the official canon of US religious history seeks continuity with a European migration narrative. So any aspect that breaks with that continuity, such as the Latino experience, tends to be excluded from the story. Because

---

25. See Juan Francisco Martínez, *Los Protestantes: An Introduction to Latino Protestantism in the United States* (Santa Barbara, CA: ABC-CLIO, 2011).

26. Hjamil A. Martínez-Vázquez, *Made in the Margins: Latina/o Constructions of US Religious History* (Waco: Baylor University Press, 2013).

of this tendency, Martínez-Vazquez argues that Latina religious history needs to offer a counternarrative to this official understanding of religion, particularly Protestantism, in the United States. This counternarrative needs to "focus on the deconstruction of the canon, so that the target picture it created is dismantled."[27] Historians need to be intentional about understanding the theory, the paradigm of knowledge, that stands behind the way the history of religion in the United States is being told.[28]

From his perspective, Latina religious histories need to be constructed as "subaltern" readings. Because they are not included in Eurocentric interpretations, Latino-based histories need to create their own spaces that counter the dominant narrative and invite Latinas to reinterpret their own histories for their own sake and for the sake of the larger narrative that needs to include what has been previously excluded.

This history is a counternarrative. It provides a different understanding from that of the official canon of US religious history. Specifically, it invites Protestant historians to recognize the role of Latino converts as more than just "new" expressions of the dominant religious expressions. In the official history, Latino Protestants may be an interesting side note, but their role in US Protestantism is not crucial and can be told within the "official canon." But this telling recognizes that Latino Protestant history cannot be subsumed under US Protestant history, as commonly told.

This book also offers a "subaltern" understanding of Latina religious expressions by questioning the common narrative that all Latinas are Catholic, that Latino subculture is best maintained through Catholic faith expressions, and that Protestant faith cannot be truly expressed or lived out through a Catholic "language" such as Spanish. It also questions the analyses that want to connect conversion to Protestantism to the process of assimilation of Latinas into majority culture.

This book is also a counternarrative in that it challenges those who attempt to tell the Latino story without taking their faith seriously or that assume that faith can be separated from other aspects of Latina identity. This author, a subaltern, a Latino Protestant believer telling the story from within the community, assumes that this story cannot be effectively told without including the faith narrative that undergirds what it means to be Latina and Protestant.

But that story is also told from the periphery to the center. Latino Prot-

27. Martínez-Vázquez, *Made in the Margins*, 3.
28. Martínez-Vázquez, *Made in the Margins*, 5.

estants have historically been on the margins, and that is where their faith commitment developed and was strengthened.

In *La fe a la periferia de la historia*, author Juan Driver posits that movements of revival and renewal in the life of the church usually happen on the periphery of official church structures.[29] They have often happened among people who have little formal power, but who believe that God continues to work in the world and that God wants to work through them. He tracks the history of various renewal movements, drawing out commonalities and arguing that one should look to peripheral places to see God at work in new ways.

So this story is told from the periphery where Latina Protestantism developed. It is the story of people who can only effectively tell their story as one of encounter with God and the difference that has made in their lives. It is about how a specific people have experienced God in the midst of their specific story. But it is also the story of those who believe that their encounter with God can have an impact on others, that they can be agents of revival and renewal in the churches of the United States.

So throughout this book, history, migration, lived faith, and cultural adaptation interact and serve as the framing for this story. In the next chapters, these issues will serve as the outline for each historical period. The story will be told by looking at the history from a macro level. But in each chapter specific people from the period will serve as examples of how Protestant faith was lived out in the Latino community during the time being studied.

Latina Protestants experience God within these frames and negotiate their identities in the midst of these encounters. So it is here that the story is told.

---

29. Juan Driver, *La fe en la periferia de la historia: Una historia del pueblo cristiano desde la perspectiva de los movimientos de restauración y reforma radical* (Guatemala City: Ediciones Semilla, 1997).

Chapter 3

Conquest, Americanization, and Evangelization (1848–1900)

The Treaty of Guadalupe Hidalgo (1848), which ended the Mexican-American War (1846–1848) and gave the United States control of half of Mexico's territory (what is now the southwestern United States), also granted US citizenship, and the promise of respect for their property rights, to those who chose to stay in the ceded territory. Though many chose to migrate south into Mexican territory, about one hundred thousand people remained and became US citizens. (In the Texas border regions, some people opted to try to have it both ways. They kept their homes north of the Rio Grande, which was now the border, but established new communities on the south side, just in case.) All these people were formally Roman Catholic, though a (very) small number had already been attracted to the Protestant faith through contacts with people from the United States or because they had lived in the United States. It would be among these conquered people that US Latino Protestantism would be born.

The Mexican-American War created a great deal of tension in the United States, particularly among Christians from the North. (Congressman Abraham Lincoln called the war immoral, proslavery, and a threat to republican values.)[1] On the one hand, there was a strong pacifist tendency among some

---

1. Abraham Lincoln, "Abraham Lincoln Speech: The War with Mexico," January 12, 1848, in *The Collected Works of Abraham Lincoln*, ed. Roy Basler, vol. 1, *1824–1848* (New Brunswick, NJ: Rutgers University Press, 1953), 431–32, accessed March 29, 2017, http://www.animatedatlas .com/mexwar/lincoln2.html.

This chapter draws heavily on my book *Sea La Luz: The Making of Mexican Protestantism in the American Southwest, 1829–1900* (Denton: University of North Texas Press, 2006). Used by kind permission of the publisher.

leaders, particularly Quakers and Unitarians, so they were strongly opposed to the war. But many Protestant leaders also expressed the regional tensions of the period. For some northerners, the war—and the westward expansion it would make possible—was an attempt by southerners to expand the number of slave states and to limit the political influence of the smaller states of the Northeast. There was also the concern that war and expansion would create a national desire for conquest and would push the country toward despotism. Some Christian publications reported on the atrocities committed by US soldiers in Mexico and recognized that it would be hard to convince Mexicans of the superiority of the American way of life if they saw this type of conquest and destruction.[2] On the other hand, those who favored the war saw it as self-defense, following President Polk's declaration that Mexican soldiers had killed US soldiers on US soil. And one denominational report of the period, reflecting on the war, stated that "victory and conquest have ever followed the preaching of the cross."[3]

But opposition to the war and questions about its morality all ended once the war was over and the United States took over the land. Though there had been strong opposition to the war, there had never been much opposition to the US controlling the Southwest. For most, the opposition had to do with the method (war) and the political impact (expansion of slave states). Most US Protestant leaders seemed to agree with Josiah Strong, who stated in 1858 "that God, with infinite wisdom and skill, is training the Anglo-Saxon race for an hour sure to come in the world's future."[4] Even preachers who were strongly against the war agreed that Anglo-Saxons "have the saving ideas of Science, Freedom, and Christianity, that are able, if diffused, to keep the life-blood flowing, in strong and pure tides through their own hearts, and also to stir the deep sleep of paganism with fresh and waking pulses of regeneration."[5]

Most US Protestant leaders were convinced that it was the destiny of Anglo-Saxons to control the Southwest, so even those who opposed the war with Mexico felt that God had used it to bring his plans to fulfillment.[6] There was a general sense that God had predestined the Anglo-Saxons to expand and that God used the war (whether seen as good or bad) as a means for

2. Abiel Abbot Livermore, *The War with Mexico Revisited* (Boston: American Peace Society, 1850), 212.

3. Methodist Episcopal Church, South, Minutes of the Annual Conference, 1851, 12.

4. Josiah Strong, *Our Country: Its Possible Future and Its Present Crisis* (New York: Baker and Taylor Co., 1858), 174.

5. Livermore, *War with Mexico Revisited*, 210.

6. Annual Report of the Methodist Episcopal Church, South, 1851, 12.

that expansion. Because the Mexicans were "semibarbarous" and "miserable," they needed the evangelizing and civilizing influence of the Anglo-Saxon race.[7] Although the war with Mexico was wrong, "from the hour that the American flag floated over the City of Mexico, a new destiny awaited all those portions which were brought under Anglo-Saxon rule."[8]

The First Converts

The first known Protestant missionary contact with a Mexican of the Southwest occurred in Mexican *Tejas* in 1829. There were no converts and no other known contacts until after 1848. The first known Latino converts were reported in New Mexico (Peralta/Socorro area) and Texas (Corpus Christi) in the early 1850s. Baptist missionaries reported the establishment of a few congregations among the *neomejicano* converts during this period, and the Southern Methodists also attempted to organize a group of Latina converts around Corpus Christi into a congregation, but all these efforts ended when the Civil War began (1861). The Baptist missionaries all left the region, and the Methodists put formal mission efforts on hold until after the war.

The end of the Civil War (1865) ushered in the beginning of a new western migration. The new land taken from Mexico and the discovery of gold (1849) in California had created the first movement of people westward. But it was not until after the Civil War that the massive westward migration began. New migrants meant that new Protestant churches needed to be established, giving denominational home mission agencies a great deal of work. Those agencies put the bulk of their energies into establishing churches for the people from the East migrating west.

While some mission leaders called for the evangelization of Mexicans of the Southwest, others questioned whether they should even be evangelized. There were those who stated that they did not deserve the gospel, since they had fought against the Americans during the Mexican-American War. But mostly home mission leaders felt that the task of establishing churches for the Anglo migrants was so large that there would not be enough energy for a Mexican mission effort. This population was seen as very small and

7. Theodore Parker, "The Mexican War," *Massachusetts Quarterly Review* 1 (December 1847): 51.

8. Hollis Read, *The Hand of God in History; or, Divine Providence Historically Illustrated in the Extension and Establishment of Christianity*, 2 vols. (Hartford: H. E. Robins, 1858), 177.

secondary to the core task of Protestant home mission efforts. Even those who were in favor of evangelization of the Mexican population often felt that this task was important because the "Mexicans" should be given the gospel before they disappeared as a people as the "strong" Anglo-Saxon population took over the Southwest.[9]

Motivations for Mission

Though the Treaty of Guadalupe Hidalgo granted the Mexicans of the southwestern United States citizenship, the general view among Protestant missionaries was that they were unfit for this new role. In fact, many stated that granting them citizenship cheapened the value of being a US citizen. They were Roman Catholics, which already made them questionable as citizens for many Protestants, and they were also seen as technologically backward in many important ways. They were "mentally weak" because their religion had never encouraged them to think for themselves. They were lazy and had little initiative. They had fallen behind while civilization advanced in many parts of the world.[10] Many Protestants felt that they were clearly incapable of becoming good citizens of the United States.

From the perspective of the Protestant missionary (and that of many US Catholics), Mexican Catholicism was a significant part of the problem. Most Protestants already questioned Roman Catholic faith, but Mexican religious practice was seen as particularly problematic. As described by an early Presbyterian missionary in New Mexico, "The Roman Catholic Mexican worships the mother of Christ, his grandmother, his father, his grandfather, his heart, his side, his cross—in short, anything or any person, not Christ himself. They pluck the diadem from the brow of King Jesus in order to give it to the Pope of Rome."[11] This analysis of the "Mexicans" meant that Protestant missionaries saw their work among the Spanish-speaking people of the Southwest as bringing together evangelization and Americanization. From the perspective of many of the missionaries and mission agencies, being a good Protestant Christian and being a good American citizen were closely linked. Therefore, their missionary task included both goals. Good Anglo-

---

9. *Baptist Almanac* (Philadelphia: American Baptist Publication Society, 1851), 19.

10. *Baptist Almanac*, 23–24.

11. Robert M. Craig, *Our Mexicans* (New York: Board of Home Missions of the Presbyterian Church, USA, 1904), 33.

American Protestants understood the task as part of their responsibility of lifting up backward peoples.[12] Related to this goal was the task of taking the Protestant message into Mexico. Since it was very difficult for Protestant missionaries to enter Mexico after the US takeover, the Mexicans of the Southwest could serve as a bridge. At the very least, they could be a training ground for the missionaries as Protestants found the way to enter Mexico to do missionary work.

Protestant Missionary Efforts in the Nineteenth Century

The new western migration after the end of the Civil War also marked the beginning of new Protestant missionary work in the Southwest. The Civil War, or the events leading up to it, had created North-South splits in many Protestant denominations, many of which lasted well into the twentieth century. Denominational mission efforts in the Southwest would mostly fall along the geographic lines marked by the Civil War. For the most part, "Northern" denominations would work in New Mexico, Colorado, and California, while "Southern" denominations would work in Texas.

New Mexico/Colorado

During the early years of Protestant mission work, the new territorial divisions of the United States did not fit the lived experiences of the existing populations. The prime example of this was the region of northern New Mexico and southern Colorado. The people in this area had been part of the same political entity during the Spanish and Mexican periods, so they were closely linked. Protestant missionary efforts among the *neomejicanos* of the region during most of the nineteenth century tended to treat this area as one, as in the Spanish and Mexican periods, even though it was now part of two different US entities, the state of Colorado and the territory of New Mexico.

The first Protestant missionaries among the Spanish-speaking people were the Baptists. They began working in central New Mexico around 1850. Soon after their arrival, there was also a short-lived Methodist missionary presence in the area. A key person in both missionary efforts was a converted

12. Melinda Rankin, *Twenty Years among the Mexicans: A Narrative of Missionary Labor* (Saint Louis: Christian Publishing Co., 1875), 23.

Catholic priest named Benigno Cárdenas. He had been a priest in the region who had been suspended by Bishop Lamy and who met the Methodists and agreed to work with them. Because both the Baptists and the Methodists focused on a strongly anti-Catholic message, a person like Cárdenas seemed crucial to both efforts. The Baptists tried to recruit him, but he continued to work with the Methodists, even after the few Methodist missionaries left the region in the early 1850s.[13]

The Baptists reported 112 baptisms during their time in New Mexico. The first Latino Protestant converts in the Southwest were Baptists, and the first Latina Protestant churches were the Baptist churches established in Peralta and Socorro, New Mexico. Baptists reported a number of small congregations in the region throughout the 1850s. But the anticipation of war caused all the missionaries to leave the region before 1860. Some of these small congregations survived without outside missionaries. Because Baptist missionaries did not return to the region, after the Civil War these congregations joined the Methodist denomination, though some of the converts continued to identify as Baptists.[14] The descendants of some of these converts would reorganize themselves as Baptist churches once there was a Baptist presence in the area after 1900.

The first (Northern) Presbyterian missionary to arrive in New Mexico to work among *neomejicanos* found one Latino Protestant, José Ynés Perea, who had become a Protestant when he had studied in the United States. A small congregation was organized in Las Vegas, New Mexico, in 1870, and eventually Perea became the first *neomejicano* to be ordained to the Presbyterian ministry. Through these initial contacts the Presbyterians came in contact with *Penitentes* who were frustrated with the new US Catholic hierarchy in New Mexico and were open to joining them. A number of *cofradías* (*Penitente* brotherhoods) became Presbyterian congregations, and some *Penitente* leaders became Presbyterian lay pastors.

A unique part of Presbyterian mission efforts was the establishing of schools in many small communities in the region. It took many years after the US takeover before public schools were established in many of the smaller *neomejicano* communities. People wanted schools for their children, and many were open to having a Presbyterian school with a single female

---

13. Martínez, *Sea La Luz*, 55.

14. Thomas Harwood, *History of the New Mexico Spanish and English Missions of the Methodist Episcopal Church from 1850–1910*, 2 vols. (Albuquerque: El Abogado Press, 1908), 1:52–53.

teacher in their communities, since these women were not seen as a threat to their way of life. Women's missionary societies funded these schools and teachers, often in opposition to the desire of home mission executives who wanted their efforts to go into helping the children of the Americans who were migrating into the Southwest.

In some communities the establishment of a school opened the door to sending a more formal missionary and to establishing a church. Single female teachers became the vanguard of the Presbyterian mission effort in the region. Though most communities would eventually have public schools, Presbyterians continued establishing and supporting schools in the area until well into the twentieth century. A significant number of Latino Presbyterian church members and leaders in the region attended a Presbyterian school at one time or another. At their apex in 1890, Presbyterians had forty schools in the region.[15] These efforts produced a growing number of small Latina Presbyterian congregations, many of them led by lay ministers. By 1900 there were twenty-nine Latino Presbyterian congregations with 908 members.

Though the Presbyterians were not the largest group among the Latinas in the territory of New Mexico, they were unique because of the importance they placed on education. Not only did they establish many schools, they also developed several training programs for pastors, since they placed great importance on an educated clergy and only those who had formal education could be ordained. (This is one reason why there were so few ordained Latino Presbyterian ministers during this period.)

The most important institution established for pastoral training of Latino pastors during the nineteenth century was the College of the Southwest, in Del Norte, Colorado. The college was established in 1884 offering programs in general education to both English- and Spanish-speaking students. In 1890 the college established a training program for Mexican American evangelists. It graduated its first class in 1893. Though the college survived only until 1901, when it was closed because of financial problems, it had a significant influence on Latina Presbyterianism in the Southwest. Many key leaders of the first part of the twentieth century graduated from this school, with the most famous alumnus being Gabino Rendón (of which,

---

15. Ruth Kerns Barber and Edith J. Agnew, *Sowers Went Forth: The Story of Presbyterian Missions in New Mexico and Southern Colorado* (Albuquerque: Menaul Historical Library of the Southwest, 1981), appendix 1, "Presbyterian Missions Schools in New Mexico and Colorado," 159–60.

more in the next chapter). A survey done of forty of its Spanish-speaking graduates found that "8 had become ordained ministers, 10 were evangelists, 9 were teachers, 4 were editors, 4 were ministers' wives, 3 were merchants, 1 was a lawyer, and 1 was in the employ of the government."[16]

The Methodist (Methodist Episcopal Church—MEC) work in the region during the nineteenth century is largely the story of Thomas and Emily Harwood. They arrived in La Junta, New Mexico, in 1869 with the intention of working among the English-speaking people. But they found the work among the Spanish-speaking population "far more encouraging" and began a ministry in the region that would last over forty years.

Thomas Harwood kept a detailed ministry diary that would later be published as the *History of the New Mexico Spanish and English Missions of the Methodist Episcopal Church from 1850–1910*. Harriet Kellogg also wrote a biography of Emily Harwood (*Life of Mrs. Emily J. Harwood*) soon after her death in 1903.[17] These documents provide an extensive picture of Methodist work in the region and of the normative role that the Harwoods played in interpreting Methodist ministry among the Spanish-speaking people to the larger Methodist world.

The Harwoods had a low view of the current state of the Spanish-speaking population. According to them, *neomejicanos* were a "slumbering people," a population with little desire to progress. They were backward because they had lived far from the centers of civilization, did not have access to the Bible, and had not had religious freedom. From the Harwoods' perspective, this population did not have good hygiene or good manners.[18]

According to Thomas Harwood, "Intellectually, morally and religiously . . . [New Mexico] was one of the darkest corners of Christendom. While the march of civilization had taken grand strides, almost everywhere else, New Mexico had fallen behind. Why? For want of Bibles, schools and proper instruction. These wanting, there could be but little advancement on any lines of material progress. But we must not be too severe, since we do not know what New Mexico might have been without the Roman Catholic religion."[19] Nonetheless, the Harwoods were very committed to the community. They

16. Andrew E. Murray, *The Skyline Synod: Presbyterianism in Colorado and Utah* (Denver: Golden Bell Press, 1971), 37.

17. Harriet S. Kellogg, *Life of Mrs. Emily J. Harwood* (Albuquerque: El Abogado Press, 1903).

18. Harwood, *History of the New Mexico Spanish and English Missions*, 1:215, 251.

19. Harwood, *History of the New Mexico Spanish and English Missions*, 1:19.

were convinced of the importance of the Protestant message as the answer to the spiritual needs of the *neomejicano* population. But this was a message closely linked to Americanization. From their perspective, these two things naturally came together.[20] If the people accepted the Protestant message, they would also desire to progress and learn the more advanced "American" way of doing things. If the missionaries could accomplish this, then the people could become good American citizens.

The Harwoods demonstrated the level of their commitment to the people and to the preaching of the Protestant message by being the only missionaries to make a long-term commitment, remaining as missionaries until the first part of the twentieth century. As a result, they were largely responsible for the growth of Methodist churches in the region.

As part of the early work in the region, Thomas Harwood connected with the Baptist congregations in the Peralta/Socorro area formed in the 1850s, and all of them joined the Methodist denomination with the blessing of one of the Baptist missionaries who had remained in the area as a businessman. During his years as a missionary, Harwood was a circuit rider, traveling to many of the small communities in the territory and starting new congregations. He also trained a number of the converts as circuit-riding evangelists and preachers who served in many small towns. Many of these lay preachers were later ordained and became the key leaders among Latino Methodists in New Mexico and throughout the Southwest. Harwood also worked with Methodist leaders, both in the United States and in Latin America, to develop Spanish-language publications that were a key part of the evangelistic efforts. By 1900 the Methodist Episcopal Church had fifty-eight Spanish-language churches in New Mexico with 1,537 members.[21]

The Congregational Church also did missionary work among *neomejicanos* during the nineteenth century. The Congregationalists never had many churches in the territory, so they did not have a strong presence. They attempted to follow the Presbyterian model of starting schools, but did not have the financial base for this. The missionaries never reported any churches during the nineteenth century, though there were a few *neomejicano* converts listed as members of the Congregational Church in Albuquerque.

---

20. Harwood, *History of the New Mexico Spanish and English Missions*, 1:206, 305.

21. Juan Francisco Martínez, "Origins and Development of Protestantism among Latinos in the Southwestern United States, 1836–1900" (PhD diss., Fuller Theological Seminary, School of World Mission, 1996), 221–22.

Texas

Missionary work among the Mexicans in Texas was largely done by denominations that already had English-language churches in the state. The largest of these was the Methodist Episcopal Church, South (MECS). Alejo Hernández, a convert in Mexico, entered Texas and was a key player in the establishment of the MECS congregation in Corpus Christi. Other converts moved both north and south of the Mexican border and established churches in both Texas and northern Mexico. The links between Texas and northern Mexico became the bridge for missionary work on both sides of the border. The MECS established "border" districts and conferences, denominational bodies that spanned the US-Mexico border. One superintendent oversaw churches on both sides, and pastors could be assigned churches on either side. Because many people had family on both sides of the border, this created a synergism that benefited ministry in both the United States and Mexico. But it also reinforced the idea that "Mexicans" in Texas were foreigners, not really a part of the United States.

As the transnational border conferences developed, more of the ministry focused on the Mexican side of the border. This served as the basis for the development of Methodism in Mexico, but it also limited the ministry on the US side to a certain extent. Nonetheless, by 1900 there were seventeen Spanish-language MECS congregations in Texas with 1,450 adult members.[22]

The Baptist General Convention of Texas (BGCT) began work among the "Mexicans" of Texas in the 1880s. There had been stated interest in working among them since the 1850s, but actual ministry got started after Baptists were already working in Mexico. Through the late nineteenth century various Baptist associations in Texas would have reports "on Mexican and colored population" during their annual conferences. Some years there would be much enthusiasm about what might occur, while other years the reports were not very hopeful. In 1880 one of the associations reported on what the Methodists were doing and stated that "some of these Mexicans are Baptist in principle, and would unite with us if an opportunity were offered." Interestingly, two of the early Latino Baptist preachers had formerly been Methodists, one from Mexico and the other from New Mexico.[23]

But the nineteenth-century ministry was a bit sporadic. Extant reports from the various Baptist associations that worked among the Spanish-

22. Martínez, "Origins and Development," 162–63.
23. Martínez, "Origins and Development," 170–78.

speaking population give great numbers one year and almost none the next. By the end of that century, Baptists had a small presence in Texas (nine churches with 360 members).[24] Nonetheless, Baptists continued to grow in Texas throughout the twentieth century and would eventually constitute the largest Latino church group in Texas and the second largest in the United States. Today Texas is one of the few places among the Spanish speaking of the world where Baptists constitute the largest Protestant denomination, by far, and where even the Pentecostals do not have nearly as significant a presence as they do in most of the Spanish-speaking world.

The work of the (Southern) Presbyterian Church, US (PCUS) among the Spanish-speaking population of Texas began in Mexico. A congregation in Matamoros, Tamaulipas, began a congregation in their sister border city of Brownsville, Texas, in 1877. In 1886, José María Botello (also Botelló in some records), an elder in the Matamoros congregation, moved to San Marcos and began a congregation that was later accepted into the West Texas Presbytery. Walter Scott, a pastor born in Mexico of Huguenot parents, served alongside this congregation and worked with the presbytery to oversee the establishment of other congregations. Henry Platt, who had been a missionary in Colombia, also helped train Spanish-speaking pastors.[25] By 1900 there were eight organized congregations with 517 members.[26]

The Disciples of Christ began working in San Antonio in 1899. Their presence in the Southwest would continue to be small through the middle of the twentieth century. They would begin to grow with the Puerto Rican migration after World War II (see next chapter).

The Rest of the Southwest

The Mexican populations of California and Arizona were relatively small during the nineteenth century, and so there were few congregations established during this period. Presbyterians established churches in southern California, and the MECS established churches in Tucson and some mining communities east of Tucson. The Adventists also established one congrega-

---

24. Martínez, "Origins and Development," 176, 277.

25. Henry Pratt is most well known in the Spanish-speaking world for his translation of the Bible into Spanish. His *Version Moderna* was published by the American Bible Society in 1893 and revised in 1929.

26. Martínez, "Origins and Development," 167–68.

tion in Tucson in 1899.[27] Protestant ministry in these regions would remain small until after the Mexican Revolution began, when new migration into southern California and southern Arizona occurred.

The Eastern Seaboard

While Protestant mission work in the Southwest was mostly among people who lived in the region at the time of the US takeover, the missionary efforts on the eastern seaboard focused on immigrants. These populations were small and were mostly from Cuba, Puerto Rico, and Spain. There is very little record of these efforts before the beginning of the twentieth century, though there were Protestant missionary efforts among Latinas in New York and in Florida during the 1890s. One congregation was established in New York in 1898, the Iglesia Hispano-Americana, though little is known about it and 1912 is usually mentioned as the date when Latino Protestant churches were first established in the city.[28]

Latino Protestantism at the Beginning of the Twentieth Century

As the nineteenth century came to a close, there were 149 Spanish-language Protestant congregations with 5,572 adult members reported in the Southwest. There were also some converts on the eastern seaboard, with one congregation reported in New York, though little is known about the church or its membership. Members were spread across the following states or territories.[29]

	Members
New Mexico	2,521
Texas	2,378
Colorado	462
California	115
Arizona	96

27. Martínez, "Origins and Development," 257–70, and Manuel Vásquez, *La historia aun no contada: 100 años de Adventismo Hispano* (Nampa, ID: Pacific Press Publishing Association, 2000), 36.

28. See Gastón Espinosa, *Latino Pentecostals in America: Faith and Politics in Action* (Cambridge, MA: Harvard University Press, 2014), 260.

29. Martínez, "Origins and Development," 373.

According to denominational reports, Latino Protestants were part of the following denominations:[30]

Methodist Episcopal Church	1,699
Methodist Episcopal Church, South	1,487
Presbyterian Church, USA	1,464
Presbyterian Church, US	517
Southern Baptist Convention	360
Congregational Church	45

Latino Protestant churches were all small, with few churches reporting more than fifty members. Most of them were located in the small, isolated, predominantly Latina communities of northern New Mexico, southern Colorado, and central Texas. There was almost no Protestant presence in what would become the major Latina urban centers of the twentieth century. These churches had few Latino ordained pastors. Many of them were led by missionaries or by lay pastors. Most of the Latino pastors had very little formal education and only minimal theological and ministerial formation. Nearly all the congregations were poor and provided small salaries to their pastors and minimal funds to their ministries. They depended on financial support from their denominations, something that created tensions with denominational leaders and tended to encourage a level of dependence and lack of local responsibility for the ministry of the congregations.

Because many of the congregations were located in isolated communities or villages, there was little potential for growth. By the end of the nineteenth century, some of these communities, particularly in northern New Mexico, were already feeling the impact of a changing economy. People were leaving these villages and looking for new economic opportunities in the cities or in California.

These early Protestant communities left few written records. Protestant missionaries wrote most of what we know about them. But they were already demonstrating some characteristics that would become a part of the developing Latina Protestant identity.

All Latino Protestants from this era were converts. They all had a conversion narrative (*testimonio*), many of which contained the same elements. The common themes were (1) a background of cultural Catholicism that had not brought them an encounter with God, and sometimes included a broken

30. Martínez, "Origins and Development," 307.

lifestyle; (2) a strong encounter with God usually through hearing the Bible preached or through reading it; (3) a resultant change of life on a personal level, but also in being ostracized from their families and communities for becoming Protestant; and (4) a clear sense that the sacrifice was worth it. They were suffering because of their commitment to Christ, but now they had a relationship with God. They lived a better life today and would receive the benefits of their conversion in the afterlife.

Though persecution was not a strong theme among Latina Protestants during this period, several people were marginalized by their families or their communities for becoming Protestants. Probably the most public of these persecutions happened in northern New Mexico/southern Colorado. In this area three small communities were separated into Catholic and Protestant sections, with new communities forming as a result of these divisions.[31]

A common characteristic of these early Latino Protestant converts was their love for the Bible. Conversions usually happened after they had read the Bible or heard biblically based sermons. But Bibles in Spanish were not easy to obtain during this period. The Bible became a key component in the common narrative that developed around Latina Protestant identity. People told stories of specific Bibles, how difficult it had been to obtain that Bible or to keep it hidden so that it would not be destroyed; they related the process through which it was studied and the impact it had on them. A number of the more famous Bibles were named after the communities they impacted or after the people who originally owned them. A few still exist in museums as artifacts of Latina Protestantism.[32]

Robert Craig in *Our Mexicans* recounts one of the earliest recorded histories of one of these Bibles, and its evangelistic impact. He prefaces the story by stating that "we must not forget that some of the Spanish Bibles which had been brought to New Mexico by the early missionaries remained on the field and did their enlightening and converting work even after the expeditions had been expelled and the missionaries massacred." He then tells this story. "[About 1868] a Spanish Bible was found on the road some distance from Las Vegas [New Mexico]. The finder, knowing nothing of the value of the book, shortly afterward met Señor Albino Madrid and exchanged with him this Bible for a Spanish spelling-book. Mr. Madrid, being fond of reading, at once

31. Lela Wheatherby, "A Study of the Early Years of the Presbyterian Work with the Spanish Speaking People of New Mexico and Colorado and Its Development from 1850–1920" (master's thesis, Presbyterian College of Christian Education, 1942), 51.

32. See Juan Francisco Martínez Guerra, "The Bible in Neomejicano Protestant Folklore during the 19th Century," *Apuntes* 17, no. 1 (1997): 21–26.

began to study this new book, and gained from it some knowledge of the Way of Life."[33] From this initial encounter several members of the Madrid family eventually became Protestant believers, and several members of the Madrid family continued as members of Presbyterian churches well into the twentieth century. Latina Protestant believers told similar stories throughout the Southwest, though this type of *testimonio* (conversion narrative) was particularly popular in New Mexico.

An important secondary characteristic of Latino Protestantism was its attractiveness to faithful Catholics who were either marginalized by US Catholicism or found a more faithful expression of what they sought among Protestants. During the nineteenth century, the most important conversion of faithful Catholics was what happened among the *Pentitentes* of New Mexico/Colorado. This was a lay movement with roots in Franciscan third orders. It had a strong presence in the region and was very public until the coming of US citizens. *Penitentes* provided social services to the poor and needy and were also the backbone of support for the parishes. But they also practiced public forms of penance, including flogging, during Holy Week. These practices were strongly condemned by the US Catholic Church and were the object of, often, morbid curiosity by Protestants. So, after the US takeover of the Southwest, the *Penitentes* went underground.

When the Protestants, particularly the Presbyterians, arrived, some *Penitente cofradías* found spiritual support and nurture among them. Several *cofradías* developed into Presbyterian churches. Vicente Romero, a son of the priest Antonio José Martínez, became a Presbyterian lay minister and led one of these congregations.[34] Such was the relationship between Presbyterians and *Penitentes* during the nineteenth century that Alex Darley, a Presbyterian missionary, wrote a fairly sympathetic book about them, calling them "Serious Seekers by a False Road."[35]

Though Latino Protestants of the nineteenth century left behind almost no written record, we know about a few specific converts through missionary

33. Craig, *Our Mexicans*, 54–55.

34. Martínez was married before becoming a priest. He also had children after he was ordained, which he recognized. Vicente Romero was one of those sons. See "Antonio José Martínez," *Wikipedia*, last modified December 3, 2016, https://en.wikipedia.org/w/index.php ?title=Antonio_Jos%C3%A9_Mart%C3%ADnez&oldid=728008651.

35. See Alex M. Darley, *Passionists of the Southwest: Or the Holy Brotherhood* (reprint, Glorieta, NM: Rio Grande Press, 1968); Juan Francisco Martínez, "Serious Seekers by a False Road: Nineteenth-Century Protestant Missionaries' Perceptions of the Penitente Brotherhood," *New Mexico Historical Review* 83, no. 3 (Summer 2008).

reports and the few extant documents written by this first generation of Protestant believers. All have a story of conversion, refer to God's faithfulness in spite of persecution, have a sense of being a part of a small minority, and have a hope in God's future, believing that God will prize their faithfulness in glory.

José Ynés Perea became a Protestant while studying in Saint Louis. He became a core leader in the first Presbyterian church in Las Vegas, New Mexico. According to John Annin, the first Presbyterian missionary in the area, when he and Perea first met, the latter stated that "I have been praying for a missionary, and I have made vows and promises to the Lord in connection with this work. You can depend on me for any and everything that I can do to assist this mission work."[36] He was soon ordained an elder in the Las Vegas church and later became the first *neomejicano* ordained as a Presbyterian minister. He pastored several small Presbyterian congregations in New Mexico, none of which had even twenty members. Though he had a limited impact on other *neomejicanos*, he had a clear sense of God's call on his life and hoped for the day in which the Protestant message would have a broad impact among his people.[37]

Alejo Hernández was studying for the priesthood in Mexico when the French invaded that country. He left seminary to join the army and was captured by the French. While in their custody he obtained a French Bible. After escaping from the French he read an anti-Catholic book, *Evening with the Romanists*, apparently left behind by a US soldier who was a part of the army that invaded Mexico during the Mexican-American War. These experiences led him to Brownsville, Texas, to look for a Spanish Bible and to learn about Protestantism. He had a conversion experience while attending a church there. He returned to Mexico to preach the Protestant message. But the persecution was such that he returned to Texas. In 1870 he joined the Methodist church in Corpus Christi, where he became a licensed minister and served as part of the leadership that led the MECS toward a new chapter of ministry among *tejanos* and Mexican immigrants in Texas. He preached in many parts of Texas and later returned to Mexico, having the distinction of being the first licensed Mexican Methodist minister in the Southwest.[38]

Ambrosio González was one of the first converts of the Baptist mis-

36. Craig, *Our Mexicans*, 60.

37. Martínez, *Sea La Luz*, 81–82, 148–49.

38. Martínez, "Origins and Development," 433–34. There is a second version of where and how Hernández first found a Bible. According to Hamilton Horton, a contemporary, Hernández found a Bible left by a US soldier during the invasion of Mexico. Hamilton Garmany Horton File, Southwest Texas Conference, United Methodist Church Archives, San Antonio, n.d.

sionaries in New Mexico during the 1850s. He became a lay pastor and continued to pastor a congregation that survived after the US missionaries left. When Protestant missionaries returned to New Mexico after the Civil War, he and his congregation joined the Methodist Church due to the support and influence of Thomas Harwood. He exemplified the transdenominational experience of several of the early converts. Though he had a strong Baptist identity, he was able to join the Methodists because that was the only option open to him and the congregation he led.

Little is known about **Benigno Cárdenas** before 1850. He was one of the *neomejicano* priests suspended by Bishop Lamy in the early 1850s. He traveled to Rome to try to get his suspension lifted, with no success. On his way back to the United States he traveled through London, where he met the Methodists. He was attracted to their message and agreed to work with the Methodist missionaries in New Mexico upon his return. His anti-Catholic message created a stir, though few converts, because few people were willing to publicly declare themselves Protestant in the midst of an overwhelming Catholic majority. The Baptist missionaries tried to recruit him and claimed that he had been willing to accept adult baptism. He never formally joined the Baptists, though he did preach in their meetings on several occasions. He continued preaching after the Methodist missionaries left, and he baptized and performed infant baptisms, even though the Methodists never ordained him. When he was close to death he apparently attempted to reconcile himself with the Roman Catholic Church, and it is not clear whether he received extreme unction on his deathbed.[39]

These converts are representative of thousands who became Protestants, in spite of the costs, because they had a strong encounter with God through the reading of the Bible or through the preaching of the missionaries. They were willing to pay the price of being Protestant because they had a clear sense of new life in Christ, of God's call on their lives, and because they were convinced that the Protestant message would make a fundamental change in the Latina community.

As the twentieth century began, Latinas were a very small and marginalized minority in the United States and Latino Protestants seemed almost nonexistent. On the basis of what was happening at that time, it is not surprising that some missionaries spoke of the need to evangelize the community before it completely disappeared. But two key events at the beginning of the twentieth century changed the face of the Latino community, and

39. Martínez, *Sea La Luz*, 57–58.

Latino Protestantism, in particular. The Azusa Street Revival that began in 1906 in Los Angeles would serve as the focal point for the expansion of modern Pentecostalism, which would eventually become the dominant form of Protestant faith among Latinos. The second key event was the beginning of the Mexican Revolution (1910). When linked to the beginning of US involvement in World War I, the revolution created the first major migration from Mexico to the United States. The migratory movement would be the first of a cyclical pattern that has kept the Latina population vibrant and growing. And the spiritual revival would give birth to an expression of Christian faith that became very attractive to Latinos and led to significant growth in the Protestant community.

Chapter 4

Ministry among the "Northern Mexicans" (1901–1940)

The face of the Latino community and of Latino Protestantism in particular was radically changed by events occurring at the end of the nineteenth and beginning of the twentieth century. The changing economy of the Southwest adversely affected the small communities of northern New Mexico, southern Colorado, and central Texas. The Spanish-American War (1898) brought both Puerto Rico and Cuba under the direct control or indirect influence of the United States. In the Southwest, the Mexican Revolution (1910), combined with US involvement in World War I, created the first significant migratory flow from Mexico into the United States. Later, when the Great Depression started (1929), there would be a forced reverse migration. This would be the first major deportation of Mexicans by the US government back to Mexico. Part of its significance is that it would include people born in the United States.

As a result of the Spanish-American War, both Puerto Rico and Cuba became open to Protestant missionaries and quickly became Protestant mission fields after 1898. Though the history of those missionary efforts is beyond the scope of this work, this expansion would greatly influence Latina Protestantism in the United States. When people from these islands began to migrate to the United States in significant numbers in the middle of the twentieth century, a growing percentage of these migrants would be Protestant, due to the earlier work of Protestant missionaries. Also, Protestant pastors and leaders from these islands would have a significant influence on Latino Protestantism, primarily among their own people. But a growing number would become key leaders in US denominations, having a significant impact throughout the Latino community.

But the most important event for the expansion of Latino Protestantism during the twentieth century was the Azusa Street Revival that began in Los Angeles in 1906. It became the launching pad for modern-day Pentecostalism to expand into the Latino community and into Latin America. With very few exceptions, by the end of the twentieth century Pentecostalism was the predominant expression of Protestantism among US Latinos throughout the United States and in most parts of Latin America.

US Expansion into the Spanish-Speaking World—Round Two

The Spanish-American War (1898) generated a major territorial expansion of the United States into the Spanish-speaking world of the Americas. As a result of the war, Spain lost four of its last colonies: Cuba, Puerto Rico, Guam, and the Philippines. Cuba became an independent country, though under the direct influence of the United States.[1] Puerto Rico became a colony of the United States in 1899, as did Guam and the Philippines. Since then, the relationship of Puerto Rico and its citizens to the United States has been redefined several times. For example, in 1917 Puerto Ricans were declared US citizens through the Jones-Shafroth Act, which made it possible to draft them to serve in World War I.[2] Today Puerto Rico is called a commonwealth in English and an *estado libre asociado* in Spanish. The two terms do not mean the same thing, so it is not clear what Puerto Rico is as a political entity, other than that it is neither an independent country nor a state of the Union.

The major Protestant denominations that began mission work in both Cuba and Puerto Rico established comity agreements to divide the islands geographically so that they would not compete directly with each other. Though the denominations and mission agencies not involved in these comity agreements obviously did not take them into account, they did give the participating mission agencies a clear place for ministry. Several US-based denominations developed a significant presence on each island. When significant migratory flows began from Puerto Rico and Cuba, each sent Protestant migrants to the United States. But more importantly, because of this

---

1. The Platt Amendment guaranteed this until it was repealed in 1934. "Platt Amendment (1903)," Our Documents, accessed March 29, 2017, https://ourdocuments.gov/doc.php?flash=true&doc=55.

2. "Puerto Ricans Become U.S. Citizens, Are Recruited for War Effort," History Channel, "This Day in History—Mar. 02, 1917," accessed March 29, 2017, http://www.history.com/this-day-in-history/puerto-ricans-become-u-s-citizens-are-recruited-for-war-effort.

earlier mission work, a significant number of trained pastors and leaders on these islands migrated to the United States.

Continuing Migration within and into the Southwest

At the beginning of the twentieth century, the major population bases of Latinos in the Southwest were places where few "Americans" entered. For example, one of the interesting characteristics of southern Texas was that it continued to be linked to the economy of Mexico throughout the nineteenth century. Anglos from the East did not enter the region in significant numbers, though the few that did quickly took over its economy (for example, the Kings and the Kenedys, who became owners of large parts of south Texas through various "legal" and "semilegal" means). But the region was isolated from the rest of the United States and was slow in being worked into the economic grid of the country. For example, Brownsville was not linked by rail to the rest of the country until 1904.[3] The region was never a place for significant Anglo migration, and it maintained an overwhelming Latino (Mexican and Mexican American) population throughout the twentieth century.[4]

Similarly, there was limited migration from the East into northern New Mexico and southern Colorado. Throughout the nineteenth and twentieth centuries, these rural areas remained largely Hispanic or Native American in demographic makeup. Nonetheless, many of the small communities in the region began to shrink, because the changing economy made it impossible for the traditional pastoral economy of the region to sustain the population. By the end of the nineteenth century, *neomejicanos* were already migrating west, mostly to California, looking for better economic prospects. People from the small communities of the region would continue to migrate toward the cities or toward other parts of the country throughout the twentieth century.

But the most important change in the Latina population of the Southwest came with the beginning of the Mexican Revolution in 1910. The push for social change after the long Porfirio Díaz dictatorship created a massive

---

3. "St. Louis, Brownsville and Mexico Railway," *Wikipedia*, last modified October 24, 2016, https://en.wikipedia.org/wiki/St._Louis,_Brownsville_and_Mexico_Railway.

4. Toward the end of the twentieth century this would begin to change a bit as new immigrants from Central America diversified the Latino population of the region.

social upheaval throughout the country, with one of the focal points being in northern Mexico. Crossing the border into the United States became the escape valve for those fleeing the violence, or those on the losing side of battles. In places like southern and central Texas, many of these migrants already had links with the local population. The population grew due to the new migrants, keeping the ethnic makeup of these areas overwhelmingly Latina.

One of the places where this migration created major demographic changes was Los Angeles. El Pueblo de Nuestra Señora la Reina de los Ánge-les del Río de Porciúncula had been established in 1781 during the Span-ish colonial period, but it had never had a large population base. It began to grow after the US takeover and became a very "American" city during the first part of the twentieth century. Yet there had always been a Latino base in the city. The new immigrants fleeing the violence in Mexico were different from the *californios* who had lived in the region for many years. Because of their number, this new population became the face of "Mexicans" in Los Angeles. The change they brought was so significant that most of the multigeneration US-born Latino population in Los Angeles today traces its roots to the Mexican Revolution, and later migrations, and not to the earlier *californios*.[5]

These Mexican immigrants were largely welcome in the United States because they started coming about the time the country entered World War I. The United States needed laborers to take the place of the soldiers that were going to war. The Mexicans entered the workforce at the low end, working on farms or in low-salary urban jobs. Their labor became an im-portant support to the war effort, so their presence was not questioned very much, if at all.

Latinas from southern Texas and northern New Mexico had already begun to migrate to other parts of the United States looking for employment opportunities before these new immigrants arrived. During this period, some of them also became part of the annual migration patterns that took them to several western states for labor-intensive agricultural jobs. These migratory patterns would become a way of life for generations of Latinas, particularly after World War II.

---

5. "El Pueblo de Los Angeles Historical Monument," City of Los Angeles, accessed March 29, 2017, http://elpueblo.lacity.org/historyeducation/ElPuebloHistory/Mexicans/index.html.

End of the First Round of "Mexican" Protestant Mission

Some of the assumptions made about the "Mexicans" by the first generation of Protestant missionaries in the Southwest during the nineteenth century were beginning to change by the beginning of the twentieth century. The most significant change was demographic. During the nineteenth century, most Latinos in the Southwest were in small rural communities, and so most Latino Protestants churches were established in those communities. These churches were all small, and their financial bases were limited. As Latinas began to migrate toward urban areas and new immigrants entered from Mexico, the face of the Latino community would change, as would Protestant ministry.

The Northern Presbyterians in New Mexico/southern Colorado had developed a mission strategy based on establishing educational institutions in rural communities that had no public schools. This had opened doors for them in many Latino communities during the nineteenth century. Many of their Latino churches in the region were started in conjunction with the Presbyterian schools. But by the early part of the twentieth century, most communities in the region had public schools, so the need for the Presbyterian schools began to fade. Over sixty schools were started in the late nineteenth and early twentieth centuries. By 1910, only sixteen of them were still in existence, and by 1930 only seven remained.[6]

The few that survived struggled significantly, because they depended on outside funding, since the local communities could not support them.[7] Some of these remaining schools continued to play a role in the development of a Latino Presbyterian identity in the region, and some were even a key part of their local communities, particularly in rural areas. But, overall, their influence quickly faded once the government began to provide education. Moreover, many of the communities in which Presbyterians had established Latino congregations began to lose population, and even disappear, as the changing economy caused people to migrate out of the area in the first part of the twentieth century.

The other major Presbyterian educational effort in the region, the College of the Southwest in Del Norte, Colorado, described in the last chapter, had to close its doors in 1901 due to a weak financial foundation. The Latino churches

---

6. Ruth Kerns Barber and Edith J. Agnew, *Sowers Went Forth: The Story of Presbyterian Missions in New Mexico and Southern Colorado* (Albuquerque: Menaul Historical Library of the Southwest, 1981), 159–60.

7. Barber and Agnew, *Sowers Went Forth*, 159–60.

would find themselves in similar situations. Most of the churches depended on outside financial support to pay their pastors. As populations shifted, the congregations consolidated in the largest communities and cities, which caused more churches to close. But most of the Latino churches that continued during this period did so through the financial support of outside agencies.

During the first part of the twentieth century, Presbyterians in the region began to put more energy into medical work. Because of the isolated nature of many of the communities and the primitive conditions many people lived in, there was a need for basic medical services and for clinics and hospitals. The same women's missionary societies that had helped fund the schools also helped fund nurses, doctors, basic clinics, and even hospitals. The educational and medical work in the area was placed under one board. These provided important medical services for the isolated communities of the region through the 1970s, when the last of the clinics were closed or integrated into local government efforts.[8]

But even as the early Presbyterian work was closing or shrinking, new ministry efforts developed in the new population bases. The very small ministries that were started during the late nineteenth century in California became the base for much stronger ministry in the first part of the twentieth century, once the Mexican Revolution created a migratory flow. The US Board of Home Missions created a Mexican Department that officially lasted only one year. But the person named superintendent of Mexican work, Robert McLean, continued working with the presbyteries in Los Angeles and Riverside, who asked him to organize the Spanish-language work. "He recognized the magnitude of immigration across the U.S.-Mexican border and the need to minister among those recently arrived from Mexico."[9] His dream was to establish strong churches in the major Southwestern cities of Los Angeles, San Antonio, and El Paso. By 1920, a number of Latino pastors from Mexico and New Mexico had settled in the Los Angeles area and served as the key leaders in the development of new churches in the area. These ministries continued to develop until the economic collapse of the Great Depression. Most of the growth of the PCUSA among Latinos during this period was a result of this vision and energy stimulated by the migratory flow of the Mexican Revolution.[10]

8. Barber and Agnew, *Sowers Went Forth*, 131–43.

9. Jane Atkins-Vasquez, *Hispanic Presbyterians in Southern California: One Hundred Years of Ministry* (Los Angeles: Synod of Southern California and Hawaii, 1988), 3.

10. Atkins-Vasquez, *Hispanic Presbyterians*, 2–4.

Southern Presbyterians in Texas started their mission work among Latinos later than their northern counterparts and continued to see growth into the first part of the twentieth century. The Latino churches of the region established what was known as the Tex-Mex Presbytery in 1908. But the role of this presbytery was never very clear. Should it develop into a presbytery like the "Anglo" ones, or should it be a "holding tank" for groups that could not yet meet all the requirements needed to be fully recognized churches in the "regular" presbyteries? Its role became that of a conduit for financial support from the Synod of Texas for the Latino churches that could not provide sufficient financial support for their ministries. When churches became self-supporting, they joined their geographical presbytery. The Tex-Mex Presbytery was dissolved in 1955, once the existing churches joined other presbyteries.[11] Two of the unintended results of the dissolution were that new Latino Presbyterian churches were not started in Texas and several of the existing churches slowly disappeared, even as the Latina population of the state continued to grow.

Methodist Episcopal Church ministry efforts were also impacted by the changing economic and demographic realities at the beginning of the twentieth century. Thomas and Emily Harwood found whole communities that were originally from New Mexico living in California.[12] The changing economy caused people to move west, destroying the small communities in which many of the *neomejicano* Methodist churches had been established. Many of the early Latino Methodist churches died because the communities around them began to shrink in population. The older churches that remained were located in larger towns and cities that had a more stable population or new immigration. While migration was beginning to open new mission opportunities, the work in New Mexico began a serious decline.

The newer churches established in the twentieth century tended to be in areas where the new Mexican migrants were establishing themselves. The demographic shift created the need for a shift in ministry focus. As with the Presbyterians, the Methodists expanded their ministry efforts toward the new population centers, particularly toward southern California, southern Arizona, and south Texas. Migrants fleeing the Mexican Revolution became the mission focus of the Methodist work after 1910. The

11. R. Douglas Brackenridge and Francisco O. García-Treto, *Iglesia Presbiteriana: A History of Presbyterians and Mexican Americans in the Southwest* (San Antonio: Trinity University Press, 1974).

12. Harriet S. Kellogg, *Life of Mrs. Emily J. Harwood* (Albuquerque: El Abogado Press, 1903), 340.

new migrants, including a few Mexican Methodists and some ordained Methodist pastors, impacted the existing churches in the region. These served as the basis for establishing new churches and expanding the ministry. Félix Gutiérrez describes 1920–1940 as the missionary era of Latino Methodism.[13] In both the MEC and the MECS, the opportunities opened up by the migration of the Mexican Revolution led to establishing new churches and the importation of trained leaders that made it possible to sustain that growth throughout this period.

The MECS work in Texas and southern Arizona also went through significant changes as the Mexican Revolution changed cross-border relationships. During the nineteenth century, all the work on the border had been linked to work in Mexico. But that ceased making sense as the work in Mexico began to grow and as the Mexican Revolution changed the relationships in the border region. As a result, the churches in Texas were separated from the growing churches in Mexico but were not clearly connected to US churches. By 1913, the "Mexican" churches in Texas were organized into their own Mission Conference, which would be merged into what became the Río Grande Conference in 1939. The MECS continued to establish churches in Texas and Arizona, and even established congregations in southern California.

As the MEC and MECS got closer to merging, which happened in 1939, there was some concern about ministry overlap in California and Arizona. But this was resolved with the merger. In spite of the economic setbacks of the Great Depression, Methodists were able to expand their ministry among Latinas during this period. Methodists, both North and South, in both the United States and Mexico, reported a spirit of revival that created the commitment to evangelism and church planting. Pablo García Verduzco, an MECS pastor in Texas, described the environment as one in which the people shared what they had with each other and "many souls that Christ won with his precious blood would come to his feet, feeling the spiritual joy of God's salvation."[14]

From the late nineteenth century into the first years of the twentieth century, the two Methodist bodies constituted the largest denominational tradition of Latino Protestants. But they were also the tradition that lost the

13. Justo L. González, ed., *Each in Our Own Tongue: A History of Hispanics in United Methodism* (Nashville: Abingdon, 1991), 74.

14. Pablo García Verduzco, *Bosquejo histórico del Metodismo Mexicano* (Nashville: Cokesbury Press, 1933), 33. My translation of "Muchas almas que Cristo ganó con su preciosa sangre venían a sus pies, sientiendo el gozo espiritual de la salvación de Dios."

most pastors to other denominations. Several times in the late nineteenth and early twentieth century former Methodist pastors were found on the pastoral rolls of other denominations. There are reports of Methodist pastors who later worked for the Presbyterians, the Baptists, and the Seventh-Day Adventists.[15] But the largest group of Methodist pastors who left the denomination eventually became Pentecostal pastors.

At the beginning of the twentieth century, the two largest Protestant groups among Latinas were the Methodists and the Presbyterians, reflecting the missionary fervor of these groups during this period. But they would soon lose their prominence in the first part of the new century. Many other Protestant denominations would begin working among Latinos, and several of these would grow faster than the Methodists or the Presbyterians. Though both groups continued to grow in the number of Latina members through the first part of the twentieth century, the prominent role they had among Latina Protestants would begin to ebb.

New Denominational Efforts in the Southwest

The three denominational families that became the most prominent among Latinas during the twentieth century all began their work around the beginning of that century. Several Protestant denominational families began working among Latinos in the first couple decades of the century, but a small group of denominations soon outgrew the rest. Most of the ministry continued to be in the Southwest, though gradually other parts of the country would also see a Latino Protestant presence as Latinos established themselves there.

The one Protestant group that began work in the nineteenth century and continued to grow significantly throughout the twentieth century was the **Baptist General Convention of Texas**, part of the Southern Baptist Convention. The irregular growth of the late nineteenth century, described in the last chapter, gradually stabilized, and in 1910 a group of twenty-four Latino churches organized themselves as the **Convención Bautista Mexicana de Texas** (Mexican Baptist Convention of Texas). A number of Baptist associations throughout Texas worked with this new convention to estab-

15. See Juan Francisco Martínez, "Origins and Development of Protestantism among Latinos in the Southwestern United States, 1836–1900" (PhD diss., Fuller Theological Seminary, School of World Mission, 1996).

lish "Mexican" churches. Together they organized training programs for "Mexican" pastors, and in 1925 they began the Mexican Bible Institute. They also established other ministries during this period, including the Mexican Baptist Children's Home in 1944.[16]

An early Baptist leader described the condition of their churches (in Spanish), which would have been representative of many Latino Protestant churches during the early part of the twentieth century.

> For many years most of the congregations did not have buildings to celebrate their services, and had to do them in homes, in some public school classroom or hall, under trees in the countryside, along rivers, in improvised coverings or wherever possible.
>
> Since the congregations did not have a building during those times, they struggled with the issue of seats and other objects needed for the [worship] service; lighting, for example. In most cases we used candles, petroleum lamps and improvised oil lamps. . . . Nonetheless, the majestic advancement of the ministry among our people throughout the State was uncontainable; because frequently we would receive news of new conquests and encouraging advancements; among them, that of the organization of new churches, Sunday Schools, of conversions and of baptisms.[17]

The evangelistic zeal of the Baptist associations throughout the state resulted in significant growth in the number of Latina Baptists in Texas. Though the Methodists and Presbyterians continued to grow during this period, by the beginning of World War II the Mexican Baptist Convention was the largest

---

16. Joshua Grijalva, *A History of Mexican Baptists in Texas, 1881–1981* (Dallas: Baptist General Convention of Texas, 1982), 36–66.

17. Benjamín Díaz, "Compendio de la historia de la Convención Bautista Mexicana de Texas" (unpublished manuscript, n.d.), 36. The quote is my translation of the following:

> La mayor parte de las congregaciones por muchos años no tuvieron templos para celebrar sus cultos, y tenían que hacerlos en las casas, en alguna aula o salón de escuelas públicas, en arboledas del campo, en los ríos, en improvisadas enramadas o donde se podía.
>
> En tanto que no tenían templo las congregaciones de aquellos tiempos, luchaban con el problema de asientos y de otros objetos necesarios para el culto; el alumbrado por ejemplo: En la mayoría de los casos nos alumbrábamos con velas, lámparas de petróleo y hasta con improvisados candiles. . . . No obstante ello, el majestuoso avance de la obra entre nuestro pueblo en todo el Estado era incontenible; pues frecuentemente se tenía noticia de nuevas conquistas y alentadores adelantos; entre ellos, la de la organización de nuevas iglesias, de Escuelas Dominicales, de conversiones y de bautismos.

migrant workers justly so that they would be attracted to the gospel. This included paying them equally, treating them fairly, alleviating human suffering, providing social services and Christian schools, and evangelizing them.[31] It also meant that the historic Protestant denominations needed to work together to support Latina migrant workers more effectively because of the "guerilla sects." "The fanatical earnestness of the Pentecostal people, the Holy Rollers, and the Seventh-Day Adventists, the persistent propaganda of Mormons" were seen as negatively affecting the Latino work of the denominations linked to the HMC.[32] Though the historic denominations had more resources, and were still larger than the other movements at that time, it was clear that these "guerilla sects" were becoming more attractive to Latinas than the historic Protestant denominations.

New York—Second Focal Point of Protestant Ministry

The first place where significant ministry among Latinos developed outside of the Southwest was New York City. There had been some outreach efforts there in the late nineteenth century, but only one church was established. In 1912 the New York City Mission Society began working among Spanish-speaking immigrants, mostly from Spain and the Caribbean. The society later established the Church of the Good Neighbor. This was the first recorded Latino congregation in the city and later became a "mother church" for many other Latina churches.[33] The number of Latino churches grew as the Latina population increased. By 1937 there were fifty-five Spanish-speaking congregations in the city. Six of them were affiliated with the New York Mission Society, eighteen were part of various Pentecostal denominations, and the rest were of other denominations, including the Christian and Missionary Alliance, the Seventh-Day Adventist Church, various Baptist groups, the Lutheran church, the Methodist church, and the Presbyterian church.[34]

31. Home Missions Council, *Fifteenth Annual Report of the Home Missions Council and Council of Women for Home Missions* (New York: Home Missions Council, 1922), 219.

32. Home Missions Council, *Eighteenth Annual Report*, 170.

33. Holland, "A Chronology of Significant Protestant Beginnings in Hispanic Ministry in the USA."

34. Frederick L. Whitam, "New York's Spanish Protestants," *Christian Century* 79, no. 6 (February 7, 1962): 162.

Ministry in Other Parts of the United States

During the 1930s, the (Old) Mennonites, the Mennonite Brethren, the Church of God (Anderson, Indiana), and the Salvation Army all started Latino churches in the United States. By this time there were small pockets of Latinos in Chicago and in parts of the Midwest that slowly became the focal points of Protestant mission work in these areas. Most of these denominations were small, but so were the Latina populations in the Midwest until after World War II. This meant that most of the mission efforts among Latinas in these areas were small.

In 1930 the Home Mission Council of New York published the book *The Northern Mexican* by Robert McLean. Most of the book is dedicated to describing the "Mexican" population in the United States, including socioeconomic, social, educational, and religious issues. The author focuses on the Southwest but includes information about Mexican migration into other parts of the United States and mentions that some groups, particularly the Baptists, had established ministries throughout the Midwest and that the Baptists had established an association of Mexican Baptist churches outside of the Southwest. Though the book focuses on the Mexican population, it attempts to give a fairly complete report of all Latino Protestant ministries in the country, including work being done among other Latinos, though it does not clearly distinguish the various Latina ethnic and national groups.

McLean's book has a clear evangelistic focus, particularly in reference to the new migrants into the Midwest. In his concluding paragraph he states: "The northern Mexican is not adequately cared for either religiously or socially. He is a newcomer in the communities where he lives and has to put up with the most inadequate conditions and the most unsatisfactory accommodations which are to be found in the community. Because he is a newcomer in these communities, adequate provision has not been made for his religious needs."[35] The book has a complete listing of all churches and ministries, including schools and community centers, of the denominations it surveys. It reports 367 churches with 26,599 adult members. These denominations have 591 pastors, teachers, and other workers. The book also reports thirty-nine Protestant schools and forty-four community centers that focus their ministry on the Latino community. The book reports on the work of fifteen church groups but does not include any Pentecostal denominations or the Seventh-Day Adventist Church.[36]

35. McLean, *The Northern Mexican*, 23.
36. McLean, *The Northern Mexican*, 43.

	Churches	Members	Workers
Baptist, Northern	40	3,500	64
Baptist, Southern	56	3,562	31
Congregational	7	345	22
Congregational (So. Cal.)	2	125	5
Disciples	10	805	??
Free Methodist	10	300	16
Friends	2	46	2
Interdenominational	2	164	7
Lutheran	3	266	5
Methodist (North)	55	4,617	126
Methodist (South)	62	5,710	93
Church of the Nazarene	11	415	9
PCUSA	60	4,185	144
PCUS	41	2,134	26
United Brethren	6	425	19

Azusa Street—Latino Protestantism Takes on a New Face

While Protestant denominations were expanding their ministry among Latinas, the Azusa Street Revival and the churches and denominations that came out of it would radically change the face of Latino and Latin American Protestantism. Though modern-day Pentecostalism had several manifestations elsewhere in the world before 1906, it was the revival that began at the Azusa Street Mission in April 1906 that initiated the rapid expansion of the Pentecostal movement throughout the world, and into the Spanish-speaking world in particular. By the middle of the twentieth century, modern-day Pentecostalism and its various offshoots would become the most prominent expression of Protestant faith in Latin America and among US Latinas.

Because most of the early leadership of the revival was either white or African American, the story of Azusa Street, as usually told, focuses on the impact in those two communities and efforts of leaders from those communities to overcome the racial divide that separated them. But there were a number of Mexican, Mexican American, and other Latin American converts during the first years of the revival. Some of them would later serve as pastors, missionaries, and founders of churches and denominations throughout Latin America and the Spanish-speaking United States. Non-Latino converts also went out from Azusa Street to Latin American countries and played key roles in the establishment of Pentecostalism there.

Some of the early Latino converts, such as Abundio López and Juan Navarro Martínez, were given licenses for ministry in 1909 by William Seymour, the founder of the Azusa Street Mission. At least three Pentecostal denominations that formed directly out of the Azusa Street Revival, the Assemblies of God (AG), the Apostolic Assembly of the Faith in Christ Jesus (USA), and the Apostolic Church of the Faith in Christ Jesus (Mexico), had Latino leaders that had been converted during the revival.

Many of the early Latino converts to Pentecostalism eventually joined the AG when it organized in 1914. This was particularly true in Texas and other parts of the Southwest. In southern California, many other Pentecostal movements developed, which meant the AG did not have as large a presence there during the early part of the twentieth century.

The expansion of the Pentecostal message among US Latinos and in Latin America during the early years happened largely through the work of independent Pentecostal preachers. Little is known about many of these early leaders, but they had a significant influence on the growth of Latina Pentecostalism, particularly in Texas and California. Itinerant preachers took the Pentecostal message to places where there were Spanish-speaking people. Many independent churches and movements came out of these early efforts, though eventually most of these churches and leaders joined one of the major denominations that emerged from the modern Pentecostal revivals. Some formed their own smaller denominations, and others would later develop as Pentecostalism grew and diversified.

Even though the early leaders of the Azusa Street Revival and the Pentecostal movement sought unity, there were several types of divisions among the early converts. Two of these divisions led to the formation of the Apostolic Assembly and the Apostolic Church, respectively. One major division had to do with race. Even though one of the goals of the revival was racial reconciliation, the racial divisions of the period soon manifested themselves in the life of the early Pentecostal churches. Groups that had sought to work together soon divided along racial lines. There were also several doctrinal divisions in the early movement. The one that created the clearest long-term division among the descendants of the revival was related to the baptismal formula and the issue of how one understands the Godhead of Father, Son, and Holy Spirit. The majority of Pentecostals followed the Trinitarian formula and the doctrinal definition of the Council of Nicea (AD 325). But a significant minority were "Oneness" Pentecostals, baptizing in the name of Jesus, and stating that Father, Son, and Holy Spirit were three aspects of God, not three persons.

It was at the conjunction of these two early divisions that the first, and the largest, US Latino Protestant denomination was born. By 1912, two leaders that came out of Azusa, Juan Navarro and Francisco Llorente, had begun to evangelize the "Mexican" population in southern California. The Pentecostal Assemblies of the World, a predominantly African American Oneness Pentecostal group, licensed them and other early Latino leaders. They started churches around southern California and organized these churches into the first Latino Protestant denomination in 1925. The Apostolic Assembly of the Faith in Christ Jesus was established in the United States, and later its sister denomination, the Apostolic Church of the Faith in Christ Jesus, would be established in Mexico. Other smaller "Apostolic" movements would also develop during this period as other converts took the "in the name of Jesus" baptismal formula with them as they preached the Pentecostal message in new areas.

The Apostolic Assembly grew as its original members took the Oneness message to various parts of the United States and Mexico. In 1930 it officially incorporated as a separate denomination and cut formal links with the Pentecostal Assemblies of the World. By 1940 it had sixty churches throughout the Southwest, in spite of the deportations after the Great Depression. During the early years it was closely linked to its sister church in Mexico, a cross-border relationship that lasted until the 1980s.[37]

Another denomination that was born indirectly out of the Azusa Street Revival, and had an early Latino presence, was the International Church of the Foursquare Gospel started by Aimee Semple McPherson. By 1925 it had Sunday school classes in Spanish. Francisco "El Azteca" Olazábal preached at some of the meetings, and a young convert who would later be known as the actor Anthony Quinn was also an early preacher. During the late 1920s and through the 1930s, it established Spanish-language congregations in southern California, Texas, and other parts of the Southwest. By 1944 there were sixty-three Latino congregations in the Foursquare Church.[38]

---

37. Martínez Guerra and Luis Scott, *Iglesias peregrinas en busca de identidad*, 102.

38. Juan Francisco Martínez, *Los Protestantes: An Introduction to Latino Protestantism in the United States* (Santa Barbara, CA: ABC-CLIO, 2011), 78. See also Jim Scott, "Foursquare Hispana—Part 2," *Features*, last updated April 30, 2013, http://www.foursquare.org/news/article

The Church of God (Cleveland, Tennessee) is the Pentecostal denomination with the second-largest Latina presence in the United States today. Its roots are in the Holiness movements of the nineteenth century, and so it predates Azusa Street. It began its first Spanish-language congregation in Raton, New Mexico, in 1911. By World War II it had divided its work among Latinos into two major regions, one based in San Antonio for ministry west of the Mississippi River, and the other based in New York for work in the East. Because of the growth of Latino churches, it would continue dividing into new districts throughout the twentieth century.

The Church of God of Prophecy split from the Church of God in 1923. It did not begin ministry among Latinas on its own, but connected to one of the independent Pentecostal movements that developed during the early years of Pentecostalism. The first Latino churches that would later join the denomination began as independent Pentecostal churches in 1933 around Riverside, California. Two pastors, Eduardo Rodríguez and José Jiménez, started several churches in the area and organized them into the Movimiento Libre Pentecostal in 1935. This group of churches was invited to join the denomination in 1945 and became the core of its Latino congregations.

Throughout the Southwest, small groups of Latino Pentecostal churches joined together into clusters of churches like the Movimiento Libre Pentecostal. Many of them would eventually join larger denominations. But, as the Pentecostal message spread into the Latina community, many converts without official credentials from existing denominations would begin preaching and establishing churches. Others would leave existing churches to spread the message into new areas. This would lead to many more converts and to a growing number of mini-denominations and independent churches.

Signs of Racial Tension among Pentecostals

The relationship between Anglo leaders and Latino converts clearly demonstrated a power differential. In most Protestant denominations, Latino congregations were financially dependent on the Anglo leadership. Occasionally there seemed to be overt tensions between Latinos and Anglos, but in most denominations Latinos had little power and their churches tended to be

/foursquare_hispana_part_2; James C. Scott Jr., *Aimee: La gente Hispana estaba en su corazon* (Seattle: Foursquare Media, 2010).

small and weak. Because of the power differential, most Latinas accepted the leadership of the Anglo missionaries.

This was different among the Pentecostals. Many of the early Latino Pentecostal preachers established their own churches and had never depended on Anglo support. Because of these early efforts, some Latino leaders established loose networks of churches and some advocated for the formation of Latino-led movements. Some of these remained independent. But most Latino pastors either were originally licensed for ministry by one of the existing denominations or were encouraged to join it. Many of these independent preachers joined the Assemblies of God. And the AG was one of the first Pentecostal movements to license missionaries to work among Latinos. It was in this denomination that racial tensions would have the clearest negative impact.

Though many Latino preachers and Anglo missionaries from the AG worked among the Spanish-speaking people, eventually the tensions of the 1920s became focused on the work of three key people. Henry Ball, a missionary in Texas, organized some of the new independent Pentecostal churches and pastors under the AG. He became well known because of his long-term leadership among Latinos in the AG, where he published Pentecostal materials in Spanish, prepared new pastors for ministry, and translated and compiled the first widely used hymnal for Spanish-speaking churches, *Himnos de Gloria*. But he is also well known for his tensions with some of the first generation of Latino AG leaders.

Alice Luce was a key leader in Latino AG work in California. She worked with other missionaries to establish Latino AG churches in southern California. The work these missionaries did was not as successful as in Texas during the early years because several Pentecostal groups focused on the Latino community in that area. But she was crucial in starting a Latin American Bible Institute (LABI) in 1926 that is now based in La Puente, California. The various AG Bible institutes became a crucial part of the preparation of pastors and leaders for Latino AG churches.

The third key person in the AG Latino work was Francisco "El Azteca" Olazábal. He was a Mexican evangelist who became an AG pastor in 1918. He preached in many areas and started a church and Bible institute in El Paso in 1919. He also worked in the Los Angeles area, preaching and helping the ministry there. He became an influential leader among the "Mexicans" and led the cause to form a "Mexican" AG district. Both Ball and Luce wanted Latinos to lead their own churches and take over their own ministries. But both opposed Olazábal's actions in practice. When a majority of Latino pastors voted to form their own district in 1922, Ball worked with denominational headquarters to nullify the vote.

Because of the nullified vote, in 1924 a group Latino Pentecostal pastors, led by Olazábal, organized the Interdenominational Mexican Council of Christian Churches (Pentecostal) that later became CLADIC (Concilio Latinoamericano de Iglesias Cristianas) because other, non-Mexican, Latinos also became a part of the movement. Some of the early leaders eventually returned to the AG, but the split demonstrated the very real problem between Anglos and Latinos, even in denominations where Latinos led their own churches and funded their own projects. It would not be until 1939 that a Latino would be named leader of the Latin American District of the AG.[39] But the tensions would also be internal to the Latina community. After Olazábal died suddenly in 1937, a group of Puerto Rican leaders in New York, who had also been influenced by Olazábal, formed the Asamblea de Iglesias Cristianas (AIC) in 1939, splitting from CLADIC. From their perspective, CLADIC focused on the "Mexican" population of the Southwest, and they decided to focus on Puerto Ricans in the Northeast.[40]

Impact of the Great Depression

Prior to the Great Depression there was a slow but steady growth in the number of Latino Protestants. A number of Protestant denominations began Latina ministry during this period—indeed, all the denominations that would play a major role during the twentieth century. The migratory movements linked to the Mexican Revolution and World War I increased the Latino population, mostly in the Southwest.

But that migratory flow slowed down once World War I was over (1918) and the Mexican Revolution ended (1921). But the situation that affected migration from Mexico the most was the beginning of the Great Depression (1929). The Mexican workers who had helped the country during the war years were now seen as competition for the few existing employment opportunities. The economic tensions created by the Great Depression fueled a strong nativist movement in the United States. Many people said that white men should have priority as jobs became available. Several cities and

39. Gastón Espinosa, *Latino Pentecostals in America: Faith and Politics in Action* (Cambridge, MA: Harvard University Press, 2014), 164.
40. Espinosa, *Latino Pentecostals in America*, 268.

counties passed ordinances making it virtually impossible to hire Mexican Americans and Mexican immigrants for public works projects. They also pushed to deport foreign workers, mostly Mexicans and Mexican Americans.

As a result, government policy changed, and over five hundred thousand Mexicans were deported during the 1930s. This included a number of Latinas that had been born in the United States. The methods of deportation were fairly brutal, as people were forcibly rounded up and returned to Mexico in railcars, often with little food or water.

The massive size of the deportation, given the size of the Latino community of Mexican descent at the time, had a very negative impact on Latino Protestant churches. Many denominations lost pastors, key leaders, and churches in the midst of this deportation process. The AG reported losing over one hundred Latino churches during this period.[41] Other denominations also had to close churches, though most of the loss was felt by the Pentecostals, who worked among the poorest, those most likely to feel the direct impact of nativist attitudes.

But the deportations also exposed the racial tensions that existed among US Protestants. Mission agencies were very interested in evangelizing the "Mexicans," but they did not see a relationship between this and defending them when their rights were trampled. Henry Ball and other AG leaders reported that this attitude made it difficult for the churches to evangelize among Latinas. He also said the tough socioeconomic climate made it difficult for many Latino pastors to continue in ministry. They became a part of the migrant labor force that sought work wherever it could be found.

In general, during this period Latino Protestants had very small and insignificant roles within their denominations. Because they were such a small part of most denominations and since most non-Pentecostal Latino churches had some level of dependence on Anglo churches or on denominational structures, there were few direct challenges to the existing structures and their underlying assumptions. The only place where that was different was among Pentecostals. Their message of reconciliation and their self-supporting status created a different dynamic in which Latinas could not easily be ignored. It is not surprising that in this environment issues of Latino self-governance first developed and the changing economic realities of the Great Depression created the most tensions.

So the Great Depression created the first slowdown in migration from Mexico and the first major deportation back to Mexico. Many denomina-

41. Espinosa, *Latino Pentecostals in America*, 156.

tions also slowed down their ministries among Latinos. It would not be until the new migratory flow linked to World War II that these Protestants would regain a sense of mission to Latinos, particularly to those in the Southwest.

But the changes in the economy also created the beginning of a new migratory movement among US Latinos. Temporary or cyclical migration would become a life pattern for many Latinas from poor communities throughout the Southwest, with people from south Texas and northern Mexico, in particular.

This type of migration would define life for generations of families who followed agricultural jobs throughout the Southwest and into the Pacific Northwest. These patterns would affect many families. But they would also mean that ministry had to be done in new ways. Eventually, many of these migrant families settled in new parts of the United States, places where labor opportunities seemed to provide a brighter economic future.

Who Are the Latino Protestants at the Time of World War II?

During the first four decades of the twentieth century, the number of Protestant denominations working among Latinos continued to expand. The Pentecostals were also already working, but they were often not "seen" by Protestant leaders of other denominations. As the number of churches and ministries developed, different reports demonstrated that the number of Latino Protestants was growing, even if they were a small minority in the Latino population and an even smaller minority in their denominations. Some reports are detailed by denomination, so one can find out if a particular denomination is missing from the list. But other reports are more general, limiting the usefulness of the information. Nonetheless, these reports point to a slow but steady growth among Latino Protestants.

As stated earlier, the most complete report of Latino Protestantism during this period is Robert McLean's *The Northern Mexican*. The report demonstrates that the Latina Protestant community is not very large, even as a percentage of the Latino population. And overall, Latinos are still an invisible population by the late 1930s. Most are either in isolated population pockets, like south Texas, northern New Mexico, or the border regions, where they are not "seen," or they are a small portion of the population of larger cities, such as Los Angeles or New York.

The Latino Protestant churches that were developing at this time were outside the realms of influence in Protestantism. Most Latina Protestants were poor and their congregations were heavily dependent on denominational support. The major exceptions were Latino Pentecostals. While Protestant denominations were developing church structures that attempted to look like the dominant culture and were difficult to maintain by poor Latinos, Pentecostals were developing structures that were financially self-supporting from the very beginning. Leaders with limited formal theological education often led these churches. This limited the impact of such leaders, but it made it easier for churches to find pastors. This difference made it easier for Pentecostals to evangelize and establish new churches.

Latino Identity and Protestant Convictions

By this time the historical record is substantial enough that we can begin to see the contours of Latino Protestantism through the faces of its key leaders. This is the first generation of which we have more of a written record, including books, articles, and testimonials. Though they are linked to many denominational traditions, they have in common the experience of a personal encounter with God, being ostracized for their faith by the Latino Catholic majority, and living out their faith as part of a doubly marginalized community.

The conversion stories begin to take a couple of different forms during this period. On the one hand, the stories of conversion through Bible reading or through hearing the Bible being preached continued. On the other hand, the Pentecostal revivals put a greater emphasis on a direct encounter with God, often linked to physical or psychological healing and an ecstatic experience, such as speaking in tongues. These Pentecostal experiences empowered people to preach the gospel to others, and to make major sacrifices to take its message to the people. But the Pentecostal experiences also drew some people from one form of Protestantism into Pentecostal faith, much as they did in the English-speaking world. Though most of the Latino Pentecostal converts had left Catholicism, a few were from other Protestant traditions. There were also cases of movement from one Protestant denomination to another.

The reality of being a doubly marginalized community stands out during this period. Protestant mission agencies made increasing efforts to evangelize Latinas, and their efforts produced some results. But the nativist attitudes meant that Anglo Protestants did not always welcome Latinos. There was also a clear sense that Latinos could not lead their own churches, and so they were always seen as dependent on Anglo leadership. This racialized tension was seen throughout the Protestant world, including among Pentecostals, where Latinas had more of a voice in their own churches.

Conversion to Protestantism continued to create tensions with the Catholic majority in Latino communities. While there were occasional direct attacks on Latino Protestants or their churches, there was not much direct persecution in the United States, as there had been in the nineteenth century and as had continued in parts of Latin America. However, the social costs of becoming a Protestant believer continued strongly during this period; it meant being marginalized in the Latina community for being a Protestant and among Protestants for being Latino.

Nonetheless, Protestant converts were convinced, like the missionaries, that the message of the gospel would make a spiritual change in their lives and a social change in the Latino community. Though they had started in simple and primitive circumstances, they were able to make great strides because of the impact of the gospel in changing lives and raising the living standards of the converted.

José Celestino Rodríguez was originally from New Mexico. He was part of the last graduating class of the College of the Southwest in Del Norte, Colorado.[42] He moved to southern California before 1920, where he joined with other Presbyterian pastors from Mexico, and other parts of the Southwest, to lead the growing number of Latino Presbyterian churches in the region. Southern California Presbyterians were able to grow during this period because of the migration from Mexico and, to a lesser extent, from New Mexico and Texas. Rodríguez pastored several churches in the area until he retired in 1941.

One of the first Latino Seventh-Day Adventist pastors, **Marcial Serna**, had been a Methodist pastor before he converted to the Adventist faith in 1899. He was a pastor in Tucson, Arizona, and was approached by Adventist colporteurs that did not speak Spanish. Through a series of conversations, including a public debate, Serna became convinced that Saturday was the day of rest and that he should become a Seventh-Day Adventist. He became the first baptized convert in the region. In 1900 he became a licensed minister and, until his death in 1935, started several Latino churches in various parts of the Southwest. He played a key role in the early development of the Seventh-Day Adventists among Latinos in the Southwest, and is an example

---

42. Barber and Agnew, *Sowers Went Forth*, 68.

of one who converted from Catholicism to a form of Protestant faith and then, later, to a different form of Protestantism.[43]

The role of **Francisco "El Azteca" Olazábal** as an early Latino Pentecostal leader needs to be stressed. He was raised as a Methodist in Mexico and migrated to the United States as a young man. After a period of rebellion, he returned to the church and prepared for ministry as a Methodist pastor. He pastored a number of congregations in the United States and was ordained to Methodist ministry in 1916. A couple who had helped him commit to Methodist ministry attended the Azusa Street Mission and became Pentecostal. They reconnected with Olazábal in 1917 and prayed for his sick wife, Marina. She was healed, and they had a Pentecostal experience. He was ordained to AG ministry in 1918.

Olazábal was a dynamic evangelist who preached in many parts of the Spanish-speaking United States. He led the efforts to have Latino leadership in the AG. His actions led to a split with the AG, though he continued to influence Latino Pentecostalism until his death in 1937. He preached in many countries and influenced the development of Pentecostal churches and movements led by Latinos. Many of his disciples became leaders in various Pentecostal denominations, including the AG. He can legitimately be called the most influential Latino Protestant leader of his generation.

Romana Carbajal de Valenzuela was an early convert within the Apostolic (Oneness) thread of Pentecostalism. She had a Pentecostal experience in southern California and became a preacher of the Pentecostal message. The message had such an influence on her life that she returned to Mexico to preach to her family. A number of family members and others converted. As a woman, she could not pastor a congregation. So she worked with a converted Methodist minister who had been baptized in the name of Jesus and later became the pastor of the congregation she had started. It was through her evangelistic work that the Apostolic Church of Faith in Christ Jesus developed in Mexico. Her preaching also led to the conversion of Pentecostals that joined other movements. She is particularly important because she preached and evangelized, and was a key player in the founding of a denomination that did not ordain women.[44]

One of the first books written by a "Mexican" about Latino Protestantism in the United States was Pablo García Verduzco's *Bosquejo histórico del*

43. Vasquez, *La historia aun no contada*, 31–35.

44. "Nuestra Historia," Iglesia Apostolica de la fe en Cristo Jesús, A.R., accessed April 14, 2017, http://www.iafcj.org/conócenos#historia.

Metodismo Mexicano, published in 1933. Rev. García represents the period in which the Methodist Episcopal Church, South worked on both sides of the US-Mexico border, using transnational conferences to oversee the work. García was born in Mexico but heard the Protestant message in the border city of Eagle Pass, Texas. He was later ordained to ministry in Texas but served in some churches in Mexico. Of his forty-five years of ordained ministry, thirty-seven were spent at churches in Texas. Interestingly, his first wife was Mexican American. After she died he remarried, this time to an Anglo woman. The vision and reality of transnational Methodist ministry were lived by **Pablo García Verduzco.**[45]

The early work of the Church of the Nazarene among Latinas included two key women, one a convert and the other a missionary (Maye McReynolds). **Santos Elizondo** traveled to Los Angeles in 1905 to be treated for an illness. While there she heard the gospel and was converted through the ministry of McReynolds. She attempted to preach to her family in Arizona but was rebuffed. In 1907 she returned to her husband in El Paso. He physically abused her to try to get her to recant and return to Catholicism, but later he was also converted. She tried to present her testimony in existing churches but was told she could not speak because she was a woman. Nonetheless, she felt that God was calling her to preach, and so she started preaching in the streets. Through her pioneering work the first Latino Nazarene congregation in Texas was started in El Paso. She then crossed the border into Ciudad Juárez, where she started a children's home and later another congregation. She continued preaching and serving in the area for the rest of her life.

Latinos and Pentecostalism

The beginning and growth of Pentecostalism among Latinos marked a profound change among Latino Protestants. While most Protestant ministry among Latinas was based on models of dependency, Pentecostalism began to break that assumption. Latinos were seen in US society as people unable to take responsibility for their own churches and structures. It was assumed that Anglos needed to be in charge. Yet Latina Pentecostals were empowered by their encounter with God and began to take on full agency. They established and sustained their own churches; they evangelized others at their

---

45. Garcia Verduzco, *Bosquejo histórico del Metodismo Mexicano,* 47–49.

own initiative and at great personal cost; and they became cultural agents reframing the Pentecostal message in their own idiom.

One of the places where cultural agency was most clearly seen was in hymnology. All Latino Protestants were singing translated hymns at this time, including the Pentecostals. But the Pentecostals were singing them with guitars and changing the beats of the songs so that they felt "Latino." More importantly, Latina Pentecostals began to write their own hymns during this period. Those songs traveled both ways across the US-Mexico border as Pentecostals took their faith with them, changing the flavor of Latino Protestantism.[46]

The title of Ramírez's book, *Migrating Faith*, is an apt descriptor of how Latino Protestantism expanded during this period. A migratory people had encounters with God and began to develop their own expressions of Protestant faith in the midst of their migrations. As they migrated they took their faith with them and preached it to others. This concept of migration as mission would be crucial as Latino Protestantism moved into its next stage.

46. Daniel Ramírez, *Migrating Faith: Pentecostalism in the United States and Mexico in the Twentieth Century* (Chapel Hill: University of North Carolina Press, 2015).

Chapter 5

Migrant Workers, Citizens, and Exiles (1941–1964)

The period from the start of World War II to the 1965 immigration act saw the beginning of another series of significant changes in the Latino community. On the one hand, US-born Latinos, including people from Puerto Rico, fought in World War II and gave their lives for their country. There was a growing sense within the Latina community that if they were willing to die for their country, they should also gain the benefits of citizenship. The GI Bill opened educational opportunities for many, and there was a sense that Latinas should and could gain the benefits of citizenship. For these Latinos it meant using education as a means of becoming "good" citizens and being able to fit into US society. Because of the historical link between evangelization and Americanization among many Protestant missionaries, many Protestants assumed that education would give Latino Protestants the potential of becoming model citizens.

But for many other Latinas, the possibilities of a better future were linked to internal migration. Many Mexican Americans and Puerto Ricans became part of a migrant labor force. Some moved into urban areas while others moved from place to place following the temporary labor needs of industrialized agriculture. They also began to settle in new parts of the United States. But they were also in the same labor pool as many other people who were looking for new opportunities through many of the same labor options.

Some of those who looked for new opportunities were new migrants from Latin America. World War II had created new migratory patterns from Latin America. The need for temporary workers to take the place of the soldiers going to war reopened the door to Mexican laborers through the Bracero Program that started when the United States entered the war and continued until 1964. Through a number of signed agreements between the

United States and Mexico, temporary workers came north, mostly to work in agriculture. But these agreements did not provide for all those who wanted to work in the United States. So this period also saw an increase in undocumented workers, and their massive deportation.

The temporary agricultural workers that came into the country presented expanding opportunities for Protestant ministry. But they also raised questions about their treatment and what rights US migrant workers should have in relationship to the temporary workers.

The end of the war also saw the beginning of significant, and constant, Puerto Rican migration to the mainland, what has been called the "Great Migration," particularly to the Northeast. What had been small Puerto Rican ethnic enclaves in the 1930s would become significant neighborhoods in New York and elsewhere by the 1960s. Some Puerto Ricans would also join the ranks of agricultural workers through a number of government agreements.

Events outside the United States, in which it had a role, also helped change the face of the Latina population, once again. The Cuban Revolution in 1959, which overthrew a US-supported dictatorship, and the communist takeover of the island, became the reason for the creation of the air bridge between Havana and Miami of the 1960s that eventually brought hundreds of thousands of Cubans to the United States, all entering legally as political refugees. The US invasion of Santo Domingo in 1963 created a similar situation for Dominicans, though the migratory pattern there developed more slowly. Each new wave of immigrants presented new ministry opportunities and challenges for Protestant churches. And because of earlier Protestant mission work in the Caribbean, the Cuban and Puerto Rican migratory waves also brought the first significant group of Latin American Protestants and Protestant pastors. Many of these migrants joined existing churches, but many became the foundation of new congregations. These migratory waves also provided a generation of trained leaders who would impact a number of Protestant denominations, particularly the same denominations that had earlier sent missionaries to Cuba and Puerto Rico.

The focus of Protestant work among Latinas also began to change in this period. Historic church groups, such as Methodists and Presbyterians, had claimed the largest number of Latino Protestants in the nineteenth and early part of the twentieth century. But as evangelicals and Pentecostals expanded their ministries, this balance began to change. By the time of the 1965 immigration act, the Assemblies of God and the Southern Baptist Convention ranked first and third among denominations in number of Latino members, and other Pentecostal and evangelical denominations continued in a growth trajectory, beginning to overtake the historic denominations in Latino churches and church members.

Historically, in the 1960s the mainline denominations began a membership decline in the United States that continues to this day. Some of these denominations would continue to grow in number of Latinas as the Latino population increased in the United States. But eventually the membership decline in these denominations would be seen among Latinos as well. Also during the 1960s, the differences in ministry philosophy among Latinas between evangelical and mainline churches would become more pronounced and would adversely impact the growth of Latino churches in the latter denominations. Reports about Latina Protestantism during this period tended to focus on the work of the mainline Protestant denominations, but, little by little, researchers began to recognize the growing influence of evangelicals and Pentecostals among Latinos.

Braceros and Migrant Workers

The massive economic downturn of the Great Depression created the political environment that "justified" the massive deportation of Mexican workers, including US citizens of Mexican descent. But World War II created a new massive labor shortage, and the United States again looked south for a solution. Through a series of agreements with the Mexican government, the United States allowed temporary Mexican laborers (commonly called *braceros*, "those who work with their arms" or "manual labor") to enter the country to fill an important labor gap, particularly in the agricultural sector. The United States sought to address a labor shortage while Mexico hoped to modernize the state of rural Mexican laborers. These workers did some of the work that the drafted soldiers left undone, particularly in the Southwest.[1]

Though the program was started to help with the war effort, and as a way for Mexico to informally participate in the war, most of the almost five million workers that participated in the program from 1942 to 1964 entered the United States during the 1950s, particularly after 1954. During the 1940s the agreements did not provide enough visas for all the workers who wanted

---

1. See Ana Elizabeth Rosas, *Abrazando El Espíritu: Bracero Families Confront the US-Mexico Border* (Oakland: University of California Press, 2014), for an analysis of the impact of the Bracero Program on Mexican families.

to enter the country, nor to satisfy all the employers who wanted cheaper Mexican labor. So the number of undocumented workers grew during the war period, even as the Bracero Program allowed a significant number of Mexicans to enter the country legally.

By the end of the war, there was a growing undocumented Mexican population in the United States. Agricultural interests wanted more Mexican labor, so new laws were passed to renew the Bracero Program until 1964. But while the US government was signing agreements for more temporary workers, it was also taking actions against the undocumented. By 1954 the United States had begun another period of massive deportations of Mexican workers, a policy known as Operation Wetback.[2] Accounts differ as to the number of people deported during this operation, but as many as 1.5 million people were repatriated to Mexico. In spite of this repatriation, new people continued to migrate from Mexico. The interests of US agriculture and the needs of rural Mexican laborers intersected to create extensions of the Bracero Program. But those interests also drew more workers than allowed by the various temporary worker programs, and so undocumented workers continued to enter the United States.

Because of the temporary nature of their legal status, braceros and undocumented workers tended not to establish any roots in the country. Most of them left families in Mexico, which they supported through their labor in the United States. They hoped to improve their lives through earning extra income and investing in their lives in Mexico. But they saw their future in Mexico. The braceros had legal documents but very few legal rights. Their status was limited and depended on their employer. They remained in the States until their labor contract ended, and then returned to Mexico. Most lived in labor camps and had little time for activities other than work. So these workers did not establish many structures, religious or otherwise. The Protestant missionaries that ministered among them focused on providing basic services and inviting people to faith. But they did not expect braceros to be at the center of new churches. The churches that focused on inviting people to faith tended to encourage the converts to take their faith back to their communities in Mexico. These converts established many new, mostly Pentecostal, churches back in Mexico.

Because of the expanding interests of large-scale industrial agriculture, the need for low-skill, low-wage migrant workers continued to grow during

2. "Operation Wetback," *Wikipedia*, last modified March 2, 2017, https://en.wikipedia.org/wiki/Operation_Wetback.

this period. The braceros and the undocumented met part of the need. But many people born in the United States also joined this labor force, including many Mexican Americans, particularly from south Texas. These people lived in small communities that could not provide sufficient work for them. So, many US-born Latinos also became migrant farm workers. Like their Mexican counterparts, they began as temporary migrant workers. They followed the labor patterns of seasonal agriculture around the United States. Some developed regular seasonal migratory patterns while others looked for the best work opportunities.

Braceros, the undocumented, Latino migrant workers, and other poor people from the United States were in the same labor pool. Because they faced many of the same challenges, the ministry efforts of Protestant missionaries toward them were similar. They were all temporary workers who needed the same types of support services. But it also became clear to the missionaries that US-based migrant workers and temporary workers from Mexico were different in significant ways and needed different types of ministry support.

Little by little a growing number of Mexican and Mexican American farm workers began to permanently establish themselves in the rural areas where they worked during the agricultural season. By the early 1960s, there were new Latino communities in places like the Yakima Valley of Washington, the San Joaquín Valley of California, and in Nebraska, Iowa, and other parts of the central United States. Others, attracted by the opportunities of better employment and a brighter future, migrated into the cities of these regions.

These people were often competing with other temporary workers for jobs with very low wages and very primitive working conditions. Those coming from Mexico might have deemed this "tolerable," since most of them were planning to return to their home country where they lived in extremely primitive conditions. So Protestant missionaries began to realize that they needed to address each of these communities differently.

Some of these new Latino communities were established in places with little Roman Catholic presence. So the principal spiritual support often came from Protestant pastors and missionaries. Pentecostal lay pastors were often among the migrant workers, so they quickly established congregations among these growing communities, spreading the Latina Protestant presence into these new areas. Some of the evangelical denominations also began ministry in these communities, expanding the Latino Protestant presence far beyond the Southwest or Northeast.

The denominations linked to the Home Missions Council also expanded their ministry into these new areas. They had a broader focus and commitment than many of the Pentecostal and evangelical denominations. These domestic laborers had families whose needs they had to address, but usually very few social support systems. They needed more than temporary spiritual support. "The rights of the domestic agricultural migrants are a legitimate concern of the North American Protestant churches. The domestic migrant is a citizen of the United States; he has the responsibility of maintaining his family while he travels, and his wages are usually low compared to the cost of living. He, in short, has a wide range of education, economic and social needs."[3] These various workers often competed for the same jobs, and this tended to depress wages for all. Braceros and the undocumented were at the bottom of the labor pool, since they had the fewest rights. One place where Protestant ministry among Latinos began to take a very different direction, depending on the theological orientation of the denomination, was among braceros and migrant workers. Some denominations, mostly evangelical and Pentecostal, preached to them and provided them with basic resources. But some liberal Protestant (and Catholic) organizations raised broader concerns. Many of them worked for migrant worker rights, and they opposed the law (Public Law 78) that served as the basis for the Bracero Program of the 1950s because it provided very few rights for farm workers. Some organizations, like the Migrant Ministry of the National Council of Churches,[4] worked with farm workers to help them organize and deal with the unjust working situations created by Public Law 78. During the 1950s, these same Protestant leaders helped labor organizers as they established farm labor unions and worked against the Bracero Program. Some of these efforts would serve as precursors to the farm labor movement of the 1960s.

The Protestant organizations that worked for workers' rights might appeal to religious faith as a basis for their commitment, but they did not tend to invite people into a faith commitment. Since most Latinas were Catholics, at most they were invited to draw on their existing faith commitment. So while some mainline groups struggled against the Bracero Program, other churches and ministries worked with the workers and invited them into a faith commitment. Many of these converts would return to Mexico as Prot-

---

3. Jack Taylor, *God's Messengers to Mexico's Masses: A Study of the Religious Significance of the Braceros* (Eugene, OR: Institute of Church Growth, 1962), 20.

4. Leo Grebler, Joan W. Moore, and Ralph C. Guzman, *The Mexican-American People: The Nation's Second Largest Minority* (New York: Free Press, 1970), 501.

estants (often Pentecostals) and would become the core of new churches in their communities of origin.[5]

On the other hand, braceros also had specific spiritual and social needs.

> The bracero is in a unique situation. . . . The bracero will be in our country for only a short time and then return to his homeland. . . . The needs and challenges of the braceros are basically spiritual. The bracero is a person without true Christian foundations. His faith and reliance is in the forms, ceremonies, rites and idols of a Christo-pagan Roman Catholicism. . . . As a stranger in a foreign land away from his family and surroundings which had buttressed him in this empty faith, he searches for security. . . . These braceros can have the peace and confidence of a clean heart and a pure conscience before God. . . . This is the most important thing the church has to offer these strangers with their camp.[6]

There are many studies on the conditions faced by braceros and on their impact on the US economy. But studies of their religious perspectives are more limited. Clearly they did not tend to establish their own churches, since they were temporary workers and most returned to Mexico. But they did take their faith with them. Though the vast majority were Catholics, a growing number were Protestants or became Protestants during their time in the United States or, at least, developed a more positive attitude toward Protestantism. Some of them joined existing churches when they returned, while others started new congregations. But even those that did not become Protestants (the vast majority) tended to have a more positive view of Protestantism when they returned to their communities.

Migration into the Northeast and Elsewhere

While one wave was moving north and west from Mexico, another started after World War II from Puerto Rico. The fact that they were US citizens made it easier for Puerto Ricans to come to the mainland. Soldiers from the island had served in the war, and had seen the mainland and were attracted

---

5. Because my parents became pastors in south Texas toward the end of the bracero period, I personally had occasion to go to church with braceros. The church my parents pastored held church meetings focused on the bracero community.

6. Taylor, *God's Messengers*, 21–22.

to its promises. Labor contractors recruited on the island for employment opportunities in New York. From 1940 to 1950 the Puerto Rican population that moved stateside quadrupled in size, and then did so again from 1950 to 1960. There were about seventy thousand Puerto Ricans in the United States in 1940. By 1960 the population had reached almost nine hundred thousand.[7] This growth would continue with further migratory waves and with more and more people of Puerto Rican descent born in the States. This pattern would continue throughout the rest of the twentieth century and into the twenty-first century.

In 1947 the Puerto Rican government created the Farm Labor Program to help farm laborers from the island find work in the United States, particularly the landless peasants. In conjunction with the US government, it created a temporary work program not unlike the Bracero Program. These workers were commonly known as *los tomateros* (the tomato pickers), though they worked in various types of agricultural jobs. At its height in 1968, over twenty-two thousand seasonal agricultural workers moved from the island to meet agricultural labor needs throughout the Northeast.[8]

The vast majority of the migrants from this period settled in New York, giving rise to the term *nuyoricans* to describe Puerto Ricans who were born, or lived, on the mainland. But by the 1950s there were also Puerto Rican communities in other parts of the Northeast and Midwest, the largest of which were in Philadelphia, Chicago, and other cities of the region. Some of these Puerto Ricans brought their faith and churches with them, while Protestants also expanded their ministry efforts into this growing segment of the Latina community.

Because Puerto Ricans were US citizens by birth, and Puerto Rico was a US territory, Puerto Ricans could freely move anywhere in the States. So they were not immigrants in any legal sense of the term. But clearly something was different, and that difference was reflected in how they were perceived when they moved stateside from the island. Because of the unique status of the island, they were considered immigrants in the popular understanding

7. Carmen Teresa Whalen, "Colonialism, Citizenship, and the Making of the Puerto Rican Diaspora: An Introduction," in *Puerto Rican Diaspora: Historical Perspectives*, ed. Carmen Teresa Whalen and Victor Vazquez-Hernandez (Philadelphia: Temple University Press, 2005), 3.

8. Jorge Duany, "The Puerto Rican Diaspora to the United States: A Postcolonial Migration" (paper presented at the workshop on Postcolonial Immigration and Identity Formation in Europe since 1945: Towards a Comparative Perspective, International Institute of Social History, Amsterdam, November 7, 2008), 3, https://centropr.hunter.cuny.edu/sites/default/files/past_events/Jorge_Duany_Puerto_Rican_Diaspora.pdf.

of the term. This new group added a new face to the Latino population. But because, unlike most Latina immigrants, they did not need a visa to enter the United States, they were unique within the Latina community as well.

The Puerto Rican population continued to expand rapidly, but their migratory patterns followed a slightly different logic, depending on the political and economic situation on the island and the opportunities stateside. The largest part of the population was located in New York, so that is where most Protestant ministry efforts were located. There were Puerto Rican Protestant churches and ministries throughout the Puerto Rican diaspora population. But it was Latino Protestantism in New York that received the most attention, so that is the area of which we know the most.

Exile Communities and Another Face of Latino Reality

The Cuban Revolution (1959) created a migratory bridge from Cuba to the United States, particularly into southern Florida. There had been some migration from Cuba to the United States before that time, but the changes brought on by the Castro regime created a flow of refugees. The United States opened the door to receive all who wanted to leave the now communist nation, and an "air" bridge was established between Cuba and the United States that continued through most of the 1960s. The United States gave those fleeing immediate legal status and provided them financial and educational support. Over the next fifteen years over five hundred thousand Cubans settled in Greater Miami. Others went elsewhere in the United States, establishing significant Cuban communities in places like New Jersey and southern California.[9]

Many of the first people that came saw themselves as exiles, people who hoped soon to return to Cuba once the Castro regime was overthrown. Many in the first wave of the 1960s were from the middle and upper classes and were highly educated. Also, many Cubans who had strong faith commitments left because of the antireligious direction the revolution took.

Cuban exiles represented new ministry opportunities for Protestant denominations, but among these exiles were educated and experienced pastors and leaders already prepared for ministry and church service. Even as Cubans changed the face of Miami, they also had a significant impact on

9. "Cuban Americans," *Wikipedia*, last modified March 15, 2017, https://en.wikipedia.org /wiki/Cuban_Americans.

Protestant ministries among Latinos. Several mainline denominations and church groups, such as the Methodists, the Presbyterians, and the Disciples of Christ, received many ordained pastors from the island who started new churches and became pastors of existing ones. Some eventually took leadership positions in their denominations. Because they were already seminary educated and ordained to ministry, they became a boon to denominations that had high requirements for ordination and found it hard to prepare enough leaders for their Latino ministries. But because they came with more education and with leadership abilities, they eventually were overrepresented as leaders in Latino Protestant churches. Their impact would mostly be felt after 1965 (see next chapter), but their presence began to have an influence during the period covered by this chapter.

A smaller wave of exiles started coming to the United States in 1963 from the Dominican Republic, as part of the process of ending the political tensions there. Many settled in New York City. Their impact would mostly be felt in the latter part of the twentieth century as the community continued to grow. But because the earlier immigrants had entered the country legally as exiles, they used family reunification laws to bring others into the United States legally, and so there are not a large number of undocumented Dominicans in the United States.[10]

The Cuban refugees and, to a lesser extent, the Dominicans provided another type of change to the face of the Latino community. Immigration law and practice favored the Cubans. The vast majority, to this day, are given immediate refugee status when they land on US soil. They receive social support as they establish themselves in the country. Because most of them also had more education than other Latinas, they were able to take advantage of these benefits to establish themselves quickly in the United States. Because of the favorable reception, they tended to interpret their US experience much more positively than other Latinos who did not qualify for legal status or who worked in very unfavorable circumstances.

The migration of educated, middle- and upper-class people from Latin America also influenced Protestant ministry and changed the face of many Latino churches. Throughout the nineteenth and early part of the twentieth century, the implicit, and often explicit, assumption of Protestant missionaries was that Latina ministry was ministry to the poor and mostly uned-

10. Chiamaka Nwosu and Jeanne Batalova, "Immigrants from the Dominican Republic in the United States," Migration Policy Institute, July 18, 2014, http://www.migrationpolicy.org /article/foreign-born-dominican-republic-united-states.

ucated. Many of the first Cuban exiles were educated and able to play an important role in Florida as soon as they arrived. They needed initial support to establish themselves in the United States, but the US government provided that. Because they were starting from a very different perspective than most Latinos, they served to diversify the US Latina community and to change how Protestants thought about ministry in the Latino community. Cuban Americans would soon be leading their own congregations, in mainline and evangelical denominations, and expanding their leadership base among the denominations they belonged to in Cuba.

Latina Protestantism in the Northeast

Protestant missionaries and church planters followed the expansion of Puerto Rican migrants into the Northeast after World War II. The small number of Protestant churches that existed before the war greatly increased in proportion to the rapid growth of the Puerto Rican community. US denominations expanded their ministry among the newcomers, as did the Pentecostal groups. Also, several new Latino Pentecostal groups were born during this period.

Protestants also migrated in growing numbers, including pastors and leaders who either established churches or became the leaders of the new congregations. The pastors of many of the Pentecostal churches established in New York had been formed on the island and had started their ministry there. Missionaries started most of the other Protestant ministries. But the island also provided pastors and leaders for churches of the US-based denominations that had a presence in Puerto Rico. The mainline denominations that had started ministries on the island drew on experienced pastors and leaders who had developed in the churches there to serve both as pastors and as leaders within the denominational structures. This pattern would continue throughout the twentieth century.

The increasing ministry opportunities also gave birth to new movements and denominations. The largest one that developed during this period was indirectly born through the work of the AG. That denomination had started work in Puerto Rico and established the Iglesia de Dios Pentecostal. That denomination sent workers to New York, and the churches it established joined the local Latin District of the AG. One of those churches, La Sinagoga, was started in 1925. Rev. Albelardo Berrios, who had been a pastor in Puerto Rico, was called to pastor that church in 1951. In the midst of the debates over the status of Puerto Rico and its relationship to the US AG headquarters, the Puerto Rican churches in New York often had more affinity to the church in Puerto Rico than to the AG. In 1954 Berrios led his church and some other congregations to form the Concilio Latinoamericano de la Iglesia de Dios Pentecostal de Nueva York (CLANY). Frederick Whitam, writing in 1962, reported that CLANY had thirty-two churches and 2,350 adult members.

The tensions brewing at the time concerned the US headquarters of the AG and its relationship to the Puerto Rican churches. Should the churches in Puerto Rico be treated as a "national" church and become a "sister" denomination to the US AG, or should they become a district within the US AG? The implications of this decision were many, including what role the Puerto Rican churches would have among Puerto Ricans migrating to the United States. If they formed a US district, then any church or district on the mainland would need to join the local district and pastors would need to transfer their credentials to that district. But if the Puerto Ricans were a national church, they could send their pastors and missionaries to form churches among the new migrants and those churches could maintain links to the island. Another issue involved ecclesiology, with the US AG following a congregational model and the Puerto Rican church using an episcopal model.

Because of the tensions with the AG leadership in the United States, most of the churches in Puerto Rico eventually decided to become their own denomination, and in 1957 they organized themselves as the Iglesia de Dios Pentecostal, Movimiento Internacional (often referred to as MI). However, some churches in Puerto Rico stayed with the AG, creating what eventually became a district of the AG. CLANY maintained fraternal links with the churches in Puerto Rico but never joined the new denomination. Eventually, MI began sending pastors to organize churches among the Puerto Rican population and elsewhere. So today there are AG churches in Puerto Rico linked to churches on the mainland, and CLANY and MI churches in various parts of the United States. The unclear status of Puerto Rico, combined with nationalism, cultural differences, and different styles of leadership, created two new Latina denominations within the Pentecostal fold.[11]

The most complete published report on Latina Protestantism in New York appeared in *Christian Century* in 1962. In "New York's Spanish Protes-

---

11. See Gastón Espinosa, *Latino Pentecostals in America: Faith and Politics in Action* (Cambridge, MA: Harvard University Press, 2014), 240–60.

tants," Frederick Whitam reported on the growth of Protestantism among the Spanish-speaking, mostly Puerto Rican, population. The subtitle describes the growing influence of this population: "They Constitute a Community Not Peripheral and Transitory, but Vigorous and Firmly Established." The article describes the growth of the Protestant community, which is closely linked to the migration of Puerto Ricans into the region. The number of churches reflects the growth. In 1937 there were 55 Spanish-language Protestant churches in New York, and by 1960 there were 430.[12]

This report includes significant information about Protestant ministry among the Puerto Rican population, including different ministry models. Whitam mentions Spanish-language churches, Spanish-language ministries in English-language congregations, and English-language churches that have Latino members. According to Whitam, the most successful, by far, are the Spanish-language congregations. About half of the article describes the growing number of Pentecostal congregations. Over half of the Latino churches in New York (240) are Pentecostal, and the largest churches are all from one of the Pentecostal denominations. The largest Latino church is Juan 3:16 in the Bronx, with seven hundred members.[13] Though he is not Pentecostal, Whitam recognizes that the churches that are growing the most, that have the strongest local leadership, and that are self-supporting are the Pentecostal churches.

At the end of the article, Whitam points to a question that will continue to impact Latino Protestant churches as they successfully lead people to faith and into a better lifestyle.

> Spanish Protestantism has added a new and vigorous dimension to Protestantism in New York. Yet its future is not clear. As the proportion of Puerto Ricans in the city increases, leadership will increasingly be assumed by members of the group, as it was assumed in the past by the sons of Italian and Irish immigrants. Then the Puerto Rican Protestant will be confronted not so much by the nagging problems of inadequate housing and racial discrimination as by the beguiling problems of his progress as a citizen. Then he will seek to discover whether his religion is relevant to the experiences to which his changed status gives rise. And he may be called on to discover its relevance to the problems of the new migrants

12. Frederick L. Whitam, "New York's Spanish Protestants," *Christian Century* 79, no. 6 (February 7, 1962): 162.

13. Whitam, "New York's Spanish Protestants," 162.

who come from some as yet undetermined land to work at the jobs which drew his fathers from their island homes.[14]

Whitam raises an important issue related to the changing needs of the community and how, and whether, Protestant churches will effectively respond to them. But he works from the perspective of assimilation, not taking into account both the constant migration from the island and the structural racism that has made it difficult for Puerto Ricans to assume leadership within the city. Yet the question is crucial. How would churches established by migrants respond to new immigrants and to the changing realities of their members?

Though most Puerto Ricans went into Greater New York City, others settled in the Northeast. Protestant churches also established ministries among this population, though there is limited information about churches and ministries outside of Greater New York City during this period. But by the late 1950s, there were Puerto Rican Protestant churches wherever new migrants had established themselves in the Northeast.

Growth of Latino Protestantism through 1964

Migration fueled the growth of the Latina community after World War II and was one of the key sources of Latino Protestant growth. But increasing numbers of nominal Catholics were also brought into the Protestant fold, both in the United States and in Latin America. The evangelistic efforts of Protestant pastors, lay leaders, and missionaries both in the United States and in Latin America created small but clear demographic shifts.

By the early 1960s Latina Protestantism was already developing a distinctive identity that was different from US Protestantism in general. The "guerilla sects" of which the Home Missions Council had lamented (see previous chapter) were gaining many more converts than the historic Protestant denominations. Latino Protestants were already more evangelical and more Pentecostal than the US Protestant population, though most leaders in historic denominations and church structures had not yet fully comprehended the scope of this difference, as reflected in the few extant reports about Latino Protestantism during this period.

There is one major published study of "Spanish" Protestants during this period. In their book *The Mexican-American People: The Nation's Second*

14. Whitam, "New York's Spanish Protestants," 164.

Largest Minority, authors Leo Grebler, Joan Moore, and Ralph Guzman include a chapter on Latino Protestants (written by Joan Moore). They begin the section on denominational statistics with the statement that "statistically, Protestantism is not important in the Mexican-American population."[15] They conclude this because in urban areas like Los Angeles and San Antonio, which have large Latina populations, "only 5 percent of those professing a religion are Protestant," and in the United States, only 3 percent of the Mexican American population is Protestant, according to the study they quote.[16]

They recognize several problems with the study they use. For example, the statistics do not distinguish Mexican Americans from other "Spanish Americans." They also include only those people in segregated congregations and not those who attend integrated churches (Anglo congregations that have Latina members). Also, only one Pentecostal body, the Assemblies of God, is accounted for in the study. The chart published in the book includes the following information:

	Members	Churches	Percentage of Churches in Southwest
Assemblies of God	29,054	392	77
Methodist	28,000	221	81.7
Southern Baptist	28,000	559	95.3
American Baptist	7,950	106	54.7
Presbyterian USA	6,604	94	74.5
Seventh-Day Adventist	5,000	68	64.7
Presbyterian US	2,842	38	100
Disciples of Christ	1,851	18	50
Lutheran–Missouri Synod	1,245	7	100
Evan. United Brethren	972	14	78.6
United Lutheran Church	604	4	0.0
Congregational	543	7	71.4
Church of God (Anderson)	465	7	100

The report is fairly incomplete and is based on a brief survey done by the National Council of Churches (NCC). The study leaves out Pentecostal groups like the Church of God, the Church of God of Prophecy, the Foursquare Church, CLANY, and the Apostolic Assembly, all of which have more

15. Grebler, Moore, and Guzman, *The Mexican-American People*, 487.
16. Grebler, Moore, and Guzman, *The Mexican-American People*, 487.

churches than some of the denominations listed. It also does not include non-Pentecostal groups like the Church of the Nazarene, the Friends, the Christian and Missionary Alliance, Churches of Christ, the Free Methodists, the Mennonites, and the Mennonite Brethren, all of which had more Latino churches by 1960 than some of the members of the NCC listed. Also, the numbers of some of the larger groups (particularly the Methodists and Baptists) are based on the estimates of denominational leaders and not on statistical reports. Given other reports for the period, it is likely that the Methodist numbers are too high.

The data about the percentage of ministry in the Southwest points to the geographic concentration of the Latino population. Most Latina Protestants are located in the Southwest because that is where the vast majority of the Latino population is located. As already mentioned, the other region with a significant Latina population, at this time, was the Northeast.

Nonetheless, this study gives a picture of the changing face of Latina Protestantism by this period. By this time, the Assemblies of God was already the largest Latino Protestant denomination in the United States, and the only one that was "entirely indigenous" (fully self-funded and led by Latino pastors, including Latino superintendents of Latina districts). Local Latina congregations were not dependent on any denominational support from "Anglo" churches or national structures. All the other denominations in the report provided some financial support for the "Spanish" churches, though the study does not have any numbers for the Seventh-Day Adventists.

The analysis of the authors clearly points toward a "mainline integration" orientation. They study the three largest church groups (Methodist, Presbyterian, and Baptist, not including the Assemblies of God) through the lenses of three stages of development: the missionary stage, the segregated stage, and the integrated stage. In this vision evangelization and Americanization are very clearly linked. The various stages mix mission with integration into US denominational structures as the progression that should be expected.

Nonetheless, the authors analyze Protestant missionary work among the "Mexicans" through the conflictive lenses of mission and of social norms in the United States. "Protestant denominations are simultaneously institutions of the dominant society and also religious bodies." This is a problem because the "Mexicans" have been and continue to be seen as "pariahs" within US society. The picture presented is not unlike the situation faced by the missionaries of the nineteenth century. The linked goals of evangelization and Americanization create a tension where, often, neither is effectively addressed. Some denominations are willing to evangelize Latinos but leave them in their own structures (more conservative denominations), while others (liberal) try to provide social services. Social services become the "conscience palliative" for more liberal Protestants. But if most Protestants see "Mexicans" as "pariah people," then there is little hope that these efforts will provide Latinos inclusion in the social structures of dominant society by becoming Protestants.

The authors conclude that

> It seems highly likely that the "Americanizing" goals of the early missionaries would have required a major effort on the part of the denominations to include the Mexican Americans. Neither the original religious goal of extending Christianity to the "unchurched" nor the secondary goal of acculturating the foreigners has been or can be substantially accomplished by activities [social services] that are peripheral to the goals of the organizations as these activities must necessarily be. Denominational goals are being subsumed to ecumenical goals, which will surely weaken the organizational structure of Christianity for some years to come. This "new hope" of religious liberals therefore appears to offer limited possibilities to pariah people for their inclusion into the important social institution of dominant society that Protestantism once was.[17]

Though issues related to assimilation and Latina religious identity will not yet loom large, this study also alludes to the difference between Latinos who attend predominantly Latino Protestant churches and those who attend "integrated" congregations. This is an issue that developed the moment Anglo Protestants reached out to Latinos in the nineteenth century. Since evangelization and Americanization are both goals, it is not clear what role Latino Protestant churches would have. If Latinas develop their own structures and religious identity, how do they fit in US society? Should the "end goal" be integration, the development of indigenous congregations, or something else?

The study focuses on the development and ministry of what the authors refer to as the major denominations, Presbyterian, Methodist, and Baptist. It also uses the Migrant Ministry of the National Council of Churches as a model of what liberal churches are doing. But apart from the Southern Baptist Convention, it is the denominations "outside the mainstream," to borrow the term used in the book,[18] that are already defining Latina Protestantism as significantly different.

17. Grebler, Moore, and Guzman, *The Mexican-American People*, 504.
18. Grebler, Moore, and Guzman, *The Mexican-American People*, 504.

The authors do not place a great deal of emphasis on this, but they do recognize that the Pentecostal churches do not depend on outside financial support and that they lead their own churches. They recognize that more liberal denominations are placing more emphasis on social work. But they also address the complexities of the US Protestant mission, particularly as related to the major historical denominations. The link between evangelization and Americanization has made it difficult for the churches to accomplish either. And "pariah people" like Mexican Americans cannot find access to the social structures of US Protestantism.[19]

The study also addresses some of the complexities and contradictions faced by denominations that worked among Latinos during this period. It states that traditional denominations have created paternalism and that Pentecostal denominations tend to be more successful in reaching the "hard-to-reach." But the authors point to the difficulty of actual relationships between Latinas and the Protestant population at large. They divide the denominations into three major categories on this issue. The groups they call "paternalistic," such as the Presbyterians, provide more social services but tend to implicitly exclude Mexican Americans from equal-status participation in the church's life. Churches that provide more space for Latino leadership, such as the Baptists, tend to struggle between paternalism and self-determination. The independent Latina Pentecostal groups of the period solved this issue through ethnic exclusiveness. Latinos were in charge of their own churches, but they had only marginal connections with Anglo Protestants. The authors conclude that these types of groups were outside the mainstream of US Protestantism, but they were able to gain autonomy and support their own churches and leaders.[20]

According to this study, by 1960 the AG already had the largest Latino membership. It would not drop from that position. The Southern Baptist Convention would eventually become the second in Latino membership, and the Seventh-Day Adventist Church third. Also, the authors refer to the Apostolic Assembly in their analysis of "Spanish" Pentecostalism but do not include any statistics about it. This study was done before mainline denominations began their decline in the United States, so it is not surprising that the historic denominations would have a prominent role in it. But this would be the last national study in which mainline denominations were considered the principal groups in the Latino community.

19. Grebler, Moore, and Guzman, *The Mexican-American People*, 504.
20. Grebler, Moore, and Guzman, *The Mexican-American People*, 505.

The Ministry of the Major Denominations

Latino Methodists described the period from 1914 to 1939 as the critical years. Internally, neither the MEC nor the MECS was able to develop structures that worked for its Latino churches. Externally, the changing attitudes toward Mexicans after the Great Depression made ministry more difficult. There was a sense that ministry among the Spanish-speaking population had no clear direction.

This changed when the major Methodist denominations merged in 1939. The conferences in Texas and New Mexico were merged into one, which created tensions because of the cultural differences between them and because the Texas conference was so much bigger than the New Mexico one. But the merger also created new conference support for Latino ministries. The period from 1940 to 1954 has been called the golden era of Latino Methodism. Materials were developed in Spanish, and a number of lay ministries were established. The churches of the new conference grew over 50 percent during this period, and a growing number of Latino churches also became self-supporting. Churches in California and Arizona were organized into a Latin Provisional Conference and also saw steady growth. "All these statistical measures and reports reflect a vigor and vitality seldom matched in United Methodism."[21] According to Dr. Alfredo Náñez, this growth did not come from strategic plans or methodologies, but from a spirit of renewal and revival.[22]

But in the early 1950s the Annual Conference in the California/Arizona area called for integration of the Latino churches into the larger conference. The goal was to provide more financial support for these churches. The churches of the Provisional Conference were merged into the large body in 1956. This began a decline in the Latino churches, as fewer people participated in the integrated activities such as the women's ministry or youth camps. From 1957 to 1967 the number of Latino churches in the conference declined from twenty-nine to nineteen, and the membership dropped by 20 percent. By the late 1960s, it had become clear to both Anglos and Latinos that integration had failed. "Integration seen as Angloization is an outmoded concept among Mexican Americans and no longer can be tolerated by our Latin churches."[23]

21. Justo L. González, ed., *Each in Our Own Tongue: A History of Hispanics in United Methodism* (Nashville: Abingdon, 1991), 54.

22. Alfredo Náñez, *Historia de La Conferencia Río Grande de La Iglesia Metodista Unida* (Dallas: Bridwell Library, 1980), 106-7.

23. González, *Each in Our Own Tongue*, 81-82.

The Presbyterians saw slow but steady growth through about 1940. The PCUS and the churches in southern California also had a bit of a golden era in the 1940s and early 1950s. But the PCUS in Texas began to decline when the Tex-Mex Presbytery was dissolved in 1955. The paternalistic model described by Grebler, Moore, and Guzman had applied to the PCUS work from the very beginning of the presbytery in 1908. The denomination wanted to develop Latino churches that would have the same financial and leadership base as the Anglo churches. It also provided regular financial support for the churches that could not support themselves in the same way as the Anglo congregations, because of the socioeconomic difference. The Synod of Texas pushed toward integration as a way to address the disparity, but the effort failed. So by 1964 Latino Presbyterian churches in Texas were shrinking, even as the Latina population was growing and as other Protestant denominations expanded their ministry.[24]

The situation in New Mexico/Colorado was similar. The churches in the region were not growing, and the social service ministries were in decline. The churches in southern California and Arizona also suffered from the attempts to integrate them, or their ministries, into the larger presbyteries. "While this achievement supported the goal of equality, it weakened the sense of community among Hispanic Presbyterians."[25] By the mid-1960s, there was also a sense among Latino Presbyterians that integration efforts had failed and that a new model was needed for future ministry.[26]

While the Presbyterians and Methodists were going through a period of loss, the Baptists in Texas were beginning a growth spurt. When the Mexican Convention met in San Antonio on June 22, 1942, they reported having 125 churches and missions with a total of 8,606 members. During this period the denomination established several ministries for children and schools for preparing pastors. It also established a convention magazine, *El Bautista Mexicano.* The "Mexican" churches worked closely with the Baptist associations in the state and established churches throughout. The Anglo associations often provided subsidies for the Spanish-language ministries. Because of their close association, the Mexican Baptist Convention voted to merge with the Baptist General Convention of Texas in 1964. That year the conven-

24. R. Douglas Brackenridge and Francisco O. García-Treto, *Iglesia Presbiteriana: A History of Presbyterians and Mexican Americans in the Southwest* (San Antonio: Trinity University Press, 1974), 112–25.

25. Jane Atkins-Vasquez, *Hispanic Presbyterians in Southern California: One Hundred Years of Ministry* (Los Angeles: Synod of Southern California and Hawaii, 1988), 5.

26. See Brackenridge and García-Treto, *Iglesia Presbiteriana,* 197–225.

tion reported 418 churches and 33,530 members.[27] These numbers were only for Texas and did not include the Latino Southern Baptist churches in other parts of the United States, though the largest number of Southern Baptist Latino churches was in that state.

The other major denomination mentioned by Grebler, Moore, and Guzman, the AG, was also experiencing growth. The significant splits of the 1930s and the 1950s had affected the Latino districts, particularly the Spanish district of New York. But the AG was ready to grow among the new migrants brought by the Bracero Program and Puerto Rican migration. The first Latino superintendent of the Latin District, Demetrio Bazán, was elected in 1939. He was superintendent for twenty years and saw Latino ministries grow substantially during this time. When he started in 1939, the AG had 170 churches with 3,765 members.[28] Bazán encouraged an evangelistic drive and a significant autonomy among the churches. For example, he encouraged the mostly Puerto Rican churches in the New York area to form their own district, instead of being under the mostly Mexican American district he led. They became the Spanish Eastern District in 1956. By 1957 the AG had 321 churches with 19,490 members throughout the United States.[29]

Having Latinas lead and support their own congregations gave them a great deal of autonomy in the AG. Pastors often held more than one job because their churches could not support them full time. But they also had more freedom to expand ministry and to plant new churches. Latino AG leaders also promoted education through the Latin American Bible Institutes and developed an increasing amount of literature in Spanish for the churches. Toward the end of his public ministry, Bazán encouraged José Girón to serve as his secretary, and in 1959 Girón became the superintendent.

Other Protestant Denominations circa 1964

While the focus of formal studies was still on the larger Protestant denominations, the other denominations that would have a prominent role by the end of the twentieth century were expanding their ministries into new areas and growing at a steady rate. Their growth went largely unreported outside

27. Joshua Grijalva, *A History of Mexican Baptists in Texas, 1881–1981* (Dallas: Baptist General Convention of Texas, 1982), 69, 121.

28. Espinosa, *Latino Pentecostals in America*, 169.

29. Espinosa, *Latino Pentecostals in America*, 173.

of denominational settings, but they demonstrated the changes occurring in Latino Protestantism. Several of those denominations had begun their "Latino" ministry in the Southwest closely linked to Mexico. In one way or another the acculturation of the Mexican American, the growth of Protestantism in Mexico, and the demographic changes within the Latina community in the Southwest required the denominations that were growing to rethink how work in the United States and in Latin America would connect (or not).

Up to 1945 the Spanish-language ministry of the Church of the Nazarene worked as one "district" across the US-Mexico border. In 1942 the "Mexican" work had been divided into two districts, cutting north-south, with both districts having work on both sides of the border. In 1945 the San Antonio–Monterrey district was divided according to the national boundary, though ministry continued to cross the border. This created two US-based Latino districts, the Texas-Mexican District and the Pacific Southwest Mexican District (which was linked to Mexico until 1972). The mission board sent many missionaries into the Spanish-speaking areas, strengthening both districts. In 1963 the Pacific District named the first Latino superintendent, Rev. Juan Madrid.[30] When he began ministry in the Western District, the Church of the Nazarene had fourteen churches and 503 members.[31] Later the church established a third Latino district, and many Anglo districts also established Latina churches.

During this period the Church of God also began to expand its Latino ministry. It was linked to its missionary work in Latin America. During the 1940s and 1950s, it began a Spanish-language publishing house, printed a Sunday school curriculum, and based a Bible institute in San Antonio. Students from the Bible institute helped establish and lead congregations in various parts of Texas, even as most of them were preparing to serve in Latin America. During this period the work in the United States was not clearly distinguished from mission in Latin America. In 1962 the Church of God established a separate district to oversee Latino work west of the Mississippi River, which marked the formal separation of the work in the United States from the work in Latin America.[32] By this

30. Orlando Serrano, "Historia de la Iglesia del Nazareno Hispana" (unpublished manuscript, n.d.), 23.

31. Serrano, "Historia de la Iglesia del Nazareno Hispana," 22.

32. Esdras Betancourt, *En el espíritu y poder de Pentecostés: Historia de la Iglesia de Dios Hispana en Estados Unidos* (Cleveland, TN: Vida Publication and Centro Estudios Latinos Publicaciones, 2016), 60.

time there were already churches in small clusters in the Southwest and the Northeast. These districts would continue subdividing as the number of Latino churches continued to grow. Though the United States would develop its own Latino leadership, denominational ministries would continue to work closely between US Latinos and Latin America throughout the twentieth century.

The Apostolic Assembly reflects a different issue by this time. In 1950 the assembly elected a US-born presiding bishop, Benjamín Cantú. During his tenure (until 1963) the denomination started more than forty new churches and opened churches in new states. But it was also during his tenure that differences between the US and Mexican Apostolic denominations began to develop.

Though the two denominations had started together and were committed to seeing themselves as one church in two countries, clear differences started developing. Even though the pioneers of both saw themselves as Mexicans, US-born Mexican Americans were different from their Mexican counterparts. Acculturation to life in the United States and a US education exacerbated the cultural differences between the groups. Each group started developing its own distinctive identity, accentuated by the different legal systems in each country and the cultural differences between Mexicans and US-born people of Mexican descent.

Even though the two denominations shared a common history and theological roots, and had a commitment to work together, over time the national and cultural differences created increasing tensions. The issue would be further complicated by migration. The groups had agreed that migrants would join the church in their new country. But migration was mostly from Mexico to the United States. Mexico almost always lost members in this arrangement. Also, because of the increasing cultural differences, the migrants would not always feel that they were getting the pastoral support they had received in Mexico. Though the crisis was averted during this period, the Mexican denomination (Apostolic Church) eventually decided to start churches in the United States, and vice versa.[33]

The Seventh-Day Adventists also experienced steady growth during this period, following an expansion pattern not unlike that of the AG. The first Latina churches developed in the Southwest, but in 1927 the Adventists be-

---

33. Juan F. Martínez Guerra and Luis Scott, eds., *Iglesias peregrinas en busca de identidad: Cuadros del protestantismo latino en los Estados Unidos* (Buenos Aires: Kairos Ediciones, 2004), 106.

gan a Latino church in Denver, in 1928 in New York, and in 1930 in Chicago. These churches served as the basis for ministry in these areas. Their next major expansion was in 1958 when they established churches among Latinas in Miami and Philadelphia. Because they had churches in Puerto Rico, they also benefited directly as people left the island after World War II. By the 1960s their presence was mostly concentrated in the Southwest (see the Grebler, Moore, and Guzman chart above) but would continue to expand throughout the United States.[34]

A small denomination like the Mennonite Brethren presents another issue that began to develop throughout Protestant ministry. The MBs were a small, mostly rural denomination. In 1937 they sent a missionary couple from Kansas, Harry and Sarah Neufeld, to work among the Spanish-speaking people of south Texas. The Neufelds chose to begin their work in very small agricultural communities west of McAllen, several of which had fewer than five hundred people. Through the investment of the churches in Kansas, a number of missionaries established themselves in these communities and started small churches there. By the 1950s they had small churches in eight communities and had also started a Christian school.

The costs of maintaining this ministry began to weigh heavily on denominational leaders. The people in these communities could not maintain the ministries established by the denomination, much less support a private school. On top of that, in the 1950s many people from these communities joined the internal migration from south Texas to other parts of the United States, leaving some of these communities almost like ghost towns. During the early 1960s the denomination closed the school and pulled out most of the missionaries. For a while it seemed like all the churches might completely disappear. Only when the churches changed their ministry model so that the local population could support the churches were these congregations able to find their footing.[35]

The assessment of Grebler, Moore, and Guzman in relationship to Latina Protestant ministry held true throughout all of Protestantism. With the exception of the Pentecostals, all denominations tended to develop ministries that were dependent on a constant flow of denominational support. The working assumption among most Protestants, liberal or conservative, was

34. See Manuel Vasquez, *La historia aun no contada: 100 años de Adventismo Hispano* (Nampa, ID: Pacific Press Publishing Association, 2000).

35. See Juan Francisco Martínez, "Ministry among United States Hispanics by an Ethno-Religious Minority: A Mennonite Brethren Case Study" (ThM thesis, Fuller Theological Seminary, School of World Mission, 1988).

that ministry in the Latino community needed to be "for" the community, something envisioned, developed, and supported from outside. The models of church that developed were very difficult, if not impossible, for Latinas to maintain on their own. And the amount of money invested in these churches tended to create a dependency that gradually became a codependency. These patterns would be very difficult to break, but they began to be faced during this period.

On the Edge of the Civil Rights Movement

The changing environment in the United States was beginning to affect Latino Protestantism. The question of civil rights was also beginning to impact the growing Latino population. Some of the issues had to do with the substantial needs of the community. But there were also the questions of representation and voice in larger societal structures, including Protestant denominations. Though the issue would have a greater impact after 1965, many of these questions were already affecting how Protestants looked at their role in the Latina communities. The responses from the various denominations tended to follow the broad categories described in Grebler, Moore, and Guzman's *The Mexican-American People*.

The Presbyterians, both PCUS and PCUSA, worked toward integration. They sought to resolve the issue of inequality and separation by integrating the Latino congregations into the existing Anglo structures. The idea was that everyone should have access to the same resources and that Latinas and Anglos should work together more closely. But Latinos usually ended up on the outside of the structures because of the uneven power dynamics. The Anglos were not going to join Latino structures, and Latinas were not fully welcome in Anglo structures; as a consequence, Latino membership in Presbyterian churches started dropping even as the Latino Protestant community was growing.

The situation with the Methodists was a bit more complex, because there was integration in one area while there was autonomy in another. The integration that occurred in the Southwest had the same negative impact as what happened with the Presbyterians. But autonomy and the possibilities of other structures made it possible for Methodists to continue to grow, though at a slower rate than other denominations.

The denominations that were part of the Home Missions Council became part of the National Council of Churches (NCC) in the 1950s. This body placed much more emphasis on addressing social problems related to Latinos than on evangelization. And as these churches developed a more ecumenical focus, they also decided to play down evangelization so as to minimize the tensions with Roman Catholicism.

These denominations linked to the NCC tended to focus more of their energies on the social problems faced by Latinas. They were still trying to "lift" the Latinos and to socialize them into dominant society. While the impact of the social gospel on liberal Protestantism prompted them to address the social problems of Latinos, the Americanization goal pushed them toward integration.

Most of the social work addressed needs like education and medicine or the immediate needs of migrants. The NCC also had the Council on the Spanish-American Work, which focused on evangelization. But the Migrant Ministry of the council pushed beyond that. Its concerns were much more oriented toward social justice than toward evangelization or the church.[36]

More will be said in the next chapter, but it is clear that the concerns for civil rights and social justice tended to orient the historic Protestant denominations toward actions that adversely affected their evangelization efforts among Latinas. Integration did not lift Latinos within Protestant structures very much. A focus on social problems did not draw many Latinas to Protestantism. So, as the historic denominations focused more on social justice issues, they tended to do it in such a way that evangelism among Latinos was often adversely affected. Not only that, but Latina Protestant churches also suffered from the good intentions of the Anglo leadership.

Evangelical denominations did not see their role as directly addressing social issues. They preached the gospel and called people to faith, but only provided social services as a secondary concern, if at all. They helped people in need but did not address civil rights or social injustice. They also did more work in drawing people to faith and gave Latino churches some level of autonomy but did not usually allow Latinos to take leadership within the larger denominational structures. So they saw some level of growth.

The Pentecostals gave Latinos the most space to develop as leaders. They addressed the immediate needs of their members, but were also the churches that were most on the margins of society. Latinos usually did not have a voice and were just beginning to see the importance of civic activities, such as voting. Most Pentecostals did not see themselves as potential agents in the social order. Their needs were immediate, and their hope was in the

36. Grebler, Moore, and Guzman, *The Mexican-American People*, 500–504.

God that would walk with them today and provide justice in life eternal. The hymnology of most of the churches pointed to a future day when there would be rest from labor, but today one lived in a hard world. "El mundo no es mi hogar" (The world is not my home) was one of those songs that helped people interpret their situation.

Most Latino Protestant churches developed on the edge of the civil rights movement. Many liberal Protestants would fight for their rights, but most Latinos would not join the fight. Latino Protestant churches might be a space for Latina leadership development, but in this generation not for leaders that would impact the social order. Those who developed leadership skills would either address social issues on the fringe of their churches or would be "encouraged" to leave. And so Latino Protestant leaders developed outside of the social realm, and Latina Protestants who sought to make a change often found themselves on the fringe of their churches.

A Pentecostal Vision for Latinas

The book *The Mexican-American People* points to another issue that would continue to differentiate Latina ministry by historic denominations from that done by Pentecostal churches. The working assumption of most US denominations was (and often continues to be) that poorer Latinos could not take full and complete responsibility for their own religious structures. Denominational executives assumed that Latino churches should look like their "Anglo" counterparts, even though the structures might reflect a middle-class status that most Latinos did not live. Because of this, Latinos might take immediate leadership of congregations, but usually under the tutelage and financial support of Protestant denominations. Few Latino churches in US denominations ever became strong and healthy by denominational benchmarks during this period. Grebler, Moore, and Guzman recognize this when they talk about the paternalism seen in several US denominations.

Pentecostals worked from a different set of assumptions from day one. It was leaders from among the people that did ministry. The types of ministries and churches that were established looked like the people. Leaders came from within the community, so they were from the same social class and had similar assumptions about what it meant for a church to financially support its pastor. Most of the churches had little, if any, financial support from outside. These types of churches were self-supporting from the beginning and did not depend on outsiders to develop and grow. Even as many denominations were spending a great deal of money to do ministry for Latinas, Latino Pentecostals were doing ministry from within and with the community.

These churches broke the implicit, and sometimes explicit, assumption that evangelization and Americanization went together. Pentecostal churches were started either by Latinos or by people that were on the margins of the social structure. So they did not have access to power, nor did they assume that gaining that access was part of their task. Though there were tensions over leadership and control of structures in Pentecostal denominations, the models of ministry used did not create dependency and did allow Latinos to lead their own churches. These churches became one of the few places where working-class and poor Latinas could be in charge of their own structures and could develop churches that they could support.[37]

The Expanding Backgrounds of Latino Protestantism

Throughout the nineteenth and into the first part of the twentieth century, the vast majority (over 95 percent) of Latinos in the United States traced their lineage to Mexico or to the Southwest from the Spanish colonial period. Today a bit over 60 percent have that background. That demographic shift began during this period, with the significant migratory growth of Latinos from other parts of Latin America. Most of the migrants from the Caribbean islands of Puerto Rico, Cuba, and Hispaniola settled on the eastern seaboard, so the various communities tended to be fairly separate from each other. Throughout this period Latino churches tended to be national background-specific churches (i.e., "Mexican" or "Puerto Rican"). But because of the new migrations, there would begin to be more significant encounters between Latinas from different national backgrounds, creating the space for a common term, "Hispanic" or "Latino," which would be debated during this period and become officially "normative" with the 1970 census.

The encounters of the various Latina groups would also begin to influence Latino Protestant churches. The Pentecostals encountered each other first through migration and in evangelistic ministry. Though Mexicans and Puerto Ricans tended to be in different parts of the country, they encoun-

37. See Juan Francisco Martínez, "What Happens to Church When We Move *Latinamente* beyond Inherited Ecclesiologies?," in *Building Bridges, Doing Justice: Constructing a Latino/a Ecumenical Theology*, ed. Orlando O. Espín (Maryknoll, NY: Orbis, 2009), 167–82.

tered each other in migratory work situations and in ministry. As various denominations began to work in both communities, the presence of both communities expanded in their churches.

An important contribution that occurred because of migration was the arrival of educated clergy from Latin America. Educated clergy met the expectations of historic denominations for ordination. But they also provided a level of leadership in Latino Protestantism that had not previously been common. Importing pastors made it possible for ministry to expand more quickly, particularly in light of new migration. Because of these educated leaders from different countries and theological backgrounds, Latinos, little by little, began to develop an expanding view of their role and their influence in US Protestantism.

Faces of the Period

Gabino Rendón was the most prominent face of the Presbyterian work in northern New Mexico and southern Colorado during the late nineteenth and early twentieth century. In a sense he is representative of what happened to that generation of Latino Protestant leaders from historic Protestant denominations. Rendón was born in the nineteenth century and was a graduate of the College of the Southwest in Del Norte, Colorado. He was a pastor through much of the first half of the twentieth century. In 1953 he wrote an autobiography, *Hand on My Shoulder*,[38] in which he tells about his work but focuses mostly on the early part of the twentieth century. Toward the end of his life he preached a sermon on his life and ministry, "Mientras miro los años pasar" (As I see the years pass),[39] most of which deals with the early Presbyterian work in the late nineteenth and early twentieth century. It is clear that the most significant events of his life and ministry happened then, and little of significance afterward. Even though Latino Protestantism was growing at the time of his writing, he seems only able to tell the story of what was lost and not of what might be coming. Latino Presbyterianism among *neomejicanos* was clearly in decline, which seems reflected in his memoirs. But his memories are those of commitment and sacrifice. "Blessed

38. Gabino Rendón, as told to Edith Agnew, *Hand on My Shoulder* (New York: Board of National Missions PCUSA, 1953).

39. Gabino Rendón, "Mientras miro los años pasar" (unpublished manuscript, preached on August 20, 1961, or September 20, 1961, Gabino Rendón file, Menual Historical Library, Albuquerque).

and adored Lord, you have been so good to me to allow me to present these humble words of your faithful servants that for many years worked hard to walk and sometimes going without food. But we preached the gospel and we trusted only in your power to produce growth."[40]

The contrast between what was happening among mainline Protestants and what was happening with Pentecostals stands out in the difference between Rendón and **José Girón**. Girón also grew up in the Latino Presbyterian Church, in Del Norte, Colorado, but took a very different route thereafter. The pastor of his church, Manuel Sánchez, who had also studied at the Presbyterian College of the Southwest in Del Norte, identified Girón as a potential pastor and tried to get him to study for ministry. In 1932 Girón attended a Pentecostal service and received the baptism in the Holy Spirit. The evangelist that had preached in the service soon recommended him for ordination in the AG. He was ordained and began an AG church in Del Norte. He later became an itinerant evangelist and then a church planter, establishing eight churches in New Mexico and Colorado. While serving as a substitute teacher in Taos, New Mexico, he studied by correspondence at a Bible institute. In 1947 the second superintendent of the Latin American District, Demetrio Bazán, named him as his secretary. He served in that role until he was named the third superintendent in 1959. During his tenure (until 1971) he encouraged each of the Latino conventions of the AG to adopt its own constitution and by-laws. At the end of his tenure, the AG reported 403 Latino churches, 827 ministers, and twenty-five thousand members. As part of his vision, the national Latino district was divided into four Latino districts and accepted by the General Council of the AG. Bazán became superintendent of the Pacific Latin District (today the Southern Pacific District). Because of his influence, Latinos gained a clear role in the General Council of the AG.

Rev. Leoncia Rosado Rousseau, a.k.a. **Mama Leo**, moved to New York City with her husband, Rev. Francisco Rosado, from Puerto Rico in 1935. They served as evangelists among the Puerto Rican population and then started Iglesia Cristiana Damasco. They were influenced by the ministry of Francisco Olazábal. When her husband was drafted into the military, Mama Leo became the pastor, probably the first Latina Pentecostal pastor in the United States. The ministry she and her husband developed focused on gang members and drug addicts. One of the most well-known converts of their ministry was Nicky Cruz (who will be mentioned in the next chapter).

40. Rendón, "Mientras miro los años pasar," 13.

The Concilio Latinoamericano de la Iglesia de Dios Pentecostal de Nueva York (CLANY) was started by a Puerto Rican pastor, **Abelardo Berríos**. He was converted in 1940 on the island, where he began to minister under the leadership of an experienced pastor. He was ordained to ministry in 1947 and in 1951 received a call to pastor a church of mostly Puerto Rican immigrants in New York. He arrived there in the midst of the tensions between the AG and the Pentecostal Church of God of Puerto Rico. He led his church and a group of other churches to form CLANY, and led the new organization for many years. He became a role model for a younger generation by earning university degrees in the 1970s and 1980s.[41]

As Latinos took leadership of their churches, as they shared their faith with others, as they moved into new areas, they developed a vision and a way of being Protestant that were unique to minorities in the United States. In the midst of the complexities of being Latina in this country, they were learning to be Protestant Christians, who learned to serve Jesus in culturally specific, appropriate ways.

41. "Nuestro Fundador" (in Spanish), Concilio Latinoamericano de la Iglesia de Dios Pentecostal, Inc., accessed March 18, 2017, http://clany.org/index.php?option=com_content&view=article&id=7&Itemid=291.

Chapter 6

New Faces among Latino Protestants (1965–1985)

Immediately following World War II and into the 1960s, new communities joined the Latino population in the United States so that it started to possess the diversity we experience today. Most of the national-background groups that are under the umbrella "Hispanic" or "Latina" began to have a significant presence in the United States during this period, except for the Central Americans, who would begin to enter in significant numbers in the 1970s and 1980s, and the Colombians, who would not gain a significant presence until the 1990s. The increasing diversity of the Latina community after 1965 would also be reflected in the increasingly diverse shape of Latino Protestantism, both in national background and because of additional Protestant denominations and movements that would begin to work among Latinas.

Significant during this period was the increasing role of immigrant Protestant leaders from Latin America in Latina Protestant churches. As Protestantism began a period of rapid growth in Latin America, a larger percentage of immigrants to the United States were already Protestants. But most crucial during this period were the Cuban, Puerto Rican, and, later, Central American pastors that migrated to the United States. In addition to making the US Latino community more ethnically diverse, these new immigrants took on important leadership roles in US denominations and strongly shaped the face of Latina Protestantism throughout the rest of the twentieth century and into the twenty-first.

Though the 1965 immigration law would be crucial in redefining Latin American migration, the migratory patterns it codified into law were set before the act was signed. In many ways the law merely set the legal parameters for what was already happening. This act would legally recognize the immigration from Latin America, something that had not been accounted for in previous legislation. But other issues would also play into the immigration equation. Because Puerto Rico was a part of the United States, migration from the island to the mainland would be influenced by its unique set of issues. Also, the law did not directly address the migratory patterns set in place because of the East-West conflict, such as Cuban or Dominican refugees (this would happen through subsequent legislation). The continued intervention of the United States in Latin America, because of the Cold War, set in motion new migratory patterns from Central America, something that would not be directly addressed until the immigration law of 1986.

Changing understandings of how racial and ethnic groups should interact in the United States also impacted the growth or decline of Latino Protestant churches. The denominations that had emphasized integration had lost Latina members, yet a small but growing number of Latinos were choosing to worship in English. Most of the historic denominations started declining in size, something that also slowly impacted Latino congregations. Also, the growth of Pentecostal and evangelical churches drew some people away from the historic denominations, as people sought out expressions of faith and church life that seemed to speak more closely to the Latino experience. On the other hand, new migration from the Caribbean, in particular, brought new members and new leaders into some of the historic denominations and church groups, particularly the Presbyterians and the Disciples of Christ.[1]

Changing Immigration Policies

The Immigration and Nationality Act of 1965 (also known as the Hart-Celler Act) changed the face of the United States. In spite of the profound changes it created in the demographic makeup of the country, that was not its original intent. Up to that time immigration had been based on a national quota system that favored countries that already had immigrants in the United States. The practical effect of the existing law was that people from northern European countries found it easier to enter the United States, while people from Asia were practically excluded. (People from Mexico, in particular, and other parts of Latin America had not been accounted for in previous immigration laws.)

---

1. See Paul Barton, *Hispanic Methodists, Presbyterians, and Baptists in Texas* (Austin: University of Texas Press, 2006), and Daisy L. Machado, *Of Borders and Margins: Hispanic Disciples in Texas, 1888–1945* (Oxford: Oxford University Press, 2003).

The 1965 act reflected growing changes in the United States because of the civil rights movement. There was growing opposition to laws that focused on national quotas, because they had a discriminatory impact, even against people from southern Europe, where many newer immigrants were coming from. The new law put the focus on family reunification and seeking skilled labor and ended the national quota system.

The proponents of the law, including President Lyndon Johnson, stated that very little would change, in practical terms, in the demographic makeup of the United States. But this act had the opposite result. Previous laws had practically excluded people from Africa and Asia, but this law made it possible for a significant growth in immigrants from the Philippines and, after the end of the Vietnam War, for a significant migratory wave from (formerly) South Vietnam. It also opened the door, for the first time in US history, for significant migration from other parts of Asia.

But the most significant impact, for our purposes, was on immigration from Latin America. From the time of the US takeover of the Southwest, there had been migration from Mexico, with a steady flow beginning after the Mexican Revolution. But permanent migration had not been accounted for in previous laws. The new law permitted family reunification for people from Mexico, so that families could use cross-border generational links that already existed for new legal migration. The events in Cuba and the Dominican Republic that encouraged emigration were supported by the 1965 act, which gave people from those countries clearly defined legal access to the United States.

The demographic changes brought by the immigration act were felt in the next three decades. From 1965 to 1995 over 18 million people migrated to the United States legally. Whereas before 1965 over 50 percent of immigrants were from Europe and 6 percent from Asia, three decades later, 31 percent were from Asia (1.4 million from the Philippines and 800,000 each from Korea, India, and Vietnam) and only 16 percent were from Europe. But the largest group of new immigrants was from Latin America—4.3 million legally from Mexico and about 800,000 each from Cuba and the Dominican Republic. The law also created the environment for the later migrations from Central America.[2]

Though the largest migration from Latin America originated in Mexico, the migratory patterns developed because of the 1965 law were particularly significant to Latino Protestantism because of the Protestant migrants from

2. "U.S. Immigration Since 1965," History Channel, accessed March 20, 2017, http://www.history.com/topics/us-immigration-since-1965.

Cuba and Puerto Rico. Many of the Protestants from Cuba were linked to historic church groups, such as the Presbyterians and Methodists, and included a small but important number of pastors, theologians, and leaders who had been educated in Protestant institutions and seminaries on the island. They quickly joined the ranks of leadership in their respective denominations, and the immigrants that were already Protestants joined existing Latino churches or became part of new church projects in the areas in which they settled.

A similar situation developed with Puerto Rican Protestant pastors. Because they did not have to go through the immigration process, they could be recruited directly by their respective denominations on the mainland to pastor Latina churches. On the other hand, various Puerto Rican Pentecostal groups sent pastors and missionaries to start new churches among diaspora Puerto Ricans and other Latinas. Movement between the island and the mainland strengthened Latina churches in the United States and kept them linked to their sister congregations in Puerto Rico.

Latino Protestant Growth by the Numbers

By this period, denominational reports no longer accurately reflected the number of Latino Protestants that had migrated to the United States. The historic denominations continued to prepare detailed reports, but many other denominations did not keep such exact records. Also, apart from the denominational reports and some studies of specific regions, there was no extensive study of Latino Protestantism during this period that attempted to keep track of all the denominations and churches that were starting Latino churches. Therefore, it is difficult to get a broad picture of the growth and diversification of the community from 1965 to 1986, though one can see clear patterns through the extant reports. Another difficulty was that denominational records reported only the number of adult members, with varying degrees of accuracy. They did not account for those who simply identified as Protestants, including children and nonmembers.

One of the most significant studies of Latino Protestants during this period was done by Clifton Holland, *The Religious Dimension in Hispanic Los Angeles: A Protestant Case Study*.[3] The goal of the study was to determine the size of the Latino, mostly Mexican or Mexican American, Protestant

3. Clifton L. Holland, *The Religious Dimension in Hispanic Los Angeles: A Protestant Case Study* (South Pasadena, CA: William Carey Library, 1974).

population of Los Angeles County in 1970. The study is very complete and includes general demographic information, short histories of the Latino ministry of the principal denominations represented in the region, and a list of all the known Latino Protestant churches in the region. He identified 227 churches and thirty-eight Spanish-language departments in English-language churches. According to the reports of those churches and denominations, there were 14,930 adult members, with the average church size being 71 members. The church groups with at least ten Latina churches in Los Angeles County were as follows:

	Churches	Members
American Baptist Churches	28	2,390
Southern Baptist Convention	24	1,600
Assemblies of God	18	1,080
Independent Pentecostal	17	1,020
Latin American Council (CLADIC)	15	900
United Methodist Church	14	1,540
Apostolic Assembly	12	1,000
Seventh-Day Adventist Church	11	880
Presbyterian Church USA	10	615
Church of the Foursquare Gospel	10	600

Although the largest groups were Baptists, there were more Pentecostal churches among Latinos in Los Angeles County than other ecclesial families (Holland identified 80 churches). What seems unclear is the number of AG churches reported. There were already 142 churches in the Latin Pacific District by 1971, so it is not clear why Holland identified only 18 churches in the county. But other than that issue, this seems like a very good snapshot of Latino Protestantism in the county during that period.

Holland analyzes the state of Latino Protestantism in the region. He concludes that

A series of related factors in the origin and development of the Hispanic Protestant Church has contributed to the creation of a multiplicity of introverted congregations: (1) the general hostility against Protestants in Mexican American barrios, especially of Catholic relatives and neighbors; (2) the Fundamentalist ideology—with its accompanying ascetism, hyper-individualism and anti-Catholicism—which characterized most Anglo Mexican missions "specialists" and which was generally adopted by

Hispanic Protestants; (3) the exclusiveness and competition between various Protestant groups, especially between Pentecostals and between the Seventh-Day Adventists and all other Protestant groups; (4) the cultural imperialism, and paternalism demonstrated toward the Hispanic Church both by the Anglo middle-class church and by the Anglo denominational Establishment.[4]

Holland developed PROLADES (Programa Latinoamericano de Estudios Socriorreligiosos), which became a research institute that studies religion in Latin America and Latinos in the United States. In 1983 Ildefonso Ortiz of World Team used a similar methodology as Holland in the Miami-Dade area and produced "Directory of Churches, Organizations and Ministries of the Hispanic Evangelical Churches in Miami-Dade." The study identified 222 Latina Protestant churches and missions that were part of the following groups: Southern Baptist Convention (37), independent Pentecostal churches (31), Assemblies of God (17), other independent churches (15), United Methodist Church (14), independent Baptist churches (13), Church of God (Cleveland, Tennessee) (9), Lutheran churches (9), Presbyterian churches (8), Episcopal churches (6), and the Pentecostal Church of God (6).[5]

In 1986 PROLADES provided technical assistance to AHET (Asociación Hispana para la Educación Teológica) to conduct a new study of nine counties in southern California. Lou Córdova, who worked with the US Center of World Mission (Pasadena, California), produced the *Directory of Hispanic Protestant Churches in Southern California*. Though it covers a larger area than Holland's study, one can compare the number and types of churches to realize how much growth and change happened during this period. According to the directory, there were 1,048 Latino Protestant churches in the nine-county region.

Los Angeles	687
Orange	80
San Diego	75
San Bernardino	65
Riverside	52

4. Holland, *Religious Dimension*, 442–43.

5. Clifton L. Holland, comp., "A Chronology of Significant Protestant Beginnings in Hispanic Ministry in the USA," PROLADES, last revised July 31, 2003, http://www.prolades.com/historical/usa-hisp-chron.pdf.

Ventura	29
Kern	26
Imperial	22
Santa Barbara	12

The breakout of church groups was as follows (listing only the largest groups):[6]

Assemblies of God	124
Apostolic Assembly	108
American Baptist	97
Seventh-Day Adventist	68
Southern Baptist	67
Foursquare	48
Church of God (Cleveland)	45
Church of the Nazarene	40
Conservative Baptist	24
United Methodist	19
Presbyterian USA	18
Assembly of Ch. Churches	16

Standing out most when comparing the two studies are the following: (1) The number of churches in Los Angeles County went up from 227 to 687 during the period. (2) The number of Pentecostal churches rose much more than the other groups. (3) The historic church groups (Methodist and Presbyterian) were becoming a much smaller part of the whole by this time. (4) Four of the five largest Latino Protestant groups in the United States today were already part of the top five in southern California at this time. This study does not include an analysis of the churches, nor any history. It is only a directory, as its name clearly states.

Reports from Specific Denominations

The general patterns reflected in the two studies carried over into each of the denominations involved in ministry among Latinas during this period.

6. Lou Cordova, *Directory of Hispanic Protestant Churches in Southern California* (Pasadena, CA: AHET, 1986).

The significant growth of the Latino community after 1965 was reflected in the growth of most denominations, particularly the evangelical and Pentecostal groups.

José Girón served as the national superintendent for the Latin American District of the **Assemblies of God** after 1958. Because of the growth of this district, in 1971 Girón guided the denomination to divide it into four districts.

- Pacific Latin American District—began with 142 churches in California, Nevada, Arizona, Oregon, Washington, and Hawaii (Girón—superintendent)
- Gulf Latin American District—began with 142 churches in Texas, Oklahoma, Louisiana, and Arkansas (Josué Sánchez—superintendent)
- Central Latin American District—began with 92 churches in Colorado, Utah, Idaho, Wyoming, New Mexico, and Montana (Néstor Bazán—superintendent)
- Mid-West Latin American District—began with 37 churches in Illinois, Iowa, Minnesota, Missouri, Kansas, Michigan, Indiana, Nebraska, Wisconsin, North Dakota, and South Dakota (Zeferino Caballo—superintendent)

These were added to the two districts that already existed, the Puerto Rico District (started in 1921) and the Eastern Hispanic District (started in 1957). In 1981 the Southeastern Latin American District was established for churches in Florida, North Carolina, South Carolina, Georgia, Alabama, and Mississippi. Later (1998) the Pacific Latin American District was divided in two, with churches in Washington, Oregon, and central and northern California forming the Northern Pacific Latin American District.

This structural expansion reflected the growth of the Latino churches. In 1977 there were 481 churches and 36,000 members. The growth experienced during this period would set the stage for more explosive growth and expanded impact in the latter part of the twentieth century. In a sense, the stage was set for that new role in 1984 when Jesse Miranda was named superintendent of the Pacific Latin American District (more in the next chapter).[7]

7. Sergio Navarrete, "Los Distritos Latinos de las Asambleas de Dios en Los Estados Unidos," in *Iglesias peregrinas en busca de identidad: Cuadros del protestantismo latino en los Estados Unidos*, ed. Juan F. Martínez Guerra and Luis Scott (Buenos Aires: Kairos Ediciones, 2004), 84–85.

The **Southern Baptists** saw a similar growth pattern, reporting faster growth during this period than the AG. The most dramatic growth happened in Texas, but they established Latino churches in most of the areas where Southern Baptists and Latinas interacted. By 1980 Joshua Grijalva reported that there were 115,000 Hispanic Baptists in the United States (40,000 in Texas) and that the Southern Baptists had 1,600 churches, 600 of which were in Texas.[8]

The Mexican Baptist Convention of Texas had merged with the Baptist General Convention of Texas in 1964. This made it possible to coordinate Baptist ministries among Latinos in the state. Anglo Baptists in Texas and throughout the United States were very willing to provide funding for evangelization and church development among Latinos. The Southern Baptist model for developing and funding ministry fell somewhere between those of the AG and the historic denominations. New ministries were provided a fair amount of funding, but local ministries were granted significant autonomy. This provided extensive opportunities for ministry expansion, though it also created situations where Latino churches received outside funding for many years.[9] But the sense among Baptists at that time was that

> Unification has been tried and proven. It is God's answer to the needs of the teeming thousands of Hispanics. The problems are many but the promises of God are greater when his people attempt great things for Christ. Some of the problems are: educational opportunities for Hispanic children, fairness and equality in job seeking, continued prejudice on the part of many, the continued flood of undocumented people into the state, etc. . . . [But] unification does not mean decentralization or loss of identification. . . . The ministry may have to be monolingual or bilingual. And there may be those who will completely blend into the American culture and society. But we can all work together for Jesus' sake.[10]

The **Seventh-Day Adventists** experienced a growth pattern similar to that of other groups. They were establishing Latino churches in each of their districts (unions), expanding into new parts of the United States as Latinas moved into those areas. By 1980 they were reporting 28,400 Latino members

---

8. Joshua Grijalva, *A History of Mexican Baptists in Texas, 1881–1981* (Dallas: Baptist General Convention of Texas, 1982), 171–72.

9. Grijalva, *Mexican Baptists in Texas,* 171–72.

10. Grijalva, *Mexican Baptists in Texas,* 184–85.

in the United States.[11] New migration also benefited them because they were also growing in Latin America. Specifically, they benefited from the Mariel Cuban boatlift. One of the goals of the Cuban government in the boatlift was to get rid of "undesirables." From the perspective of the Cubans, this included Seventh-Day Adventists and Jehovah's Witnesses. Tens of thousands of those who left were from these groups.[12] This gave the denomination a new growth spurt, which, when added to other immigrants, more than doubled the size of the Latino membership by 1990 to 65,402.[13]

This period was one of steady expansion for the **Church of God** (Cleveland, Tennessee). Its work in the United States continued to be linked to its work in Latin America, particularly as it related to publications. It also drew on its Latin American base for many new leaders. Because of the close link between the work in Latin America and ministry among US Latinas, the denomination was able to capitalize on the new migrants. During this period it expanded the number of Hispanic regions as it established churches in new areas to eight, which is the current number of regions.

The **Apostolic Assembly of the Faith in Christ Jesus** underwent a period of growth, consolidation, and change during this period. Like other Pentecostal denominations, it benefited from the growth of the Latina population through new migration. It received members from its sister denomination in Mexico and also drew new people to faith. Internally, it consolidated its organizational structure by naming bishops that provided long-term stability to the denomination. But it was also during these years that it confronted the most significant tensions with its sister denomination in Mexico.

While evangelical and Pentecostal denominations were experiencing extensive growth, the mainline denominations, with almost one hundred years of ministry in the Latina community, were looking for new ways to move forward. Integration had weakened Latino presence in both the Presbyterian and the Methodist churches. In 1968 Latinos in the Southern California–Arizona Conference of the **United Methodist Church** addressed the impact of the integration model on Latina Methodists. The Ethnic Strategy Committee of the conference stated that "integration seen as Angloization

11. Clifton L. Holland, ed., comp., producer, "Historical Profiles of Protestant Denominations with Hispanic Ministries in the USA: Listed by Major Traditions and Denominational Families," PROLADES, last updated August 15, 2012, http://www.hispanicchurchesusa.net /denominations/hsusa_historical_profiles_15August2012.pdf, 208.

12. "Mariel Boatlift," *Wikipedia*, last modified March 9, 2017, https://en.wikipedia.org /wiki/Mariel_boatlift.

13. Holland, "Historical Profiles," 208.

is an outmoded concept among Mexican Americans and no longer can be tolerated by our Latin churches. . . . Rather than accepting an Anglo model, the Hispanic leadership challenged the fundamental thinking of the church and called for others in the region to adapt to the Hispanic reality. It is against this framework that the work that followed should be measured."[14]

In 1971 Latino leaders in the denomination formed MARCHA (Metodistas Representando la Causa de los Hispanos Americanos) as a caucus within the denomination to make sure that issues related to Latinos were addressed. In 1979 they organized the National Hispanic Consultation, which served to give Latinas a sense of "power and enthusiasm" within the UMC.[15] During this period Methodists produced a hymnal, *Himnario Metodista* (1973), and two smaller songbooks, *Celebremos* (1979) and *Celebremos II* (1983), that helped to bring a sense of unity to Latino UMC churches. In 1973 the Perkins School of Theology established the Mexican American Program (MAP—now called the Hispanic/Latin@ Program) "to prepare church leaders with knowledge and skills for effective ministry in Spanish-speaking contexts and cultures." This program continues to provide leadership in theological thought and serves as an advocate on behalf of Latino churches and ministries.[16]

The Presbyterian churches, both **PCUSA** and **PCUS**, found themselves in a difficult situation at the beginning of this period. The La Raza movement among Chicanos caused the denominations to rethink the "beneficent paternalism which had so indelibly characterized their missionary operations for more than a century."[17] "As the 1960s began, both the US and UPUSA churches were coming to the realization that their respective mission programs for Mexican Americans had reached a cul de sac. In the southern church this was signaled by the dissolution of Texas-Mexican Presbytery and unsuccessful efforts to integrate the Spanish-speaking congregations into Anglo presbyteries. In the northern denominations the 'retrenchment' of educational missions in New Mexico . . . indicated that the old order was slowly giving way."[18]

14. Justo L. González, ed., *Each in Our Own Tongue: A History of Hispanics in United Methodism* (Nashville: Abingdon, 1991), 82–83.

15. González, *Each in Our Own Tongue*, 156.

16. "The Hispanic/Latin@ Ministries Program," SMU Perkins School of Theology, accessed March 30, 2017, https://www.smu.edu/Perkins/PublicPrograms/MAP.

17. R. Douglas Brackenridge and Francisco O. García-Treto, *Iglesia Presbiteriana: A History of Presbyterians and Mexican Americans in the Southwest* (San Antonio: Trinity University Press, 1974), 197.

18. Brackenridge and García-Treto, *Iglesia Presbiteriana*, 197.

As both denominations started coordinating their ministry efforts, working toward an eventual merger in 1983, in 1966 they developed the Hispanic American Institute with Dr. Jorge Lara-Braud as director. In 1967 he presented a paper, "The Church's Partnership with Mexican Americans: A Proposal to Anglo Protestant Churchmen," in which he described how Presbyterians might more effectively serve among Latinos. The relationship between Anglos and Mexican Americans was changing in US society, and the militant attitude of many of the latter was felt in the General Assembly of the PCUSA when it met in 1969. Black and brown militants occupied the New York offices of the Board of National Missions and the offices of McCormick Theological Seminary in Chicago. There was also a group of La Raza churchmen formed in southern California to address issues of concern in that synod. Throughout the 1970s, other efforts were made to address the issues of the community within the larger denomination. Yet by the mid-1980s, it was unclear whether the efforts were producing positive results in Latino Presbyterian ministry. By 1987 Brackenridge and García-Treto were asking: "In the past decade the Hispanic churches of the Southwest appear to have had little, or no, growth. Can they be said to be holding their own, even given the steady decline in the membership of the church at large? . . . [Is there] the emergence of a new self-understanding of the nature and mission of the Hispanic church?"[19]

Other Denominations

During the early years of Oneness Pentecostalism, each of the major denominations focused on one ethnic group and encouraged people of other ethnic groups to join its sister denominations. In that model the Apostolic Assembly focused on Latinas, the Pentecostal Assemblies of the World focused on African Americans, and the **United Pentecostal Church** (UPC) focused on Anglos. This began to change as the UPC did mission work in Latin America and as dissatisfied Latino Apostolic members appealed to the UPC for support. In 1978 the UPC began ministry among Latinas in New York with a group of Spanish-speaking Apostolics and would expand from there. Earlier (1971) a split among Oneness Pentecostals had served as the basis for establishing the Iglesia Pentecostal Unida Hispana, Inc., in Houston in 1971.[20]

19. Brackenridge and García-Treto, *Iglesia Presbiteriana*, 239.
20. See the denomination's Web site at http://www.ipuh.us/.

Another Oneness group developed from UPC missionary work in Colombia. As the church developed in that country, it became independent from the US body. When Colombian immigrants arrived in the United States, they began the Iglesia Pentecostal Unida Latinoamericana in 1989.[21] Throughout the years, other smaller splits among Oneness Pentecostals have produced a number of smaller Apostolic or United Pentecostal offshoots among Latinas.

Trinitarian Pentecostalism experienced a similar type of situation, particularly among Puerto Ricans in Greater New York. The number of Latino Pentecostal churches continued to grow, but the work did not consolidate into the larger denominations. Many smaller groups of churches developed, such as Federación de Iglesias Pentecostales Alpha y Omega (1967).[22] Some were started in the United States while others were missionary efforts that had started in Puerto Rico. This was also seen among Latinas in the Southwest, particularly as new immigrants brought new expressions of Pentecostal faith with them, such as Iglesia del Dios Vivo "Cristo Viene" (1974).[23] This tendency would reflect a similar tendency in Latin America for new movements to develop as new leaders branched out on their own, sensing God's call to do something new.

During this period, some smaller denominations also began or expanded work among Latinas. Some of these did not split off but instead sought ways to work together. For example, both the Mennonite Church and the Mennonite Brethren had begun work among Latinos in the 1930s. Other Anabaptist/Mennonite groups, such as the Brethren in Christ and the Evangelical Mennonite Church, began working among Latinos in the 1960s and 1970s. During the late 1970s and early 1980s, these sister denominations worked together with both Spanish-language churches in the United States and churches in Latin America to develop a common Christian education curriculum (Currículo Anabautista de Educación Bíblica Congregacional) and a joint US-based magazine, *Ecos Menonitas*. These, and other joint efforts in Latin America, reflected the growth of Anabaptist-related churches among US Latinas and in Latin America.

New movements developed during this period that demonstrated that Latinos were an increasingly diverse group of people. In 1967 Sonny Arguinzoni, an ordained AG pastor, decided to focus his ministry on drug addicts and gang members in the Los Angeles area. Victory Outreach was

21. See the denomination's Web site at http://www.ipul.us/.
22. Holland, "Historical Profiles," 273.
23. Holland, "Historical Profiles," 306.

born among Latinos and has focused most of its ministry within the Latino community. Even though it has many congregations that minister primarily in Spanish, it has never seen itself as a Latino denomination and is clearly committed to ministry beyond the Latino community. Yet it is a predominantly Latina denomination that has reached out and impacted the lives of Latinos who have found themselves in the midst of destructive lifestyles. It developed a ministry model that has successfully drawn thousands of people out of drug addition and gang lifestyles around the world. Though not formally a Latino denomination, it reflected the changing face of Latino reality and spoke, and continues to speak, to an important segment of the community.

A different type of diversification among Latinas stood out as various manifestations of renewal developed in southern California. Both **Calvary Chapel** and **Vineyard** attracted Latinos from early on, and both developed Spanish-language ministries during this period. But they also have attracted many Latinos who preferred to worship in English. These movements have attracted Latinas across the spectrum of Latino identity. There are people in the English-language services who speak Spanish once they walk out of church, people who prefer to worship in Spanish, Latino leaders who lead English-language congregations, and Anglos who lead congregations that worship in Spanish.

Other denominational families also started Latino congregations, though their presence was not felt as strongly as the major denominations. By the 1980s there were Latino churches in most Protestant theological traditions. Most had small clusters of churches or congregations scattered wherever there were existing Anglo churches in the midst of new Latina communities.

Most of the growth reported by existing denominations and the new movements reflected an expansion directly linked to the growth of the Latina community and to the increasing impact of Protestantism, both among the Spanish-speaking population in the United States and throughout Latin America. But the patterns of growth also reflected the changing face of US Protestantism. It was the evangelical and Pentecostal groups that were growing, often fairly rapidly. And it was the historic denominations, some of which had a longer history among Latinos, that were either not growing or were finding it difficult to expand their ministries in the midst of the demographic expansion.

The Civil Rights Movement and Its Impact on Latino Protestantism

The civil rights movement had a significant impact on the Latina community. Though the focus of the 1965 civil rights legislation was the African American community, Latinos also rose up to question the existing order and to seek their rights. One of the areas in which their efforts produced a positive result was the 1965 immigration legislation. They also addressed issues of education, housing, policing, and workers' rights.

The issues raised by the civil rights movement affected Latino Protestantism on several levels. As Latinas were seeking recognition of their rights, Protestant churches were having to ask hard questions about their attitudes toward Latinos and toward the social issues being raised by Latinas around the United States.

Internally, Latinos were challenging the existing denominational structures. They were also seeking (or demanding) a place at the decision-making table. The earlier models of integration and assimilation had failed, and now a new model was needed. Some denominations formed Latino caucuses in which Latina leaders sought a voice; others named Latino leaders to head Latina-oriented ethnic ministries. Latinos were leaving denominations to form their own because they felt they lacked input on what was happening there. This was further complicated by the different types of needs felt by the various Latino groups in the country.

But the issues raised externally also had an impact. What role, if any, should Latino Protestants have in the social issues directly related to them? The question was particularly pertinent during the struggle over farm workers' rights and the protests in several major cities related to housing, education, and employment opportunities. Groups like the Young Lords, the Brown Berets, and La Raza Unida Party sought to galvanize Latinos toward action. One of the most well known of these efforts was the attempt by César Chávez's United Farm Workers (UFW) to organize agricultural labor in central California and elsewhere.

Different denominations responded very differently to the organizing efforts of the UFW. For many evangelicals this was something outside of their realm of understanding of the ministry of the church. They did not see a role for the church in the farm workers' movement. If they spoke to the issue at all, it was usually in a negative light, assuming that the UFW represented left-leaning interests that would not benefit the United States in general.

On the other hand, there was considerable support for the UFW among mainline denominations. The Migrant Ministry (later the National Farm

Worker Ministry) of the National Council of Churches publicly supported the UFW. Chris Hartmire, an ordained Presbyterian pastor, who served as the executive director of the ministry from 1961 to 1981, strongly supported the UFW, a position that was seen as controversial in many circles. He later resigned from this position to work directly with the union. Hartmire worked hard to connect the NCC to the UFW.[24] The NCC, the Disciples of Christ, the United Church of Christ, and the Unitarian Universalist Association all made statements in favor of the UFW at different times.[25]

These statements of public support for Latino rights occurred in the midst of other external changes within mainline Protestantism. As these churches became more interested in ecumenical relations, they were less interested in inviting Latinas to leave Catholicism, even if it was only a nominal faith for them, and joining their churches. Because most Latina Protestant converts were formerly Roman Catholic, even if only by name, this created a dilemma for mainline Protestant denominations who were strengthening links with the Roman Catholic Church at that time. What had always been understood as evangelization by Protestants was now seen by many in mainline churches as proselytizing. So even though they were working for Latino rights among farm workers and later protecting Latinos through the Sanctuary Movement, mainline denominations did not reap significant growth in Latina membership. Because this was not an issue for Pentecostals and evangelicals, they continued to draw nominal Roman Catholics into their churches while historic denominations were involved in efforts to support their civil rights.

The issue was further complicated because the people involved in these types of ministries often did not reflect the attitudes of the people in the pews. The majority of Anglos in mainline churches did not necessarily support the UFW or the Sanctuary Movement.

But the role of Latino Protestants in these types of movements was also complicated by the changing theological understanding of Latino Pentecostals about their role in society. Historically, most had been apolitical. But a few began to work on social justice issues. Reies López Tijerina, a

24. See Ronald A. Wells, "Cesar Chavez's Protestant Allies: The California Migrant Ministry and the Farm Workers," *Journal of Presbyterian History* (Spring/Summer 2009): 5–16; Pat Hoffman, *Ministry of the Dispossessed: Learning from the Farm Worker Movement* (Los Angeles: Wallace Press, 1987); Frank Bardacke, *Trampling Out the Vintage: Cesar Chavez and the Two Souls of the United Farm Workers* (New York: Verso, 2011), 121–24.

25. "Statements and Resolutions," National Farm Worker Ministry, 2017, http://nfwm .org/statements-resolutions/.

licensed AG pastor, worked land rights issues in New Mexico during the 1960s. Though his credentials were revoked by the denomination, he became an important face of the Latino struggles for justice.

There were also a few Latino AG pastors that participated with César Chávez and had an influence on his organizing efforts. Chávez was influenced by Latino Pentecostals as a child and learned from their religious commitment. Lay Latino Pentecostals participated in the Community Service Organization (CSO) and later in the UFW. Chávez himself recognized that he learned from the spirit of Latino Pentecostals and that he used some of their techniques in his union organizing. Chávez also drew deeply on his Catholic faith and the faith of people, which tended to create tensions with nonreligious liberal allies of the movement. But Chávez also lamented that he often got better support from Protestant pastors, while Catholic priests were sometimes reluctant to openly support him.[26]

There was a different type of social commitment among Protestants regarding the Cuban refugees who began to settle in the United States in large numbers during the 1960s. Because some of the refugees were already members of sister denominations in Cuba, resettlement programs of various types helped link them to the churches of their denominational background. Because many of the first generation of Cuban refugees had been in positions of power and influence in Cuba, they were prepared to become part of the fabric of society. Once they became citizens, they began voting and gradually became a major political and economic force in Miami and elsewhere. They also began to have an influence on national Spanish-language media and in the Republican Party. This type of leadership also led to strong Latino churches and to leaders in denominational structures.

But overall, Latino Protestants did not play a significant role in the civil rights movement. Latinos were marginalized in the religious structures, be they Catholic or Protestant, and had little influence on them. Most of the key Latino leaders in the struggle were formed outside of the churches, in contrast to most African American leaders of the period. And because Latino Protestants had been doubly marginalized, as a minority within a minority, most found it difficult to find a voice in this struggle. The theology of most of the churches invited Latinos to personal transformation but assumed that social transformation would happen only when Jesus returned. During this period most Latino Protestants did not see themselves as potential agents of

---

26. Gastón Espinosa, *Latino Pentecostals in America: Faith and Politics in Action* (Cambridge, MA: Harvard University Press, 2014), 334–39.

change in US society. That is why Clifton Holland's assessment of the situation among Hispanic Protestants in Los Angeles in 1970 would have applied to the majority of Latino Protestants in the United States.

> Many Mexican Americans seriously question the relevance of religious institutions—Catholic and Protestant—which refuse to stand with suppressed minorities in their struggles for social justice within American society. Have institutional churches, whether the Catholic Church or the various Protestant denominations, forfeited their right to be heard because of the lack of involvement in improving socioeconomic conditions among Mexican Americans and in bringing social justice to the *barrios* of Southern California? Social *service* is not enough, social *action* is required—that is, *changing* unjust social structures that have created and that maintain injustice for the nation's minorities, especially blacks, Indians, and Hispanic Americans. This type of corrective action is a biblical and moral imperative.[27]

US Politics in Central America and a New Migratory Wave

As stated in chapter 2, one of the key threads for understanding Latina Protestantism is migration, particularly new migratory patterns created by US intervention in Latin America. The civil wars in Central America during the 1960s–1990s created a great deal of social upheaval in the region. During this time of rapid change, many people looked to new religious expressions as a way to address the painful realities they were facing. The existing religious system, Roman Catholicism, did not seem to address their needs. For some, the Catholic Church seemed to be allied with the powers of oppression. Some people rejected religion altogether, but others were attracted to liberation theology, which seemed to offer them a way to draw from their faith experiences to address the need for profound social change.

But the civil wars and internal conflicts were happening within the global context of the Cold War. In the United States the civil wars were framed within the struggle between capitalism (or Christian faith) and (godless) communism. But for many in Latin America, the issue was injustice. For these people liberation theology seemed to offer a way forward, because it helped them draw from their faith as they struggled for change. But the

---

27. Holland, *Religious Dimension*, 415–16.

majority of the poor rejected liberation theology. Said one Maryknoll nun in Guatemala: "Liberation theology opted for the poor, but the poor opted for Pentecostalism."

People were looking for fresh expressions of faith in the midst of their suffering. Catholicism, which had been the official religion of most Latin American countries, was not seen as life giving by many people. Pentecostalism had been increasingly attractive to the poor. It provided a space for an encounter with God, a personal transformation, and a place where the poor could be subjects of mission and church. The charismatic renewal of the 1960s and 1970s created new religious expressions throughout Latin America. New religious movements developed that quickly left behind traditional Protestantism and even challenged some of the Pentecostal movements.[28]

As people were drawn to these new expressions of faith, some people tried to draw a link to the work of the CIA in the region. It is clear that some of the US missionaries shared the Cold War interpretation of the situation, and that some of the new movements were influenced by leaders in the United States. But the situation was much more complex. People were being drawn to new expressions of faith and experience with God in the midst of the violence and social disorder. In the course of a couple of decades, Protestants went from being a minuscule minority to becoming a significant presence in many countries in Latin America.

It was in the midst of the violence and the religious reordering that people started fleeing Central America during the first part of the 1980s. Because many people and politicians in the United States saw the civil wars as a part of the East-West conflict, they believed that any and all actions by the military governments to stop the advance of communism were justified, including a growing number of massacres. President Jimmy Carter had attempted to control the military support to these regimes, but the Reagan administration provided strong political, financial, and military support as these governments oppressed their people and killed hundreds of thousands of civilians. Anyone who questioned their actions was treated as a leftist sympathizer. Because of the increasing violence as governments used any means to crush the guerilla movements, many people fled their countries and arrived at the US border seeking political asylum. But because the United States was supporting the governments they were fleeing, it seldom

28. See Jean-Pierre Bastian, *La mutación religiosa de América Latina para una sociología del cambio social en la modernidad periférica* (Mexico City: Fondo de Cultura Económica, 1997), for an analysis of the development of the new religious movements.

recognized them as political refugees, even though the violence they were fleeing was much more destructive than what the Cubans had fled a few years earlier.

As a result of US government policy, many mainline Protestant churches started the Sanctuary Movement. Churches, mostly mainline Protestant churches, offered their buildings to refugees as safe havens in light of the restrictive immigration policies of the US government. Some of these churches helped people make it to Canada, where the government was accepting Central American refugees if they could prove that their lives were in danger. Over five hundred churches directly offered protection to people fleeing the violence, and many more supported their work indirectly.

The Sanctuary Movement was another example of the changing face of mainline Protestant ministry among Latinas. The churches provided this type of support, but, for the most part, did not attempt to draw the Central American refugees into them. Some churches provided spiritual support for those staying in their building, including counseling and religious services. But there were few efforts to organize them into church congregations. Many benefited from these efforts, but for the most part, those helped did not look toward these churches for long-term spiritual support. Many of those who were Catholic looked to the Catholic Church for their spiritual community. But many were from Pentecostal or evangelical churches and so looked there for a church.

So the 1980s turned out to be a time of significant growth for Latino Pentecostal and evangelical churches, reflecting growth patterns similar to those happening in the countries of origin of the new migrants. Because a growing percentage of the Central American migrants were already Protestant, they tended to join existing Latino churches, often bringing new spiritual vitality to those churches.

But some Central Americans also brought their own churches with them to the United States. Some groups, like Elim (Guatemala) and Elim (El Salvador), established churches where Central Americans from these churches were settling. As these churches grew, they expanded beyond the Central American base and began to draw Latinas from other national backgrounds. Other movements, like Amor Viviente (Honduras), partnered with existing denominations to establish churches in the United States. Still others, like Llamada Final, were started in the United States, but with leaders and church people who came from Guatemala and other parts of Central America.

Latino churches, particularly in the Southwest, received new energy from the new migrants and developed new outreach efforts toward other migrants. Though most of the Protestant migrants were from Pentecostal backgrounds, many Protestants from non-Pentecostal movements joined churches of their own denominational tradition, or found churches with similar theological framing. Protestants like those from Iglesias Centroamericanas, a Central American denomination without a direct denominational link to the United States, usually joined existing conservative, non-Pentecostal evangelical churches, though later, a few churches with a direct link to that denomination were started in the United States. Because mainline denominations had a very limited presence in Central America, Latino churches from those denominations did not benefit directly as much from this migratory wave.

By the time the issue of the Central American refugees was partially resolved with the immigration act of 1986 (see next chapter), Latino Pentecostal and neo-Pentecostal churches had experienced new growth and the strengthening of existing churches because of this new wave of immigrants. The growth of Latino Protestant churches in the Southwest during this period was largely due to the influx of Central Americans.

The New Waves from the Caribbean

Immigration from Cuba had slowed down after the "air" bridge of the 1960s ended. But the United States continued to give immediate refugee status to any Cuban who made it to the US mainland. That policy was put to the test when dissident Cubans invaded various embassies in Havana and the Cuban government allowed anyone who wanted to leave Cuba to do so, if another country would receive them. In April 1980 the Cuban government opened Mariel Harbor for boats from the United States that wanted to pick people up. From that time until the two nations came to an agreement and Cuba closed the harbor, about 125,000 people were carried to the United States from Cuba (and some from Haiti). This wave impacted Latino Protestantism because many churches responded to the need, but also because the Cuban government used the boatlift to get rid of "undesirable" people, including thousands of Seventh-Day Adventists and Jehovah's Witnesses. The "Marielitas," as they came to be called, were different in class and education from many of the earlier Cuban migrants and created new challenges for the Cuban Protestant churches, but also growth for the Seventh-Day Adventists.[29]

29. "Mariel Boatlift," *Wikipedia*.

But the Caribbean country that sent the most migrants to the United States during the 1980s was the Dominican Republic. Even though Dominican migration began in earnest after the US invasion of Santo Domingo in 1963, immigrant numbers were not very large until the 1980s. During that decade over 250,000 Dominicans were legally admitted into the country. By the 1990 census, the majority of the Dominican population in the United States was foreign-born. Most of them settled in the Northeast (over 80 percent), like the Puerto Ricans.[30]

Unique Face of Latino Protestantism

While some of the denominations with a historic presence in the Latina community were struggling to gain a new footing for mission, Latinas were opting to become evangelicals and Pentecostals. Even as mainline denominations became more concerned with issues related to Latinos, such as civil rights, the farm workers' movement, or, later, the Sanctuary Movement, Latinas increasingly joined Pentecostal or evangelical churches. In part, this is because the mainline's focus on justice issues detracted from efforts of evangelism and church establishment. Also, working alongside Catholics raised questions about whether they should draw people out of Catholicism into Protestant churches. Some historic Protestant churches attempted to address this issue by establishing more "Catholic"-friendly practices, such as including Catholic saints and virgins. While Anglicans in Latin America have historically focused on the fact that they are Protestants, many Episcopalians in the United States that wanted to reach out to Latinos focused on a "Catholic" worship style.

So, while historic denominations expanded their focus on providing Latinos social services and supported Central Americans through the Sanctuary Movement, Latino Pentecostals and evangelicals began many new churches among these same immigrants. Also, the growth of Protestantism, particularly Pentecostalism, in Latin America meant that more of the new immigrants were already Protestants. Some of them brought their own churches and movements with them, while others arrived in the United States and started new movements.

By the 1980s, Latino Protestantism was looking different from Latin

30. Sean T. Buffington, "Dominican Americans," Countries and Their Cultures, accessed March 20, 2017, http://www.everyculture.com/multi/Bu-Dr/Dominican-Americans.html.

American or US Protestantism, even though both were clearly influencing it. Though US Protestantism still had a strong mainline presence, by this time Latino Protestantism was already majority Pentecostal, with the significant exception of Texas. But Latino Protestantism was also different from that of some of the Latin American places that nourished it, because those places, particularly Guatemala, El Salvador, and Puerto Rico, were already more Protestant, and were seeing more conversions to Protestantism, than US Latinos in general.

Another important change during this period was the growing recognition of the influence of assimilation on the religious tendencies of Latino Protestants. A growing number of them were worshiping in English. Traditionally, many had assumed that becoming a Protestant was part of the adaptation process into life in the United States. But this is not necessarily the case. Yet younger Latinas were being attracted to ministries that looked different from the "traditional" Latino Protestant church. So Latino Protestantism was clearly beginning to reflect the complex identities of Latinas in the United States. New immigrants were bringing life and flourishing to the churches. But US-born Latinos were also looking toward new ministries. Latino Protestants were looking toward Latin America, toward US Protestantism, and toward Pentecostal renewal movements all at the same time they were seeking to define what it meant to be Latina Protestant. In the middle of all that, Latino leaders were beginning to find a voice in US Protestantism, even if that voice was not always heard.

People and Voices from This Period

As Latina Protestantism continued to diversify, its leaders took on very different roles and had an increasingly diverse impact. Some were known for their leadership within the Latino Protestant community, while others gained a platform beyond the community. But they were all Latino Protestant leaders who intentionally understood that their role came out of being Latina Protestant leaders.

If US Protestants from this period had been asked to name one Latino Protestant, they would have likely named Nuyorican **Nicky Cruz**. His story of conversion from a gang lifestyle to an Assemblies of God preacher is told in the 1962 best seller *The Cross and the Switchblade*. David Wilkerson told the story of his work among gang members in New York, in which Cruz was one of the key converts. (The book was made into a movie in 1970.) Cruz also wrote *Run, Baby, Run,* which focuses on his conversion. He was strongly influenced by Mama Leo and the ministry of Iglesia Cristiana Damasco (mentioned in the last chapter).

Though the story can be read as a Christian version of *West Side Story,* Cruz's testimony is a reflection of how Latino Pentecostalism would see itself. The good news of the gospel could change the life of a gang member and make him into a preacher who would help others leave that lifestyle. Cruz is a key example of creating social change through the conversion of an individual. He later followed a trajectory common among AG leaders. After his conversion he went to Latin American Bible Institute (LABI) in La Puente, California. He later became an evangelist and TV preacher. He continued ministry to gang members through Nicky Cruz Outreach.

Arguably the most controversial Latino Pentecostal preacher of the period was **Reies López Tijerina**. He was born in Texas, where he joined an AG church. He studied at the LABI in Texas and was licensed as an evangelist. He preached throughout the Southwest, but had his credentials revoked because of his increasingly fanatical style of preaching and his apocalyptic message. In the 1950s he attempted to begin a Christian commune in Arizona, but had to abandon the project due to local opposition. After this period he became aware of the issues related to the land grants in New Mexico and helped organize people to address this. During the 1960s he organized people into a political movement that took over land in New Mexico and attempted to organize a community on that land. After he was arrested and removed from the land, he and his followers attempted to perform a citizens' arrest of the district attorney who was involved in the arrest. The raid on the county courthouse in Tierra Amarilla in 1967 made him a national figure. He later joined with other civil rights leaders to address the larger issue of minority rights. His influence dwindled over time, though he continued fighting for Latino rights. Though he later officially became a Catholic (it was never an important part of his work), his style and his commitment were formed by his AG upbringing. He always maintained the passion of a Pentecostal evangelist in his concerns for social justice.

Probably the most well-known Latino theologian in the United States and Latin America is **Justo González**. He was born in Cuba, and his parents were missionaries in Latin America. He came to study in the United States right before the Cuban Revolution, and ended up staying there. Though a Methodist, he is one of the Latino leaders with a strong influence in mainline, evangelical, and Pentecostal circles. He is par excellence an example of a Cuban exile who became an important leader of Latino Protestantism as it began a growth spurt during this period.

González is known in many Protestant circles because of his extensive scholarship and his broad contribution to theology and church history. Many theology students have read his books (in English, in Spanish, and translated into other languages) on church history and the history of Christian thought. He was also one of the key voices in the development of Latino theology. He has written broadly, and his influence has been felt throughout the Latino Protestant world.

Because of his broad influence, González developed a platform still in use in the twenty-first century. During the 1980s he encouraged US seminaries to take the needs of Latino students into account. During the 1990s he helped start three organizations that continue to address theological education to this day. Hispanic Summer Program (HSP), Hispanic Theological Initiative (HTI), and Asociación para La Educación Teológica Hispana (AETH) are all programs initiated by González that will be described in the next chapter. Because he is a trusted leader in both Latino and Anglo communities, he has become an important power broker in the Latino Protestant world and in relation to the larger Protestant world, particularly in mainline churches and structures.

Joshua (Josué) Grijalva served as president of the Mexican Baptist Convention of Texas from 1953 to 1955 and from 1964 to 1966. He was recognized as an important leader by Baptists in Texas, and in 1977 he was asked to write *A History of Mexican Baptists in Texas* in preparation for the celebration of the centennial of Mexican Baptist ministry in Texas. This book became the most complete review of Latino Baptist work in the state. Though the book was mostly a review, he also addressed some issues facing Anglo and Latino Baptists as they worked together in ministry. Back in 1980 he spoke to Anglo Baptists about the role that Latinos would have among Southern Baptists (and other church groups). Even today his words sound prophetic.

Non-Hispanic evangelicals need to experience what Latinos call *concientización*, an awareness of the needs of Hispanics in the light of their culture, customs, and traditions. While the Hispanic immigrant in this country accepts the economy, education and social life, ofttimes he has left his religion back in his country. This offers opportunities for witnessing on our part.

Hispanics are often critical of the artificiality of Anglo-Americans. What Baptists say they believe is not always what they practice. Such "double standards" often confuse ethnics. Most ethnic converts generally embrace New Testament Christianity in a purer sense of the word than most traditional Protestant practitioners. Bringing ethnics into the Baptist fold can revitalize our churches.[31]

Another Cuban immigrant who had an important influence in the development of Latino Pentecostalism, particularly in southern California, was **Lázaro Santana**. When he settled in southern California, he became an evangelist linked with the Church of God. His testimony of God's power presented a message that was very attractive and was able to cross ethnic and national boundaries in southern California. Not only did he have a direct impact, but several of his children became important leaders within the Church of God.

Alberto Motessi, originally from Argentina, is most well known as a Latin American evangelist. But since the 1970s he has been based in the Los Angeles area. Though Latin America has been his principal focus, Spanish-speaking US Latinos have also been an important part of his outreach. His work crosses borders and his ministries do the same. His ministry developed a number of television programs that are broadcast, or on cable, in most countries of Latin America and in the Spanish-speaking United States. His leadership-training programs are based in the Los Angeles area and have extensions throughout the Spanish-speaking world. Though his first impact was during the 1970s and 1980s in the United States, he is still seen as an important evangelist, the Billy Graham of the Spanish-speaking world.

Jorge Lara-Braud was born in Mexico in 1931. He came to the United States to attend high school at the Presbyterian Pan-American School in Kingsville, Texas. He had a conversion experience there and joined the Presbyterian church. He studied at Austin Presbyterian Seminary and completed his PhD at Princeton. He was on the faculty of Austin Seminary when he was invited to form and lead a Hispanic American institute based at the seminary in 1966. He used that platform to address key issues related to how Presbyterians should work among Latinos in Texas and elsewhere, though he resigned in 1972, frustrated that the denomination did not seem willing to move forward with his recommendations. In spite of this, he was truly a transnational leader. After serving in Austin he became the dean of the Presbyterian seminary in Mexico, taught at San Francisco Theological Seminary, and served as the director of Faith and Order for the National Council of

---

31. Grijalva, *Mexican Baptists in Texas*, 187.

Churches. His impact was felt in Presbyterian circles throughout the latter part of the twentieth century.[32]

The inflow of new immigrant Protestant leaders made it possible for ministries to develop more quickly. The leadership pool created by new migrants benefited most of the denominations that wanted to work in the Latina community. But the inflow also delayed the issue of how best to prepare leaders from within the Latino community for the increasing diversity of the community.

During most of the twentieth century, the various groups under the umbrella Latino or Hispanic were seen as separate groups. The 1970 census officially brought all these communities under the category Hispanic. Even as the community was expanding and becoming more diverse, the US government sought to constrict it under one defining term. What united ministry across these groups had been a common language. Now it would be a perceived ethnic/racial unity. The Mexican Baptist Convention of Texas would become the Hispanic Convention. The national differences would be subsumed under this new term. But increasingly, so would the issues related to participation in US majority culture. Because of new migration, Latinas would also be tagged "eternally foreign," no matter how far back they could trace their lineage in the United States. But it would also be as Hispanics or Latinos that they would struggle to find a place at the table of US Protestantism.

How US Latino Protestantism Became Central American and Puerto Rican (Caribbean)

One of the interesting side notes about Latino Protestantism is that demographically it does not look like the Latina community at large. While Mexicans and Mexican Americans constitute over 60 percent of the Latino population, this number is not reflected in Latina Protestant church membership and is much smaller for nationally recognized Latino Protestant leaders. This is due to a number of factors, some of which developed during this period.

As mentioned throughout the chapter, a key factor in the growth of

---

32. Brackenridge and García-Treto, *Iglesia Presbiteriana*, 203–25; Jerry L. Van Marter, "Jorge Lara-Braud, Pastor, Theologian, Fighter for the Poor Dies at 77," *Presbyterian Outlook*, July 2, 2008, https://pres-outlook.org/2008/07/jorge-lara-braud-pastor-theologian-fighter-for -the-poor-dies-at-77/.

Latina Protestantism during this period was the migration of Latino Protestants to the United States. There was significant migration from localities that had a growing Protestant presence and places that already had trained and experienced Protestant pastors. First it was Puerto Rico and Cuba, and later it was countries in Central America. Though Mexico has sent the most migrants to the United States, it is also the most Catholic country in the world. It has the smallest percentage of Protestant believers of any of the major Latin American sending countries.

This creates a situation where not only are Puerto Ricans and Central Americans "overrepresented" as a percentage of the Latina Protestant population, but they are also "overrepresented" among Latino Protestant leaders. As the Latino Protestant community matured in the last part of the twentieth century and into the twenty-first century, two of the most well-known Latino Protestant leaders, Sammy Rodríguez of NHCLC and Luis Cortés of Esperanza USA, are both of Puerto Rican descent, as is Gabriel Salguero of the National Latino Evangelical Coalition (NaLEC). And the most well-known Latino Protestant theologian, Justo González, was born in Cuba. Jesse Miranda is one of the few Mexican Americans whose name might be known at the same level as these leaders.

This was not always the case, since the first Protestant converts in the Southwest were all of Mexican descent and the vast majority of all Latina Protestants were of Mexican descent through the 1970s. But, as some places in Latin America, such as Puerto Rico, Guatemala, and El Salvador, became more Protestant than the US Latina population and also sent more migrants to the United States, this "overrepresentation" became more pronounced. Before 1965 it was only the Puerto Ricans that were "overrepresented." But as Cubans and, later, Central Americans became part of the Latino community, they added to this situation. These places also sent more experienced Protestant clergy to serve Latino churches in the United States.

Given current migration patterns from Latin America, Latino Protestantism will likely continue to be more Puerto Rican and Central American than the Latino population at large. It is probable that Latino Protestant leaders will continue to reflect that reality. But it is also likely that US Latinas will continue to have a smaller percentage of Protestants than a growing number of countries in Latin America.

Chapter 7

Latino Protestants Are Finally "Discovered" (1986–2000)

The Immigration Reform and Control Act of 1986 legalized about 2.7 million people, including many Latino Protestants. Their legalized presence provided stability for the growing number of Latino Protestant churches and also the opportunity for these legal immigrants to petition for their families to come to the States. But the law also created other political pressures. By the 1990s the Clinton administration began the increasing militarization of the US-Mexico border. This changed the often temporary migratory patterns of many people and had an unintended consequence—a growing percentage of undocumented people would no longer move back and forth across the border, but would choose to remain in the United States and bring their families. During this same period, the North American Free Trade Agreement (NAFTA) created new pressures on the Mexican population, particularly the rural subsistence farmers, who were not able to compete against US industrialized, and sometimes subsidized, agricultural production. So a new generation of Mexicans left their farming lands and migrated north.

But this is also the period in which Latino Protestantism began to find a voice and be recognized as having something to say to the larger world. The development of a more clearly defined Latina theology, books by Latinos about Latina ministry, and the beginning of national Latino Protestant organizations—all these represented an expanding role for Latina Protestants within US Protestantism.

Immigration Reform and Control Act of 1986

The next major immigration reform act that had a significant impact on the Latina community was the Simpson-Mazzoli Act of 1986. This law sought to address two major issues: the status of a growing undocumented population and the need to control the job market that attracted these people to the United States. On the latter issue, this new law made it mandatory that employers check the legal status of any new employees and made it illegal for employers to knowingly hire undocumented workers.

The law also provided an amnesty (when this word was approved even by Republicans) for two groups of people, agricultural workers and those who had been in the United States continuously for at least four years. In his public statement upon signing the bill, President Ronald Reagan said this amnesty should favor those who had become a part of the fabric of the United States. People who qualified for this amnesty had to demonstrate that they did not have a criminal record, and that they had some knowledge of US history and the English language. They also had to admit guilt to being in the country illegally, pay a fine, and pay any back taxes they might owe.

The 1986 amnesty began to address the growing number of Central American refugees and the large number of Mexicans who had entered the country because of employment opportunities but had not entered legally. It provided legal stability to those who were working here and wanted to be able to do so without fear. As with other laws before it, the 1986 act did not adequately address the future flow of migrant workers. The demand for workers at the low end of the job market continued. The law did not answer the question: How would future workers find a legal way to enter the United States? It also did not really deal with employers who hired the undocumented. Many employers used subcontractors to skirt the law, while others hired people with no legal processing. It also created a proliferation of "creative documentation," which often got the undocumented through the verification process.

Because of the nature of the legalization process, the 1986 act allowed churches and other nonprofit agencies to help people complete the application paperwork. Many Latino churches became a part of this process, both to help their own church people and as a service to the community. The church members that legalized their status provided their churches with increased stability. These churches now had members more likely to stay in the United States and a more stable income base from which to support their ministries. As a result, many Latina Protestant churches saw a direct benefit from the 1986 amnesty.

As with the 1965 law, the 1986 act merely recognized what was already happening and attempted to provide a legal framework to deal with it. The older migratory patterns had not changed. The new part was that now there were also Central Americans in the mix because of US intervention in the civil wars in the region. But their presence, and their growth as part of the Latino community, changed, again, the face of the Latina community and of Latino Protestantism.

The 1986 law had a number of unforeseen results. First, the legalization process allowed for those who now had legal status to request the immigration of family members, creating a steady immigration flow for several years. Second, the two million people who did not qualify for the amnesty were now in a more precarious legal situation. Those who wrote the law assumed these people would leave. But because their labor was still needed, they developed new ways to live and work in the United States despite the new law. Third, the 1986 amnesty created the expectation for another amnesty within a few years. Since the law did not address future flow, people entered the United States undocumented, assuming that the United States would address the issue through amnesties since it did not do it through work visas. Another interesting side note is that people did not necessarily choose to become citizens after the amnesty, particularly those from Mexico. It seemed as if they wanted a legal status to work safely in the United States but still hoped to return to Mexico, so they did not become US citizens in high numbers.[1]

The 1986 law also marked a changing view of undocumented migration. A law passed in 1990 raised the cap on the number of people who could migrate to the United States. But a more open immigration policy did not create a more positive attitude toward the border. There was a sense in the Clinton administration that the border had to be more secure. So work on building and reinforcing the border fence began during the 1990s. Also, in 1996 the immigration law that was passed by Congress and signed by President Clinton increased the penalties for those in the United States without proper authorization. Border crossing without going through a legal checkpoint,

1. Nancy Rytina, "IRCA Legalization Effects: Lawful Permanent Residence and Naturalization through 2001" (paper presented at conference on the Effects of Immigrant Legalization Programs on the United States, the Cloister, Mary Woodward Lasker Center, NIH Main Campus, Bethesda, MD, October 25, 2002), https://www.dhs.gov/xlibrary/assets/statistics/publications/irca0114int.pdf.

which had been relatively easy in the past, became a deadly proposition. Fences and increased patrols near urban areas pushed the undocumented into more dangerous desert areas. Crossing the border became the business of the same mafias that were smuggling drugs north and weapons south. Dying at the border became a new reality for those trying to enter the United States without legal documentation.

When President George W. Bush was elected in 2000, he was convinced of the importance of a new relationship between the United States and Mexico. So he sought to create a more positive process for the movement of people between the two countries. As part of the commitment to work toward a long-term solution for immigration reform, he met several times with President Fox of Mexico. But the events of September 11, 2001, changed his focus, and the possibility of long-term immigration reform was lost once again.

The North American Free Trade Agreement (NAFTA) happened in the midst of all this. Signed on December 17, 1992, it opened markets but also changed the labor demands. On the Mexican side, it drew many people to the border, where *maquiladoras* manufactured products for the US market. It created freer markets for US products in Mexico. But it also created a new exodus from Mexican farms to the cities and to the United States.

Another Growth Decade for the Latino Population

While NAFTA and border security were affecting migration from Mexico and Central America, one country in South America began to send immigrants north in significant numbers during this period. Small groups of Colombians, often professionals, had migrated into the United States throughout the twentieth century. But the increased violence related to the long-term civil war, tied to drug trafficking and US intervention in Colombia to deal with it, created a massive dislocation of people within Colombia and a significant emigration from that country. Colombia became one of the world's leaders in internally displaced populations. During the 1980s and 1990s, these factors created a significant migration from Colombia, making it the leading South American country to send migrants to the United States; it stands at number fourteen in foreign-born migrants in the United States and at number seven in national background among Latinos.[2]

2. Sharon R. Ennis, Merarys Rios-Vargas, and Nora G. Albert, "The Hispanic Population: 2010," 2010 Census Brief, United States Census Bureau, May 2011, http://www.census.gov/prod

Migration kept the Latino population in a growth mode during most of this period. Legal migration into this country since the beginning of the 1990s has been about 1 million people a year, and most migrants have come from Latin America. But the biggest growth in the Latino community during this time came from internal growth—births among Latinas already in the United States. From 1980 through 2000 the Latina community grew from 14 million to over 35 million.[3] The majority of Latinos in the United States have always been US-born, but each new immigrant wave kept the focus on those more recently arrived. This has traditionally created a sense of Latinas as eternal foreigners or foreigners in their own land. But the reality of multiple-generation US-born Latinos has allowed them to become more prominent in the thinking of US Protestants, and among Latino Protestants.

Growth and Development at a National Level

The substantial growth in the Latina community during this period provided new outreach opportunities for Protestants. New immigrants provided Protestants new people to serve and also new people to invite into Christian faith, Protestant style. But these newer immigrants also strengthened Latino Protestant churches, because many of them were already Protestants. Some of them also created new denominations and movements in the United States. Their presence helped invigorate existing Latina churches and served as the base for many new Latino congregations. But their growing presence also helped Latina Protestantism by expanding the platform from which Latino Protestant leaders could develop their own voice as they entered the national stage.

But the US-born population provided their own opportunities and challenges. US-born Latina Protestants were growing up in Latino churches and being a part of the growth. But they were also asking new questions

---

/cen2010/briefs/c2010br-04.pdf; "The Colombian Diaspora in the United States," Migration Policy Institute, revised May 2015, http://www.migrationpolicy.org/sites/default/files/publi cations/RAD-ColombiaII.pdf.

3. See Campbell Gibson and Kay Jung, "Historical Census Statistics on Population Totals by Race, 1790 to 1990, and by Hispanic Origin, 1970 to 1990, for Large Cities and Other Urban Places in the United States," United States Census Bureau, Population Division, Working Paper no. 76, February 2005, https://www.census.gov/population/www/documentation/twps0076 /twps0076.pdf; Ennis, Rios-Vargas, and Albert, "The Hispanic Population: 2010."

and inviting Protestants to think in new ways about ministry in the Latina community.

Clifton Holland and PROLADES continued to develop or sponsor studies of Latino Protestant churches in different regions of the United States. In 1988 they sponsored a study in the San Francisco Bay Area that identified 157 Latino churches in the six-county area.[4] This work continued to be used in different parts of the United States, as Holland worked toward a national database of Latino Protestant churches.

PROLADES used the same methodology in conjunction with HABBM (Hispanic Association for Bilingual-Bicultural Ministries) and in 1993 developed the first national database of Latino Protestant churches since the early twentieth century (when there were very few churches to account for). The 1993 database listed 6,837 congregations, geographically distributed as follows (top eight states):

California	2,388
Texas	1,799
Florida	643
New York	353
Illinois	277
Arizona	231
New Mexico	173
New Jersey	118

These churches were part of the following groups:

Assemblies of God	1,268
Southern Baptist Convention	759
Other Baptists	447
Apostolic Assembly	444
Seventh-Day Adventists	283
Churches of Christ	248
Church of God (Cleveland, TN)	227
United Methodist Church	199
Presbyterian Church USA	143

4. Clifton L. Holland, comp., "A Chronology of Significant Protestant Beginnings in Hispanic Ministry in the USA," PROLADES, last revised July 31, 2003, http://www.prolades.com /historical/usa-hisp-chron.pdf.

Church of the Nazarene	129
American Baptist Churches	124
Foursquare Gospel	113
Evangelical Lutheran	111
Christian and Missionary Alliance	102

Holland estimated that by 1993 there were over ten thousand Latino congregations in the United States, though he was able to clearly identify only the total that he reported.[5] If there were any doubt about the theological focus of the majority of Latino churches, this study demonstrated that the direction was clearly toward evangelical or Pentecostal churches. The mainline denominations that held strong sway among US Latinas in the first part of the twentieth century kept dropping in membership and as a percentage of the Latina Protestant community. But though the majority of Latino Protestants fit in the category of evangelicals, they were very different from majority-culture evangelicals. Latino Protestantism had taken on a look of its own; it had many similarities to Latin American Protestantism but also had its own uniquenesses. What it did not look like was US Protestantism.

There would be no other national study of Latina Protestantism until the first part of the twenty-first century, so it is difficult to give exact numbers at the end of the twentieth century. But the first major studies in the twenty-first century point to a steady growth in Latino Protestant churches throughout the period. Most of it happened in the growing denominations listed in the 1993 study. But the number of denominations starting Latino churches also increased; new Latino-led movements were begun; and the number of Latin American–based movements and denominations expanding into the United States grew as well. The numerical growth of the Latina community during this period was clearly accompanied by a significant growth in Latino Protestant churches and members. The numbers reflect a significant growth in Protestant immigrants from Latin America, many converts from among nominal Catholics, and biological growth within the churches.

As the Latina community continued to grow, its religious tendencies drew increasing interest from scholars. One of the major studies of the period was conducted by the Program for the Analysis of Religion among

5. Clifton L. Holland, "Table of 20 Largest Hispanic Denominations in the USA: By Number of Congregations, 1993," PROLADES, 1993, http://www.hispanicchurchesusa.net/hsusa2 .htm.

Latinos (PARAL), developed by the Bildner Center for Western Hemisphere Studies of the City University of New York. The PARAL project organized a major conference in 1993 of scholars looking at various aspects of Latino religion in the United States. It then published four volumes on various aspects of Latina religion, including an extensive bibliography. The series was edited by Anthony M. Stevens-Arroyo.

The project did not focus on Protestantism very much, but it did recognize the increasing importance of understanding Latino religious tendencies. There are a couple of chapters that address issues of Protestantism and of Latino Catholics becoming Protestants.

In "Brevia from the Hispanic Shift: Continuity Rather Than Conversion?" Kenneth Davis, a Franciscan priest, suggests that Latina popular religion, both Catholic and Protestant, provides Latinos support that they need and a way of looking at faith that US churches, Catholic and Protestant, both need. "Pentecostalism may represent a perceived resource for the psychological, cultural, and social survival of a Hispanic who experiences both dominant society and Church authority as a threat to that survival. . . . We do not know the full consequence of the Hispanic exodus . . . but I am convinced of one thing. The mainline churches in the United States will be spiritually poorer (as well as numerically smaller and older) if they squander this opportunity to retrieve those ancient, vibrant intuitions so often preserved by our Hispanic sisters and brothers."[6]

In another important chapter, "Assumptions, Theories and Methods in the Study of Latino Religion after 25 Years," Patrick McNamara looks back on the chapters on religion in the book *The Mexican-American People* (quoted in chapter 5) thirty years after it was published.[7] The author was one of the graduate students that participated in the study. He recognizes that the book worked from an assimilationist assumption. In that perspective, "churches can be important as adaptive institutions helping ethnic group members adjust to American society," so the study focused on the role of churches in encouraging "social changes that removed obstacles to socioeconomic ad-

6. Kenneth Davis, "Brevia from the Hispanic Shift: Continuity Rather Than Conversion?" in *An Enduring Flame: Studies on Latino Popular Religiosity*, ed. Antonio M. Stevens Arroyo and Ana Maria Diaz-Stevens, PARAL Studies Series, vol. 1 (New York: Bildner Center for Western Hemisphere Studies, 1995), 207–9.

7. Patrick McNamara, "Assumptions, Theories and Methods in the Study of Latino Religion after 25 Years," in *Old Masks, New Faces: Religion and Latino Identities*, ed. Antonio M. Stevens Arroyo and Gilbert Cadena, PARAL Studies Series, vol. 2 (New York: Bildner Center for Western Hemisphere Studies, 1995), 23–32.

vancement."[8] But they did not take into account that Latinas have developed their faith and their ethnic identities independently of official church structures. McNamara concludes by stating that "a reconstructed paradigm today, then, would balance institutional analysis with a cultural approach focusing on enduring elements of folk religiosity both Catholic and Protestant."[9]

In 1998 Larry Hunt of the University of Maryland looked at the impact conversion from Catholicism to Protestantism was having on Latinos. One of the questions he sought to answer was whether becoming a Protestant was a path toward assimilation into majority culture and a loss of Latina identity. Hunt cross-referenced the data of the General Social Surveys (GSS) to ascertain whether conversion to Protestantism was linked to upper mobility and assimilation by Latinas into dominant society. He concluded that

> While there is movement away from Catholicism and a growing diversity of the Hispanic population, the most basic finding of this study is that there are few signs that Protestantism is emerging as a major force defining an upwardly mobile Hispanic middle class. Only in the case of mainline Protestantism is there evidence of a religious factor shaping mobility patterns implying assimilation and upward mobility. The fact that such dynamics are associated with kinds of Protestant affiliation that are neither numerically strong, nor where major lines of defection from Catholicism have been leading, suggests a limited role for shifts away from Catholicism as a factor in the social mobility of Hispanics.[10]

Researchers were beginning to notice the growing reality of conversions to Protestantism, the cultural adaptation of Latinos in the United States, and the loss of Latino identity among some Latinas. The implicit assumption had always been that being Catholic was a sign of maintaining Latino identity and that becoming Protestant was a marker of assimilation. But the study demonstrated that Latino Pentecostals tended to have a stronger sense of Latino identity than Latino Catholics.

The issues raised by these studies pointed to a reality that was finally getting attention. There was a relationship between faith and ethnic identity maintenance among Latinos, but that relationship was not clear. There was

8. McNamara, "Assumptions, Theories and Methods," 27.

9. McNamara, "Assumptions, Theories and Methods," 31.

10. Larry L. Hunt, "The Spirit of Hispanic Protestantism in the United States: National Survey Comparisons of Catholics and Non-Catholics," *Social Science Quarterly* 79, no. 4 (December 1998): 844.

also a growing number of Latinas worshiping in English and Latinos who were identifying as religiously unaffiliated. How did these issues interact among Latinas?

Expansion at the Denominational Level

The growth of the Latino community during this period had a positive impact on most of the Protestant denominations and movements in the community, including the mainline denominations that had been adversely impacted earlier. Though most of the growth occurred among evangelicals and Pentecostals, other denominations also benefited from the new migrations and the upward mobility of some Latinas.

The **Assemblies of God** reported massive growth during this period. In 1993 the denomination had reported 1,268 Latino churches. The next complete report was not available until 2002. By that time the Pacific Latin American District had been divided in two (1998) by adding the Northern Pacific Latin American District. The denomination reported 1,758 Latina churches with 439,866 members. From 1984 to 1992 the Pacific Latin American District had Jesse Miranda as its superintendent. He guided it through substantial growth but also used that platform to become a national leader among Latino Protestants (on which, more later).[11]

The **Southern Baptist Convention** experienced a similar level of growth in number of churches and members. The Mexican Baptist Convention of Texas had become a formal part of the Baptist General Convention of Texas and was receiving substantial support for church planting and leadership development from the state convention. At the beginning of this period, Latino Baptists were contributing $500,000 a year to Latina ministry while the Texas Convention was contributing $3,000,000.[12] As the Latino population in Texas began to diversify, leaders decided to change the name to the Hispanic Baptist Convention. Southern Baptists elsewhere in the United States continued to work where Latinas were settling, starting new Latina churches in many communities, including in many parts of the South.

11. Sergio Navarrete, "Los Distritos Latinos de las Asambleas de Dios en Los Estados Unidos," in *Iglesias peregrinas en busca de identidad: Cuadros del protestantismo latino en los Estados Unidos*, ed. Juan F. Martínez Guerra and Luis Scott (Buenos Aires: Kairos Ediciones, 2004), 84–85.

12. Alberto Reyes, "Unification to Integration: A Brief History of the Hispanic Baptist Convention of Texas," *Baptist History and Heritage* 40, no. 1 (Winter 2005): 50.

The **Seventh-Day Adventist Church** experienced the most significant growth of the principal denominations during this period. Though the growth is not carefully documented, one can notice a clear trajectory. In 1980 it reported 28,400 Latino members. By 1990 it had 65,402 members. And by 2001 it claimed 115,244 members, a growth of 400 percent over twenty-one years.[13] This growth was all the more significant because the denomination was drawing from many ethnic groups, making it one of the most ethnically diverse denominations in the United States.

As the **Church of God** (Cleveland, Tennessee) continued to grow during this period, it expanded its leadership structure and support services for the increasing number of Latino churches and pastors. In 1992 it established a national Office of Hispanic Ministries. In 1994 it established a new Latino region in the Northwest and also started a Hispanic Ministerial Institute to better prepare its pastors for ministry.[14]

The **Apostolic Assembly of Faith in Christ Jesus** continued to grow in the United States, but because a part of that growth came from members that migrated north from its sister denomination in Mexico, tensions continued to mount between the two bodies. As each national church developed its own identity, it became clear that they had different understandings of how to minister to the Mexicans migrating north. Many people from Mexico felt that the US church did not properly address their needs. So in 1990 the Apostolic Church in Mexico organized itself in the United States and began establishing churches among migrants. Within a couple of years the Apostolic Assembly in the United States legally established itself in Mexico and established churches in that country. As a result, the two sister denominations became four national denominations. Despite this situation, the denomination continued to grow. In 1994 it reported 49,000 members in 431 churches. That growth continued throughout the decade, and by 2004 it had 700 churches and 80,000 members. By that time it also had 600 churches outside the United States with 50,000 members.[15]

---

13. Clifton L. Holland, ed., comp., producer, "Historical Profiles of Protestant Denominations with Hispanic Ministries in the USA: Listed by Major Traditions and Denominational Families," PROLADES, last updated August 15, 2012, http://www.hispanicchurchesusa.net/denominations/hsusa_historical_profiles_15August2012.pdf, 208.

14. Esdras Betancourt, *En el espíritu y poder de Pentecostés: Historia de la Iglesia de Dios Hispana en Estados Unidos* (Cleveland, TN: Vida Publication and Centro Estudios Latinos Publicaciones, 2016), 183–84, 193.

15. Ismael Martín del Campo, "Asamblea Apostólica de la Fe en Cristo Jesús," in Martínez Guerra and Scott, *Iglesias peregrinas en busca de identidad*, 112–14.

One issue that stood out for growing denominations was the inadequacy of existing structures to handle the new things happening in the Latina community. For example, the **Church of the Nazarene** had developed Latino districts as a way of organizing its Latina churches. But during this period existing Anglo congregations supported the establishment of new Latino churches that were linked to existing "Anglo" districts. As described by the director of the Office of Hispanic Ministries, Roberto Hodgson,

> The mass immigration of Latin Americans in the decades of the 1980's and 1990's all across the United States motivated English-speaking districts and churches to adopt a new vision in the evangelization among Hispanics and other ethnic groups, as the church pioneers had. The districts and churches began to start missionary initiatives of evangelism towards the millions of Hispanics that arrived in the United States for various reasons. During these two decades the movement of the multicongregational and multicultural district and church models was developed. The multicongregational churches shared installations and some of the governing and financial structures. This new modality has experienced the greatest growth of Hispanic churches starting more than 150 new congregations in a decade.[16]

This was never a planned strategy, but the actions of churches that responded to the needs around them. The churches brought in pastors and leaders from Latin America to lead many of the new efforts. As a result, the new growth outpaced the existing Hispanic districts. Today, the Church of the Nazarene has many more Latino churches outside of the Hispanic districts than within them.

This reality of growth affected all denominations. The mainline churches that had lost Latino members and churches in the 1960s and 1970s gained new members from Latin America and expanded their ministries in changing urban neighborhoods. This revitalized many churches and also produced new churches. Immigrants from Latin America also brought their churches with them or started new churches and movements once they were in the United States. And denominations that had not worked among Latinos be-

16. Roberto Hodgson, "History of the Hispanic Church of the Nazarene in the United States and Canada" (paper presented at the Ibero-American Theological Conference, San José, Costa Rica, October 18, 2004), http://didache.nazarene.org/index.php/regiontheoconf /ibero-amer-theo-conf/507-iberoam04-eng-24-usa-canada/file.

gan ministries as they realized that Latinas were among their number. As the Latina community grew, Latino Protestants also found new expansive growth.

The Next Set of Ministry and Theological Publications

One of the signs that Latina Protestants had been "discovered" by the larger Protestant community was the growth of publications and conferences related to ministry in the Latino community or to Latina theology. Various denominations had published pamphlets or other small documents related to Latino ministry in previous generations. But for the first time, during this period major events were organized and publications printed that focused on ministry in the Latina community; there was an increase also in materials and activities focused on Latino Protestants in particular.

A major evangelical conference, Evangelizing Ethnic America, held in 1985, created a new nationally oriented vision among evangelical Protestants and focused on the growing ethnic diversification of the United States, particularly because of new migration from around the world. It was described as "strategic because this is the first time in the life of North American Protestantism that this kind of high-level meeting has been called which focuses *entirely* on the unevangelized ethnic groups here in our own country." Conference organizers challenged the melting-pot vision of the United States and called on the churches to have a different view. In the words of Dr. C. Peter Wagner, one of the conference organizers: "If the real America is a multitude of multicolored, multilingual, multicultural human beings, the spiritual vision for the real America is summed up in an extraordinarily challenging evangelistic task. America is a multitude to be won for Jesus Christ." The organizing committee had a Latino as chair, Baptist leader Oscar Romo; this recognized the importance of this fast-growing ethnic group, though many ethnic groups were represented at the conference.[17] This conference created energy among denominations and parachurch organizations and also brought to the fore the reality of the growing Latino community.

During this period several books were published to ignite (or reignite) interest in Latino ministry among Protestant churches, such as *Los Hispanos en los Estados Unidos: Un reto y una oportunidad para la iglesia* (1985), *His-*

---

17. Houston 85: The National Convocation on Evangelizing Ethnic America, April 15–18, 1985, conference documents.

panic Ministry in North America (1987), *The Hispanic Challenge: Opportunities Confronting the Church* (1993), and *Who Comes in the Name of the Lord? Jesus at the Margins* (1997).[18] Each book analyzed the growing Latino community, but the books differed on how Protestants should respond. A Latino Pentecostal leader wrote the first book for Latino Pentecostals. The second and third books present a more general evangelical perspective, with the latter book presenting a broader vision of what Latinas might accomplish in urban areas. The last book is written from a mainline perspective and calls out mainline churches to have a progressive vision for the margins in contrast to the orthodox vision of other churches.

During this time Latino theology also began to find a public voice in seminaries and schools of religion. Latina Protestants, particularly Pentecostals, had been reflecting on their experience with God particularly through the narratives (*testimonios*) and songs written originally in Spanish. Some of the early leaders mentioned in previous chapters called for Latino expressions of faith and developed worship expressions that reflected the unique religious experiences of Latinas. And Pentecostal expressions of faith in the Latino community tended to reflect the cultural influences of Latino reality, whereas other Protestant expressions tended to be translations of what was taught and practiced in English.

One important change during this period is that Latino Protestant thinkers began to publish their works in English. Two of the early voices that had the most impact were Orlando Costas and Justo González. Both leaders earned a place in the theological academy, which gave them a platform from which to reflect theologically from a Latino perspective. Costas raised important missiological questions. Both *Christ outside the Gate* (1982) and *Liberating News* (1989) presented a Latino take on the gospel and its implications among minority communities.[19] Costas's untimely death in 1987 left his work incomplete but opened doors for important conversations.

González is most widely known in Christian circles as a church historian. He has written several books on church history and Christian thought

---

18. José Reyes, *Los Hispanos en los Estados Unidos: Un reto y una oportunidad para la iglesia* (Cleveland, TN: White Wing Publishing House, 1985); Alex Montoya, *Hispanic Ministry in North America* (Grand Rapids: Zondervan, 1987); Manuel Ortiz, *The Hispanic Challenge: Opportunities Confronting the Church* (Downers Grove: InterVarsity, 1993); Harold J. Recinos, *Who Comes in the Name of the Lord? Jesus at the Margins* (Nashville: Abingdon, 1997).

19. Orlando E. Costas, *Christ outside the Gate: Mission beyond Christendom* (Maryknoll, NY: Orbis, 1982); Orlando E. Costas, *Liberating News: A Theology of Contextual Evangelization* (Grand Rapids: Eerdmans, 1989).

that are used in many US seminaries and throughout Latin America. His more direct impact on Latino theological reflection came with his book *Mañana: Christian Theology from a Hispanic Perspective*.[20] Several Roman Catholic authors had already been writing about Latina theology in the 1980s. But for Protestants the doors opened wide after the publication of *Mañana*.

The 1990s became the decade of Latino theology. A large number of books were published from both a Catholic and a Protestant perspective, focusing on the distinctiveness of living the Christian faith as a Latina Protestant. The two books that summarized Latino Protestantism were written or edited by González. *Santa Biblia: The Bible through Hispanic Eyes*[21] focuses on how social location affects Bible reading and the contribution Latinas can make to US churches as they seek to understand the message of Scripture for today. *¡Alabadle! Hispanic Christian Worship*[22] looks at various worship styles in the Latino community, recognizing that most Latinas, Protestant or Catholic, share commonalities in how to approach God in worship. These two books reflected a growing literature that would mature throughout the 1990s and into the twenty-first century.[23]

As Latino theology developed, it drew from a number of wells. Clearly it was influenced by Latin American liberation theology. But it was written out of the US experience. Protestant Latina theology recognized early that Pentecostalism was a key component in understanding the faith of Latinos; a key text that described that relationship was Eldin Villafañe's work *The Liberating Spirit*.[24] Also, one could not speak of Latino theology without addressing the complex and varied experiences of what it meant to be Latino.

But because of the nature of the churches and the role of the theological academy, Latina theology tended to develop in mainline circles. Most of the early voices came from mainline traditions. But even though some Pente-

---

20. Justo L. González, *Mañana: Christian Theology from a Hispanic Perspective* (Nashville: Abingdon, 1990).

21. Justo L. González, *Santa Biblia: The Bible through Hispanic Eyes* (Nashville: Abingdon, 1996).

22. Justo L. González, ed., *¡Alabadle! Hispanic Christian Worship* (Nashville: Abingdon, 1996).

23. For a more complete bibliography of the books of Latino theology of this period, see Miguel A. De La Torre and Edwin David Aponte, *Introducing Latino/a Theologies* (Maryknoll, NY: Orbis, 2001).

24. Eldin Villafañe, *The Liberating Spirit: Toward an Hispanic American Pentecostal Social Ethic* (Grand Rapids: Eerdmans, 1993).

costals and evangelicals also published their voices, the reflections did not always come out of the pews. Even as academically oriented Latino voices were writing Latino theology, Latino Protestant churches were writing their own theology through the hymns and worship songs that developed during this period. If Justo González was the voice of the Latino academy, Marcos Witt became the voice of popular worship. During the 1990s a new, livelier worship style permeated churches throughout the Spanish-speaking world. CanZion Music influenced worship, and the CanZion Institute, also started by Witt, taught thousands of worship leaders from throughout Latin America and Latino USA this new worship style. Witt became the catalyst for a major renovation of worship and influenced churches far beyond the Pentecostal churches that were most directly influenced by his style.

Another area in which Latino Protestants began to find a voice related to how to read their own history. Most of what had been written earlier about the history of Latino Protestantism was testimonial and denominationally focused. It provided details about who had done what and when and about the results of those efforts. Many denominations wrote narratives about their work among Latinas, particularly as they got ready to celebrate one hundred years of ministry. Several denominations also published memorials related to specific churches, leaders, or areas of ministry. What changed during this period is that some churches not only recorded what had happened, but they included a historical analysis of the events. Both *Iglesia Presbiteriana*[25] and *Each in Our Own Tongue*[26] analyzed the history of their respective denominational traditions, going far beyond a mere retelling of the events toward an attempt to place these histories within the larger experience of US Protestantism within their respective denominational families.

The first extant published attempt to understand Latino Protestantism in historical perspective, *Republican Protestantism in Atzlán*, was written to "demonstrate" why Chicanos were rejecting Protestantism.[27] Two initial efforts by Latino Protestants to develop a broader history of Latino Protestantism started in the 1990s. The Asociación Hispana para la Educación

25. R. Douglas Brackenridge and Francisco O. García-Treto, *Iglesia Presbiteriana: A History of Presbyterians and Mexican Americans in the Southwest* (San Antonio: Trinity University Press, 1974).

26. Justo L. González, ed., *Each in Our Own Tongue: A History of Hispanics in United Methodism* (Nashville: Abingdon, 1991).

27. E. C. Orozco, *Republican Protestantism in Aztlán: The Encounter between Mexicanism and Anglo-Saxon Secular Humanism in the United States Southwest* (Glendale, CA: Petereins Press, 1980).

Teológica (AHET) published *Hacia una historia de la iglesia evangélica Hispana de California del Sur* in 1993.[28] It was "the first united effort of *evangélico* Christians to put in order the history of Hispanic work in the United States of America," according to the introduction by Dr. José Arreguín.[29] It was a collection of narratives from denominations about their work among Latinas in southern California. This effort sought to help denominational traditions understand why Latino Protestant churches had gained or lost members through the years. The authors hoped to expand this effort to include all the Southwest, particularly those areas where there had been a Latino presence since the Spanish colonial period.

The other major effort of the period was published in 1994. *Hidden Stories: Unveiling the History of the Latino Church*[30] was also a collection of essays. Daniel Rodríguez-Díaz, one of the editors, worked with his school, McCormick Theological Seminary, to write and submit a grant proposal to Pew Charitable Trusts to gather scholars and leaders who were involved in "working on Latin Protestant Church History, to exchange information, to assess needs, and to begin planning future steps."[31] The concern of the participants was that "while Latinos or Americans of Hispanic descent have joined a variety of Protestant denominations for over one hundred and fifty years, little have [*sic*] been done to document their history. Archival materials are scattered, often preserved in less than optimal conditions, and generally inaccessible. There is an urgent need to preserve the oral history which is being lost, and the archival material which is being destroyed through inadequate preservation."[32] The scholars that came together addressed methodological issues and the relationship of culture and religion. They were also part of an early effort to start an association of church historians that was later merged into the recently established Asociación para la Educación Teológica Hispana (AETH).

Formal theological education also developed during this period, in that seminaries, the Association of Theological Schools (ATS), and denomina-

28. Rodelo Wilson, ed., *Hacia una historia de la iglesia evangélica hispana de California del Sur* (Montebello, CA: AHET, 1993).

29. My translation of "el primera esfuerzo unido de los cristianos evangélicos de poner en orden la historia de la obra hispana en los Estados Unidos de América." Wilson, *Hacia una historia de la iglesia evangélica hispana de California del Sur*, 7.

30. Daniel R. Rodríguez-Díaz and David Cortés-Fuentes, eds., *Hidden Stories: Unveiling the History of the Latino Church* (Decatur, GA: AETH, 1994).

31. Rodríguez-Díaz and Cortés-Fuentes, *Hidden Stories*, xi.

32. Rodríguez-Díaz and Cortés-Fuentes, *Hidden Stories*, xi.

tional institutions began to take the needs of Latino theological education more seriously.

The first effort at addressing these issues was established in 1974. The Asociación Teológica para la Educación Hispana (ATEH, now Asociación Teológica Hispana—ATH) was born in southern California as local institutions recognized the need to address the training needs of a growing Latina Protestant population. Fuller Theological Seminary began a program for Hispanic pastors in 1974. A number of regional theological institutions and church bodies worked together to form ATH in conjunction with ATS. Over the years it has strengthened its regional ties with Latino Bible institutes and has offered them a certification process that allows them to maintain rigorous programs that have been recognized by a number of ATS schools.[33]

In the late 1980s and during the 1990s Justo González directly or indirectly influenced the establishment of three organizations that addressed the task of theological education among Latinas. Each was started to address specific issues related to this task. As each has developed, it has tended to take on a "personality" of its own.

The **Hispanic Summer Program** (HSP) was born out of several efforts to advance "the theological education and the pastoral leadership of the ever-growing Hispanic American Church." ATS hired Dr. Cecilio Arrastía to help the theological schools of mainline denominations effectively respond to the needs of their Latino students. His initial work was followed up by a Pew Charitable Trusts–funded national study of the needs of Latina theological education. González led the study and concluded that in the "absence of a full-fledged Hispanic seminary or Hispanic program of ministerial education and training, it was decided to have a two-week summer program whose character would be such that it would serve as a Latino seminary for that short period of time." Begun in 1989, it has provided an ecumenical program of seminary-level courses taught by Latina faculty that focuses on the specific issues and needs of the Latino community. Over forty institutions are sponsors of HSP.[34]

The **Asociación para la Educación Teológica Hispana** (AETH) was founded in 1991 "to stimulate dialogue and collaboration among theological educators, administrators of institutions for ministerial formation,

33. See http://athispana.com/.

34. "Who We Are, and What We Do," Hispanic Summer Program, accessed March 21, 2017, http://hispanicsummerprogram.org/whoweare/.

and Christian ministerial students within and outside the United States."[35] Throughout its history it has promoted dialogue among those involved in Latino theological education at various levels, from Bible institutes to seminaries, and is the only place where that happens on a regular basis. It has produced basic texts for usage in Bible institutes and has served as a publishing house for books of specific interest to Latinos. Its newest projects include the establishment of the Justo González Center at Asbury Seminary–Orlando, which sponsors an annual lectureship on issues of interest to the Latino Protestant community. It is also working with ATS to develop a system of certification whereby Latino Bible institutes can operate at a baccalaureate level. Graduates of institutions that meet the criteria are then able to enroll in masters programs at ATS schools that are willing to recognize this certification.[36]

Hispanic Theological Initiative (HTI) was the third national organization formed to address issues of Latino theological education (1996). Its focus is supporting Latina PhD students who are committed to serving the academy and the church. It provides financial and mentorship support to these students in order to increase the number of Latino faculty in theological education and, thereby, "better equip US institutions to serve the growing Hispanic population."[37]

Latino Protestant Organizations

Most denominations had developed internal "Latino" conferences of churches. But these often had little voice within the larger structures and were often seen as marginal to the life of the denomination. As the number of Latino Protestants continued to grow, Latino leaders looked for new ways to have a voice in their denominations. The first efforts entailed caucuses or loose networks of Latino leaders that organized to address issues of common concern within church structures. These types of networks developed in most Protestant denominations. Many were short-lived and were often reorganized as new migratory waves brought new leaders to the fore. De-

35. "About Us," Asociación para la Educación Teológica Hispana, 2015, http://www.aeth .org/en/about-us/.

36. "Certification of Bible Institutes," Asociación para la Educación Teológica Hispana, 2015, http://www.aeth.org/en/certification-bible-institutes/.

37. "About Us," *Perspectivas*, accessed March 21, 2017, http://perspectivasonline.com/about /about-hispanic-theological-initiative-hti/.

nominations responded to the growth in the number of Latinos by expanding their "Hispanic" offices or by opening some denominational leadership positions to Latina leaders.

During this period Latino Protestants, as they found their own voice, also began to develop their own organizations that crossed denominational lines. They found that they would need to work across denominational lines and theological traditions if they were going to successfully address issues of common concern.

The most significant change during this era was in the recognition of the growth of the US-born Latino population. Up to this point each immigrant wave tended to refocus Protestant ministry back toward the immigrant population. The majority of the Latino population had always been US-born, but each succeeding immigrant wave kept ministry focus on those who had more recently arrived. But in the 1980s and 1990s Latino Protestants focused on the US-born population in ways that had not previously been seen as important.

One clear sign of this change was the development of the Hispanic Association for Bilingual-Bicultural Ministries (HABBM) in southern California in 1985, one of the first national transdenominational organizational efforts. Its target audience was second- and third-generation Latino Protestant leaders. Danny de León of **Templo Calvario** (AG) in Santa Ana, California, gained a national platform and invited Latino leaders to join him in this effort. Though short-lived, this group created the environment for and became the harbinger of later organizations. It became clear that it would take a charismatic Pentecostal leader to draw together a circle of pastors and leaders to organize for issues of mutual interest.

In 1992 Dr. Jesse Miranda, another AG leader, organized Latino pastors and leaders into the **Alianza Ministerial Evangélica National** (AMEN). In many ways this was the next step after HABBM. He brought together leaders from more than twenty Protestant denominations and over seventy parachurch organizations from the United States, Canada, Puerto Rico, and Mexico to form the principal Latino Protestant advocacy group of the period. They came together to represent the growing Latina Protestant community, to promote unity among Latino Protestant leaders, to strengthen their common work, and to develop a public voice for Latino Protestants. From 1992 through 2006, AMEN was the principal voice for Latino Protestantism. AMEN was the first Latino Protestant organization to gain national prominence. Because of Dr. Miranda's influence, Latino Protestant leaders have met with every US president since Ronald Reagan.

AMEN helped organize a number of national conferences and exchanges with the larger US Protestant community. Because of Dr. Miranda's work and the impact of AMEN, he was invited by Pew Charitable Trusts to direct a national study called **Hispanic Churches in American Public Life** (HCAPL) from 1999 to 2002. He and Virgilio Elizondo, Mexican American Catholic priest and Latino theologian, co-led this project that looked at the increasing public role of Hispanic churches, both Protestant and Catholic. This study became the most complete picture, up to that point, of the religious tendencies of US Latinas.[38]

AMEN served both as a platform for Latina Protestants and as a launching pad for a new generation of Latino Protestant leaders. Many leaders found their voice and a space for broader ministry through AMEN. A number of new ministries developed while others grew as they networked together through AMEN. The most direct descendant of AMEN is the **National Hispanic Christian Leadership Conference** (NHCLC), of which more will be said in the next chapter.

Increasing Levels of Diversification

As with previous expansions of the community, one theme that stands out during this period is the increasing diversification of the Latina community. National organizations speak of the increasing size and influence of Latino Protestantism and of the importance of developing national platforms to address common issues. Even though some organizations were pulling Latino Protestants together, the expansion of ministry was creating increasing levels of diversification.

First of all, as the Latino community continued to grow, more and more Protestant denominations got involved in ministry in the Latina community. So, even though a relatively small number of denominations represent the bulk of Latino Protestantism, there was a proliferation of smaller efforts throughout this period. Some ministries were started by small denominations that established a small number of churches, while other efforts were done by denominations that had not traditionally done ministry in the Latino community, such as predominantly African American denominations. Also, newer Protestant churches and movements in the United

---

38. Gastón Espinosa, *Latino Pentecostals in America: Faith and Politics in Action* (Cambridge, MA: Harvard University Press, 2014), 343–45.

States also started Latino ministries or congregations. Many of the newer charismatic or neocharismatic movements and many larger independent churches developed some type of specific outreach to Latinas. And as Latin American–based churches and denominations saw more of their members migrate north, many of them began churches in the United States. There is also the growth of various types of independent ministries started by Latinos themselves.

This type of diversification should not be surprising given the nature of the Protestantism that was growing among Latinas and of the diverse segments of the Latino community. This tendency was, and is, reflective of free church Protestant movements, which are the types of churches and de- nominations that are growing the most among US Latinos. As Latinas moved into new parts of the United States, they were also coming into contact with denominations that might not have encountered Latinos in the past. But this denominational and theological diversification is also reflective of the desire of many Latinas to encounter God and the spiritual in new ways.

As the Latina community continued to grow, its predominant religious expressions went in a Pentecostal charismatic direction. Most of the largest Protestant denominations with a Latino presence are Pentecostal. But most other Latina Protestant churches have a Pentecostal or charismatic worship style. What was happening in Latin America was also happening among Latinos—Protestantism had become largely Pentecostal or Pentecostalized. And that influence had gone further than Protestantism, since there was also a strong charismatic tendency in Latino Catholicism.

Another important type of diversification during this period was re- lated to acculturation. Despite significant migratory waves, the majority of Latinos have always been US-born. And acculturation has always been an issue in the Latina community. As stated earlier, even in the late 1800s, some younger Latino Protestants were more interested in being a part of "white" congregations than in staying in the Latino churches they grew up in. There were many reasons for this attraction. Certainly some Latinas saw Anglo Protestant churches as places that could nurture or support upward mobility and assimilation into majority culture. Others were there because education and a shift in language dominance to English made those churches more attractive. These Latinos had been raised as Protestants, and they wanted to continue being part of a Protestant church. But an English-language con- gregation seemed to make more sense to them.

But a growing number of Latinas were also attracted to the large char- ismatic or neo-Pentecostal churches that began to develop in the 1970s and

1980s. Many of them first heard the Protestant message in English, even if they were Spanish-dominant, usually through these types of ministries. So, many were not actually leaving Latino Protestant churches to join Anglo churches—they had never been a part of a Latino Protestant church, even those who were Spanish-dominant.

Hunt's study demonstrated that becoming a Protestant and joining a Latino Protestant church was not necessarily a sign of assimilation into dominant society. But only in 2007 would it become clear that, while more Latina Protestants were worshiping in English, the vast majority were attracted to churches that had some type of Latino identity. A Pew study of that year, *Changing Faiths*, found that the vast majority of Latinas, Catholic, Protestant, and otherwise, attended churches that had some type of clear Latino identity. It found that 80 percent of Latina churchgoers went to a church that had some Latina clergy; 87 percent went to a church that offered services in Spanish; and 74 percent attended a church that was majority Latino. Sixty-six percent of Latinas went to churches that had all three characteristics; another 21 percent went to churches that had two; and 8 percent went to churches that had one of these characteristics. Though this tendency is less pronounced among US Latinas that have been in the United States for several generations, Latinos still exhibit a strong tendency to attend churches that have some clear Latino ethnic markers. Even Latinas that worship in English seem to prefer places of worship where their ethnicity is represented in leadership or in the community.[39]

What Does a Latina Protestant Look Like?

If assimilation of Latinos had been the implicit long-term assumption or goal of some of the Protestant denominations, that assumption was losing favor by this time. But it also seemed clear that completely separate churches and denominations were not the future. Some denominations continued doing ministry from an assimilationist assumption and established "one generation" ministries. Others began to see a long-term role of Latino Protestant churches. But it was not clear by this time whether those Latina churches would worship completely in Spanish, in English, or in some type of bilingual format.

39. *Changing Faiths: Latinos and the Transformation of American Religion* (Washington, DC: Pew Research Center, 2007), http://www.pewforum.org/files/2007/04/hispanics-religion-07-final-mar08.pdf.

The new Latino churches and ministries reflected the intersection of faith, minorization, understanding of assimilation, ethnic identity maintenance, theology, and ecclesiology. Different churches and ministries were responding in very different ways to these challenges. What further complicated the issue was that Latino ministries were developing in very different ways and that one could successfully start a Latina Protestant church no matter what assumptions one was making about the future of the Latino community.

Among the many challenges raised by these differences was that many seemed to assume that their experience in the Latina community was "normative." Those involved in ministry wanted to have a sense that they were pointing toward the future, but they did not consider that there might be several futures. As the assimilationist perspective was losing ground, there were no other interpretative frameworks that would provide a single way forward for ministry among Latinos.

In the midst of this the leaders that arose during this period were often looking for a broad umbrella that could include all Latino Protestants, even as they faced the growing diversification within the community. A few of the leaders worked for a broad unity, while most worked within their specific contexts but had a broader impact.

The most prominent Latino Protestant leader of this period was **Jesse Miranda**. He was born in New Mexico and joined an AG church after his mother was miraculously healed. He studied at one of the extensions of the Latin American Bible Institute (LABI) and earned degrees at Vanguard University, Talbot Theological Seminary, and Fuller Theological Seminary. He also studied at the University of Southern California. As he developed as a leader within the AG, he took on a more prominent role within the denomination. In 1985 he became the first Latino to be a keynote speaker at a national convention of the AG. He has served as a district superintendent (Pacific Latin American District) and as an executive presbyter for his denomination. He has used these platforms to promote Latino issues and to address issues of Latino Protestants' role in society.

Miranda became the key spokesperson for Latino Protestants during this period. He met with public officials, including US presidents, and encouraged Latino Protestant leaders to engage public issues. He wrote about the plight of Latinos and helped to organize them by forming AMEN. His role became a turning point in encouraging Latino AGs and other Latino Protestants to participate in political, civic, and social action.[40] It was be-

---

40. Espinosa, *Latino Pentecostals in America*, 342–45.

cause of this platform that he was invited by Pew to lead their first major study of Latino religion, Hispanic Churches in American Public Life (of which, more in the next chapter). He continues to be involved in these issues through the Jesse Miranda Center for Hispanic Leadership, based at Vanguard University, an AG university based in southern California.

Danny de León is originally from Texas. He became pastor of Templo Calvario AG Church in Santa Ana, California, in 1976 and led the congregation into a period of extensive growth. From this platform he drew a group of leaders together and developed HABBM. Since AMEN and NHCLC were already organized, de León focused on the local congregation and its regional impact through its Community Development Corporation. Templo Calvario is currently recognized as one of the five largest AG churches in the United States.

Ray Rivera has been a pastor, professor, and community organizer in New York since 1964. He is an ordained pastor of the Reformed Church in America and served as national executive of the Hispanic Council of that denomination from 1975 to 1984. He has been involved in various types of community service and ministry throughout the years and founded the Latino Pastoral Action Center (LPAC) in New York in 1992. Rivera has used that platform to work toward a holistic understanding of the gospel and faith-based community service. He has written *Liberty to the Captives: Our Call to Minister in a Captive World* as a guide for urban ministry.[41] He was one of the founders of NaLEC (of which, more in the next chapter).

Marcos Witt was born of missionary parents who worked in Mexico. He became a gospel singer and recorded his first major album in 1986. He founded CanZion Producciones, which became a venue for his music and that of other musicians that shared his style and vision. He founded CanZion Institute to train worship leaders and has written several books on worship in the Latin American and Latino Protestant context. During the 1990s he became the face of the movement that worked to renovate worship in the Spanish-speaking world. He has used music to support Latino Protestant issues, including immigration reform, and from 2002 to 2012 pastored the Spanish-language congregation of Lakewood Church in Houston, Texas.

There have been several important leaders in the Hispanic Baptist Convention. **Rudy Sánchez** stands out during this period because of his long-term commitment and the recognition he received. He served as pastor

41. Raymond Rivera, *Liberty to the Captives: Our Call to Minister in a Captive World* (Grand Rapids: Eerdmans, 2012).

of several large Latino Baptist churches in Texas (in Houston, Dallas, and Corpus Christi) and twice served as the president of the Hispanic Baptist Convention. He also served on various boards and committees of the Baptist General Convention of Texas. His service and leadership were recognized by all Baptists in Texas when he became the first Latino chair of the executive board of the state convention in 2000.[42]

Otto René Azurdia, a Guatemalan immigrant, started Ministerios Llamada Final, a Latino movement with Latin American roots, in 1990. The Guatemalan pastor moved to the Los Angeles area in 1987 to pastor a small church. As the church grew, it decided to become the base of this new movement. Llamada Final now has churches in the United States and in Latin America, all led by Apostle Azurdia. This model of free church entrepreneurship continues to be one of the ways Latino Pentecostalism is growing.

As Latino Protestants were finally discovered, there was a lot of interest in ministry among them. But it was not clear if they could find a place at the table of US Protestantism. There was a sense that their growing presence was already creating fear among some Anglo Protestant leaders.

42. "Pastor Rudy Sanchez," obituary, *Dallas Morning News*, February 10, 2009, http://www.legacy.com/obituaries/dallasmorningnews/obituary.aspx?n=rudy-sanchez&pid=123965119.

Chapter 8

Finding a Place at the Table (2001–Present)

Throughout the first part of the twenty-first century, the number of Latina Protestants and the number of Latino Protestant churches have continued to grow. There are also more Latinos in Protestant churches that do not identify themselves as Latino. This growth has three major sources: internal biological growth, conversion growth, and new migration from Latin America. Most of the growth is happening in the largest denominations and movements, but there are Latino churches and church members in most denominations in the United States today. Given the increasing diversity in the community, it is also not always clear what should be counted as a Latino Protestant church (or even who should be counted as a Latina Protestant). Different denominations use different criteria to decide these things. On the other hand, national and regional surveys use different survey methods. That makes it difficult to translate survey results into concrete numbers of churches and members. Yet all the studies point to the fact that Latina Protestantism is growing. What is not yet as clear is the role that this growing community will have within the larger Protestant community in the United States.

Birth Rates, Growth Projections, and Changing Migration Patterns

The 2010 US Census reported that the Latino population had reached 50.5 million, or 16.3 percent of the US population. This represented a 43 percent growth from 2000. Latinas represented 56 percent of the population growth in the United States during this decade. Among children seventeen years old and younger, Latinos grew 39 percent during the decade, and by 2010 they were 23.1 percent of this population.[1]

During this decade the US Census also projected that Latinos would continue to grow as a percentage of the US population and that, around 2044, the various minority groups would together become the majority of the US population, with Latinos leading the way. Though the growth projections of the Latina community have been pared back a bit, the current expectation is for 109 million Latinos in the United States in 2050.[2]

The decade saw major changes in issues related to immigration. When President Bush was elected, he promised to work toward immigration reform. Though his priorities changed after the events of September 11, 2001, there continued to be a sense that Congress might pass a comprehensive immigration reform law that would address the estimated 12 million undocumented aliens in the country. Those hopes reached a high point when the Senate passed a bill in 2006. But the bill never moved in the House. After that the political attitudes continued to harden against the undocumented. When President Obama was elected in 2008, he also stated that he would work toward immigration reform. But he also worked hard to deport undocumented aliens. By the end of his administration, he was called "Deporter in Chief" because about 2.5 million people were deported during his time in office, more than in the previous administrations.[3]

The changing political and social situation also changed the migration patterns from Latin America. Migration from Mexico slowed to the point that Mexico no longer sent the most legal migrants to the United States. Other Latin American countries continue sending significant numbers, however, particularly El Salvador, Guatemala, Honduras, Colombia, and the Dominican Republic. Migration from Puerto Rico also increased because of the deteriorating economic situation on the island. But because of the slowdown

1. Jeffrey S. Passel, D'Vera Cohn, and Mark Hugo Lopez, "Hispanics Account for More Than Half of Nation's Growth in Past Decade," Pew Research Center, March 24, 2011, http://www.pewhispanic.org/2011/03/24/hispanics-account-for-more-than-half-of-nations-growth-in-past-decade/.

2. Jens Manuel Krogstad, "With Fewer New Arrivals, Census Lowers Hispanic Population Projections," Pew Research Center, December 16, 2014, http://www.pewresearch.org/fact-tank/2014/12/16/with-fewer-new-arrivals-census-lowers-hispanic-population-projections-2/.

3. Ana Gonzalez-Barrera and Jens Manuel Krogstad, "U.S. Deportations of Immigrants Reach Record High in 2013," Pew Research Center, October 2, 2014, http://www.pewresearch.org/fact-tank/2014/10/02/u-s-deportations-of-immigrants-reach-record-high-in-2013/.

in immigration, Latin America is no longer the region that sends the most legal immigrants to the United States.[4]

Over the last couple of years, the political environment has also become more negative toward immigrants. Because Latinos are the largest part of the immigrant population, and of the undocumented immigrant population, they have become the "poster children" for opponents of immigration reform. During the 2016 presidential campaign, Donald Trump, now the president, referred to undocumented "Mexicans" as rapists and killers, creating a strong anti-Latino and anti-immigrant stance among many in the United States. It is yet to be seen how that rhetoric will translate into policy decisions of the new administration.

How Do We Count, What Do We Count, and What Is Learned in the Counting?

During the first few years of the twenty-first century, several major studies of the state of Latina religion in the United States were conducted. There have been three studies by the Pew Hispanic Center and one by Trinity College as part of the ARIS (American Religious Identification Survey) study project. Because they used different methodologies, it is not always easy to compare their results or to have a clear sense of changes that are occurring. But they give us a panoramic view of the Latina Protestant community.

Pew Charitable Trusts funded the first broad national study of Hispanic religion in the United States. *Hispanic Churches in American Public Life* (2003)[5] studied the role of faith in how Latinas participated in US society. Dr. Gastón Espinosa managed the study, codirected by Dr. Jesse Miranda and Dr. Virgilio Elizondo. The study began by recognizing that there had been few studies of religious tendencies in the Latino community, something the study hoped to effectively address. Among the important findings for our purposes are the following:

- 23 percent of Latinas identified as Protestants, 70 percent as Catholics, 1 percent as members of other world religions (particularly Islam),

4. Jie Zong and Jeanne Batalova, "Asian Immigrants in the United States," Migration Policy Institute, January 6, 2016, http://www.migrationpolicy.org/article/asian-immigrants-united-states.

5. Gastón Espinosa, Virgilio P. Elizondo, and Jesse Miranda, *Hispanic Churches in American Public Life: Summary of Findings* (Notre Dame: Institute for Latino Studies, University of Notre Dame, 2003). A pdf is available at http://www.hispanicchurchesusa.net/hcapl-rpt-1.pdf.

and 6 percent had no religious preference (or other); less than one-half of 1 percent self-identified as agnostic or atheist.

- There seemed to be a generational tendency in the shift toward Protestantism. Latinos were leaving the Catholic Church in fairly significant numbers, but new migration kept the percentage of Latino Catholics high.

- "To put these findings in national perspective, there are now more Latino Protestants in the United States than Jews or Muslims or Episcopalians and Presbyterians combined."[6]

- Latinos tend to be attracted to a more charismatic or Pentecostal faith. This is true for both Protestants and Catholics.

- The number of Latino Roman Catholics continues to grow numerically, even as they are shrinking as a percentage of the Latino population.

- Marginal Christian groups, such as Mormons and Jehovah's Witnesses, are attractive to Latinos.

- 37 percent of Latinos self-identify as "born again," which means that a significant percentage of Catholics use that term to describe themselves.

- Politically, Latinos seem to occupy a middle space between African Americans and the white majority. On some issues they look more like the former, and on others more like the latter.

This study set the framework for other major studies funded by Pew and for other studies that looked at religion within the Latina community. The major patterns that would be seen in each of the studies were the defection of Latinos from the Catholic Church and the growth of Protestantism. Another pattern not as addressed in this first study but standing out in later surveys was the number of Latinos who would not identify as either Protestant or Catholic.

The second major Pew study, *Changing Faiths: Latinos and the Transformation of American Religion*, was published in 2007.[7] This work built upon the 2003 study but addressed a number of important issues that helped describe Latina Protestantism more succinctly. It found that 20 percent of

---

6. Espinosa, Elizondo, and Miranda, *Hispanic Churches*, 16.

7. *Changing Faiths: Latinos and the Transformation of American Religion* (Washington, DC: Pew Research Center, 2007), http://www.pewforum.org/files/2007/04/hispanics-religion -07-final-mar08.pdf.

the Latino population identified as Protestant—15 percent as evangelical or Pentecostal, and 5 percent as mainline. The study correlated these numbers by country of birth, language usage, and generations in the United States. According to the study:

- 45 percent of evangelicals/Pentecostals were born in the United States and 55 percent in Latin America.
- 65 percent of mainline members were born in the United States and 35 percent in Latin America.
- By generations, 55 percent of evangelicals/Pentecostals were first generation, 23 percent second generation, and 21 percent third generation or older. Among members of mainline denominations, the numbers were 35 percent first generation, 37 percent second generation, and 28 percent third or older.
- By language usage, 31 percent of Pentecostals/evangelicals were English-dominant, 32 percent were bilingual, and 38 percent Spanish-dominant. Among those that identified with mainline denominations, the numbers were 45 percent, 28 percent, and 26 percent.
- By place of origin among mainline Latinos: Puerto Rico 16 percent, Mexico 56 percent, Cuba 6 percent, Dominican Republic 3 percent, Central America 6 percent, South America 4 percent, and other 8 percent. Among evangelicals/Pentecostals: Puerto Rico 16 percent, Mexico 50 percent, Cuba 4 percent, Dominican Republic 1 percent, Central America 14 percent, South America 6 percent, and other 8 percent.

The Trinity College/ARIS study "U.S. Latino Religious Identification, 1990–2008: Growth, Diversity and Transformation" is difficult to compare with other studies because it uses categories not commonly used by Protestants, nor other researchers. The categories used for non-Catholic Christians are Baptist, Christian generic, Pentecostal, and Protestant sects. The study separates out the Mormons, but includes Jehovah's Witnesses in Protestant sects with Mennonites, Covenant, Churches of Christ, Adventists, and other groups. This type of categorization makes it difficult to compare and contrast the data from this study with that of other studies, and to extrapolate information that would make sense to the average Latino Protestant or to those who study religion in the Latina community.[8]

8. Juhem Navarro-Rivera, Barry A. Kosmin, and Ariela Keysar, "U.S. Latino Religious

According to the 2014 Pew report on Latino religion, "The Shifting Religious Identity of Latinos in the United States," 22 percent of Latinas identify as Protestants.[9] Sixteen percent are evangelical/Pentecostal, and about 5 percent are part of mainline denominations. The emphasis of this report is the number of Latinas that no longer identify as Roman Catholics. The Protestant percentages are not significantly different from those of previous reports, but the number of people that claim no religious affiliation has grown. According to this report, only 55 percent of Latinos identify as Catholic and 18 percent claim no affiliation. It reflects the results of the earlier studies, that 3 percent identify as other Christian, usually assumed to be mostly Mormons and Jehovah's Witnesses.

Based on the numbers reported by the 2014 report and using 2010 census data, one can conclude that about 12 million Latinos identify as Protestant (22 percent of 55 million) at this time. About 8.8 million are evangelical/Pentecostal, and the rest are from mainline churches. That part seems somewhat straightforward.

One of the complexities in describing Latino Protestants today begins when one attempts to translate those numbers into people in churches and denominations. Most churches and denominations report the number of adult members, which focuses on those with a clear commitment to the life of the church. Of course, no one would expect that the numbers of adult members will add up to the percentage of people that self-identify as Protestants. But several issues make a correlation difficult. On the one hand, there is not a clear definition of what constitutes a Latino church. Does a predominantly Latino church that does not call itself Latino count? What about an English-language congregation that has services in Spanish but not a separate "church" in Spanish? On the other hand, denominations do not usually conduct a detailed census of the ethnic background of their members. So it is difficult to count Latinas that do not attend a church clearly identified as Latino.

Clifton Holland has done the most extensive work in addressing the first issue. He interviewed church officials in the United States, Puerto Rico, and Canada, asking them to identify Latino congregations in their denomina-

---

Identification 1990–2008: Growth, Diversity and Transformation" (Hartford, CT: Program on Public Values, Trinity College, 2010), http://commons.trincoll.edu/aris/files/2011/08/latinos 2008.pdf.

9. "The Shifting Religious Identity of Latinos in the United States," Pew Research Center, May 7, 2014, http://www.pewforum.org/2014/05/07/the-shifting-religious-identity-of-latinos -in-the-united-states/.

tions or movements. He collated the information into a database with name, address, and denominational affiliation. In 2012 he identified 23,189 Latino congregations in the United States and Canada. According to the database he developed, "14,400 local churches are listed as Spanish-speaking (62%); 8,676 are English-speaking (37%); 67 are bilingual (Spanish & English) and 49 are Portuguese-speaking (the last two combined total about 1%)."[10]

Another important piece of information based on this database is where the churches are concentrated, both by denomination and by region. According to his study, the 21 largest denominations with Latino members account for about 55 percent of the churches and members, and the other 225 denominations and movements that have a Latino presence account for about 45 percent of the total.[11] The states with the most Latino Protestant churches are:[12]

California	6,396
Texas	5,655
Florida	1,635
New York	1,553
Illinois	751
New Mexico	703
Arizona	663
New Jersey	649

These numbers do not necessarily correspond to denominational reports of Hispanic churches, because many of these congregations do not have a Latino-oriented ministry as their principal focus. But it gives us the most complete listing of congregations that have some level of commitment to the Latino community.

Keeping an updated database on Latino Protestant churches will not be easy. Most of the new church plants start in very informal settings, and many never develop into a formal church. Also, many independent congre-

10. "An On-Line Handbook of Hispanic Protestant Denominations, Institutions and Ministries in the USA," PROLADES, August 31, 2012, http://www.hispanicchurchesusa.net/index-new-model.html. The number of bilingual churches seems extremely low given how many Latino Protestant churches use some English in their ministry.

11. Clifton L. Holland, "Appendix II: A Statistical Overview of the Hispanic Protestant Church in the USA, 1921–2013," in *The Hispanic Evangelical Church in the United States: History, Ministry, and Challenges*, ed. Samuel Pagan (Sacramento: NHCLC, 2016), 517.

12. Holland, "Appendix II," 514–15.

gations are started and led by people without formal denominational links and are not easily identified through "normal" channels. Some congregations and ministries exist for only short periods and may escape cataloguing. But wherever there is a Latina presence in the United States, one can find established or emerging Latino Protestant congregations. As the community continues to grow and migrate into new areas, one can anticipate a continual growth in the number of Latino Protestant churches.

Sources of Growth of Latina Protestant Churches

Most Latino Protestants have always been evangelistic and conversion-oriented. There is a clear sense among most, particularly the evangelical or Pentecostal, that God invites people from nonfaith to faith and from nominal faith to active faith. Leading people to personal conversion experiences is clearly the focus of all evangelical and Pentecostal churches. Because most non-Protestant Latinos are Catholic, or nominally Catholic, most of this growth could be interpreted as transfer growth from Catholic churches. But most Protestants would see it as conversion growth. From their perspective, people who were nominally or culturally Catholic had a personal encounter with God, through Jesus Christ. In Pentecostal circles, this is usually linked to a spiritual ecstatic experience or some type of transformative experience. This type of growth is similar to what is being seen throughout Latin America.

As has been mentioned throughout, constant migration from Latin America is an important part of the growth of the Latina community. This is also the case for Latino Protestant churches. This second important source of growth is due, in part, to the growth of Protestantism, particularly in the countries that are sending a growing percentage of the new migrants. Each immigrant wave has created new opportunities for growth in Latina churches. Though there has been a slowdown in new migration from Latin America, there continues to be a constant flow of migrants, documented and undocumented, from that region. Given the steady migratory flow, it is likely that new immigrants will continue to be an important source of growth for Latino Protestant churches into the foreseeable future. And if there were to be a new migratory wave, then that growth could see a new spike.

The third area of growth for Latino Protestant churches is biological. Yet this area of growth is the most complicated, for various reasons. Because of the effects of acculturation, some Latino Protestants leave Latino churches for English-language congregations, particularly churches with a multicultural focus. But another issue faced by Latino Protestant churches is one common to other Protestant churches in the United States. To what extent are members keeping their own children in their churches, or in any church at all? Most of the "nones" that have been identified among Latinos are former Catholics. Latino Protestant churches face the same situation as their English-language counterparts, in that they are losing a percentage of their children.

Various Forms of Self-Identifying

Latina Protestantism is a child of US Protestantism. It was Protestant missionaries that first preached to Latinos and guided the first people to conversion. Over the years missionaries have played an important part in the growth of Latino and Latin American Protestantism. Those US missionaries have been part of churches and denominations that fit into one of the categories used to describe US Protestants, mainline, evangelical, or Pentecostal, recognizing the overlap between evangelicals and Pentecostals. But those categories have not exactly fit in Latin America. Historically the term *evangélico* has described most Protestants and has been a broader term than "evangelical" in English. Also, in many parts of Latin America Protestants are called *cristianos*, as opposed to *católicos*. Since cognates are used in slightly different ways in each language, this has created some confusion, particularly with the term *evangélico* when used in Spanish. US Latino Protestants tend to use the term in multiple ways, sometimes meaning "Protestant" and sometimes meaning "evangelical," as it is used in the United States. This also affects survey data. It is not always clear whether answers to questions about self-identity are impacted by whether the surveyor uses English or Spanish first. What is clear is that Latino Protestants are much more *evangélico* than the US Protestant population is evangelical, and that some Latinas in mainline denominations would identify as *evangélico*, though they might disavow the term "evangelical."

Some of the current tensions related to numbers have to do with which terms are used and how they are defined. But sometimes there is also a tendency toward triumphalism among some Latino Protestants, as has been occasionally seen in Latin America. Because of the significant growth of Protestantism in some countries, at times there is a sense of the inevitable shift from Catholicism to Protestantism. Some Protestants have even made predictions about how soon the majority of any given country will become Protestant. In the United States there has been a tendency to describe some Catholic practices as "Protestant-like" and to "almost" count charismatic or born-again Catholics as evangelicals.

The Denominations and the Churches

Any attempt to name and describe all 225 denominations and church movements or associations in the United States that have Latino congregations would necessarily change the nature of this book from a history to a compilation.[13] Most Protestant denominations have some type of ministry focused on the Latina community and, at least, a small number of Latino churches. Many denominations that are reporting growth recognize that it is almost exclusively because of new Latina members. Clearly Latinos are having an impact on most US Protestant churches. Even as most denominations are losing members, one consistent bright spot is the number of Latinos that are providing a spiritually vibrant presence in many churches (including the Roman Catholic Church).

The earlier-cited 2012 database developed by Clifton Holland also reported on the twenty-one largest church groups and sorted them by number of members. These numbers provide a good summary of the current state of Latina Protestantism.

	Members	Churches
Assemblies of God	293,000	1,935
Southern Baptist Convention	204,000	3,228
Seventh-Day Adventist Church	167,000	1,077
Independent Christian Churches of Christ	75,000	750
United Methodist Church	63,000	823
Church of God (Cleveland, TN)	60,000	1,000
Apostolic Assembly/Church	60,000	909
United Pentecostal Church Including Colombia UPC	50,730	534
Episcopal Church	38,000	400
Presbyterian Church USA	31,000	262

13. Holland, "Appendix II," 517.

Foursquare Gospel	30,800	250
American Baptist Churches	26,757	254
Church of the Nazarene	26,430	439
CLANY	20,615	217
Disciples of Christ	19,000	200
Llamada Final	17,857	75
Asamblea de Iglesias Cristianas	17,100	180
Lutheran Church–Missouri Synod	14,250	150
Church of God of Prophecy	13,800	230
CLADIC	13,000	130
Evangelical Lutheran Church	10,095	100

The Protestant denomination with the largest Latino presence is the
Assemblies of God. Even though it is not one of the largest Protestant denominations in the United States, it is the largest Pentecostal denomination,
and the one with the largest number of Latinas. As of January 2015, the AG
reported over 2,700 Latino congregations in its fourteen Latino districts in
the United States, including Puerto Rico.[14] There are also Latino churches
in "non-Latino" districts and many Latinos in "non-Latino" congregations.
By some estimates, there may be as many Latinas in intercultural churches
as in Latino congregations.

According to denominational reports, the AG has over three million
adult members. Of these, over 25 percent are Latinas, making the AG one of
the most ethnically diverse denominations in the United States.[15] While the
"white" population is slowing shrinking, it is Latinos and other ethnic minority groups that are at the core of the AG's continuing numerical growth.[16]
Currently, some of the largest AG churches in the United States are either
Latino or predominantly Latino.[17] Because the denomination has a strong

14. "Hispanic Relations," Office of Hispanic Relations, ag.org, accessed March 22, 2017,
http://ag.org/top/office_of_hispanic_relations/index.cfm.

15. Michael Lipka, "The Most and Least Racially Diverse U.S. Religious Groups," Pew
Research Center, July 27, 2015, http://www.pewresearch.org/fact-tank/2015/07/27/the-most
-and-least-racially-diverse-u-s-religious-groups/.

16. Darrin J. Rodgers, "Assemblies of God 2014 Statistics Released, Reveals Ethnic Transformation," Flower Pentecostal Heritage Center, June 18, 2015, https://ifphc.wordpress.com
/2015/06/18/assemblies-of-god-2014-statistics-released-reveals-ethnic-transformation/.

17. For example, New Life Covenant (mostly English) and Templo Calvario (bilingual).
"Megachurches Affiliated with the Assemblies of God," *Wikipedia*, accessed March 22, 2017,
https://en.wikipedia.org/w/index.php?title=Megachurches_affiliated_with_the_Assemblies
_of_God&oldid=751244648.

presence in Latin America, it continually benefits from migratory flows of AG members from the south and also draws people from other Pentecostal traditions. Also, almost from the very beginning of the denomination, the AG has employed a leadership model in which Latinos have been responsible for their own churches. This has empowered Latinas to plant new churches as people move into new areas. This model provides a flexibility not common in other denominations. Because of this, it is likely to continue growing and remain the largest Latino denomination in the United States.

The AG is also likely to provide models of intercultural relations because of the size of the Latino presence, not only in Latino churches, but also in traditionally non-Latino churches. Because of the growing size of the Latino membership, the growing number of English-dominant Latinos, and their presence throughout the denomination, the AG has to think in ways other denominations have not yet had to about how Latinos are included and how they take leadership. The AG is likely to be a bellwether for how Protestant denominations with a growing Latina presence work into an intercultural reality.

The **Southern Baptist Convention** (SBC) is the largest Protestant denomination in the United States and second in Latina membership. Historically, most of its Latino growth has been in Texas. But the denomination also has an increasing presence in parts of the country where there is new Latina migration. The denomination reports having over 1,500 Latino churches and over 1,700 "church-type missions," the latter being new congregations that are not yet fully established. These missions are mostly located in places where there is new Latino migration and a strong SBC presence, such as in southern states.

Because Southern Baptist churches have a strong evangelistic commitment and because they are in so many parts of the United States, it is likely that they will continue to develop "church-type missions" in the areas where they have a presence and there are Latinos. Nonetheless, Latinas play a very different role in the SBC than in the AG. Because the SBC is so much larger than the AG, Latinos constitute only 3 percent of total membership. Also, most SBC Latino churches are fairly small and do not have a strong financial base. It is yet to be seen how prominent a role Latinos will have in a denomination where their presence is so relatively small. Another issue for many SBC churches is the legal status of the Latino converts. According to Richard Land, about 40 percent of the new SBC Latina converts are undocumented.[18] This

18. Elizabeth Dias, "The Rise of Evangélicos," *Time*, April 4, 2013, http://nation.time.com /2013/04/04/the-rise-of-evangelicos/.

creates a tension between the evangelistic zeal of many SBC members and the large percentage of Anglo SBC members who are against immigration reform.

The **Seventh-Day Adventist Church** (SDA) is a unique denomination in many ways. Historically, many Protestants shunned it because of its origins and sectarian theological perspectives. This has changed as the denomination has sought to identify itself as an evangelical denomination. But it is also unique because it is the most racially diverse denomination in the United States.[19] Although relatively small with fewer than one million US members, it ranks third in Latino membership; 15 percent of its members are Latino. As of 2009, the denomination reported 167,000 Latino adult members in 1,077 churches.[20] This does not include Latinas in non-Latina churches. The denomination's focus on health and education has been attractive to many Latinos.

The Seventh-Day Adventists are also the only church group that has done a major study of Latino members. *Avance: A Vision for a New Mañana* studied various aspects of belief and practice of Latina SDA members.[21] Because of its unique nature, it has served as a model for other denominations, though none have done the level of work of this study.

Because of the nature of the **Churches of Christ**, it is difficult to obtain much information about the history and growth of its Latina churches. According to a 2010 directory, it has 247 Latino congregations spread throughout the United States.[22] The independent **Christian Churches/Churches of Christ** reports 143 Latino congregations, with most of those concentrated in Texas and California.[23] This latter group of churches has a Bible institute, Colegio Bíblico, in Eagle Pass, Texas, that has prepared pastors and leaders for a number of churches and denominations in Mexico and the United States since 1945.[24]

The mainline denomination with the largest Latino presence is the **United Methodist Church** (UMC). It had the largest Latina membership

---

19. Lipka, "The Most and Least Racially Diverse U.S. Religious Groups."

20. Based on a report by Sharri Davenport of the Multi-lingual Ministries Department of the North American Division of the Seventh-Day Adventists, sent by email, February 3, 2011.

21. Johnny Ramírez-Johnson and Edwin I. Hernández, *Avance: A Vision for a New Mañana* (Loma Linda, CA: Loma Linda University Press, 2003).

22. "Directorio iglesias de Cristos en Estados Unidos de América," Editorial La Paz, accessed March 22, 2017, http://www.editoriallapaz.org/directorio_EstadosUnidos.htm.

23. See http://www.saeministries.com/index.html.

24. See http://www.colegiobiblico.net/. This is the only group of churches for which I was not able to independently verify the numbers reported by Clifton Holland.

throughout the nineteenth and into the first part of the twentieth century, before other denominations began to grow much faster. Because of the denomination's size, it is also more like the SBC than like other large Latino denominations. Latinos constitute less than 2 percent of UMC membership, even though they are close to 18 percent of the US population.

Even though the UMC has not lost Latino members at the same rate that the larger denominations are losing members, Latino congregations are suffering some of the same issues as their "Anglo" counterparts. For example, the oldest Latino District Conference of the UMC, the Río Grande Conference, merged with an Anglo counterpart in 2014.[25] Currently the denomination reports about 675 Latino churches and 150 congregations that work under a majority-culture church. These churches and congregations report a total of 63,000 members. The denomination has a national plan for reaching out to Latinos with new churches and faith communities. One of the difficulties the UMC and other mainline denominations have in starting new Latino congregations is the expectation they place on a new church-planting project. One UMC leader estimated that it would cost the denomination about $250,000 to fully establish a Latino church.[26] If this is the case, it will be difficult for the denomination to start many churches or for Latinos to take over full responsibility for their churches.

The second-largest Pentecostal denomination among Latinos is the **Church of God** (Cleveland, Tennessee). It is similar to the AG and the SDA in that it is a significantly diverse denomination, with 28 percent of members being Latino.[27] Like those two denominations, it also has a stronger presence abroad than in the United States because of its extensive missionary efforts. The Church of God reports over 1,000 Latino churches and about 60,000 adult members in those churches. Most of the churches are part of one of eight Latino-focused regions, though some work under a traditionally "Anglo" congregation or in a majority-culture region. The denomination is in the midst of significant growth among Latinas and anticipates having some 2,000 congregations by 2020.[28] Because of its significant presence in Latin

25. Heather Hahn, "Five Conferences Merge to Become Two," United Methodist Church, accessed March 22, 2017, http://www.umc.org/news-and-media/five-conferences-merge-to -become-two.

26. Emilio Müller, in charge of Latino ministries for the UMC. Statement made during a class presentation at Fuller Theological Seminary, July 24, 2009.

27. Lipka, "The Most and Least Racially Diverse U.S. Religious Groups."

28. Carlos Morán, "Breve Reseña de los Latinos de la Iglesia de Dios en los Estados Unidos" (unpublished paper by the national director of Hispanic Ministries, Church of God, 2011);

America, it can also anticipate a direct benefit from new Latin American migration.

Oneness Pentecostals have a significant presence among Latino Protestants. The **Apostolic Assembly of the Faith in Christ Jesus** is the largest of the denominations, claiming 750 churches in the United States and over 50,000 adult members. It also has 600 churches in nineteen countries around the world. Because it is the oldest Latino-founded and Latino-led Protestant denomination, it deserves a unique recognition within US Latino Protestantism. But, as mentioned earlier, tensions between the US-born leadership and the Mexican immigrants created a division with its Mexican sister denomination. So the **Apostolic Church of the Faith in Christ Jesus** (Mexico) has started its own churches in the United States. (The US-based Apostolic Assembly has also started churches in Mexico.) Currently the Apostolic Church reports over 9,500 adult members in 216 churches that are divided among six districts in the United States.[29] Both denominations have also suffered splits, and there are an undetermined number of independent churches, or small clusters of churches, that also call themselves Apostolic churches from within this same theological tradition. Because the largest Apostolic denomination in Latin America is in Mexico, both major Oneness Pentecostal groups tend to benefit when there is increased new migration from Mexico.

The **United Pentecostal Church** (UPC) is the largest Oneness Pentecostal denomination in the United States and has a growing Latino presence. Since it began Spanish-language ministries in the United States in 1978, ending years of the tacit ethnic-specific ministry agreement among the various Oneness Pentecostal denominations, it has continued to grow among Latinas. The UPC reports 350 Spanish-language congregations, and a number of congregations are being started in conjunction with existing churches. The UPC has also done mission work in Latin America.

One of the countries where the UPC was most successful was Colombia, where it has been one of the largest Protestant denominations. Because of some historical tensions between the churches in Colombia and those in the United States, many Colombian immigrants coming to the States chose to start their own denomination instead of joining the US UPC. The Iglesia

---

see also Juan Francisco Martínez, *Los Protestantes: An Introduction to Latino Protestantism in the United States* (Santa Barbara, CA: ABC-CLIO, 2011), 67.

29. "Bienvenidos," *wikiHistoria IAFCJ*, accessed March 22, 2017, http://wikihistoria.iafcj .org/Bienvenidos.

Pentecostal Unida Latinoamericana, which these immigrants started, reports over 100 congregations in this country.[30] Splits among Oneness Pentecostals resulted in the establishment of other UPC-oriented denominations, similar to the situation among the Apostolic churches. The Iglesia Pentecostal Unida Hispana, Inc., the largest of these groups, also reports over 100 congregations.[31]

The **Episcopal Church USA** reports that 400 parishes have some ministry in Spanish. This is not the same as having established churches, so the numbers are not comparable to those of other denominations. Also, it is not a denomination with much diversity. Ninety percent of its members are white, and only 2 percent are Latino.[32] But the denomination does report extensive work among Spanish-speaking people.

The **Presbyterian Church (USA)** is the other mainline denomination that has had an extensive Latino presence since the nineteenth century. Down through the years Latinos never became a core part of the denomination's constituency, and currently 4 percent of its members are Latina. The PCUSA has not grown in numbers of Latino members for several years. Currently, the denomination's work among Latinos is linked to Puerto Rico, and some of the biggest Latino churches in the denomination are on the island. In 2015 the denomination reported 318 congregations (13 Portuguese-speaking), including in Puerto Rico, with about 40,000 members.[33] Because of denominational tensions, many churches have left the PCUSA and joined other Reformed denominations, including some Latino congregations. If current trends continue, the denomination is likely to lose more Latino churches and members in the foreseeable future.

As of 2014, the **International Church of the Foursquare Gospel**, another Pentecostal denomination, reported 216 Latino churches plus 77 in the pipeline and 37 congregations that met under the leadership of an existing

30. "Congregaciones," Iglesia Pentecostal Unida Latinoamericana, accessed March 22, 2017, http://ipul.us/directorio/congregaciones-usa.

31. See the denomination's Web site at http://www.ipuh.us/.

32. Lipka, "The Most and Least Racially Diverse U.S. Religious Groups."

33. This is a drop from the 2010 report that recorded 338 churches. "Iglesia Presbiteriana (E.U.A.)/Presbyterian Church (USA) Directorio Nacional Ministerios Hispano/Latinos Presbiterianos National Hispanic/Latino Presbyterian Ministries Directory: Iglesias, Misiones, Caucuses, Organizaciones, Liderato, Seminarios y Comités" (Louisville: Oficina de Apoyo Congregacional Hispana/Latina Ministerios Etnico Raciales, and Agencia Presbiteriana de Mision/Presbyterian Mission Agency, 2015), 4, http://www.presbyterianmission.org/wp-content/uploads/National-Hispanic-Latino-Presbyterian-Min-Directory.pdf.

church.[34] The denomination established an office of Hispanic ministries in 2008. Though it is a smaller Pentecostal denomination, its Latina membership is growing. It does not have as large a presence in Latin America as other Pentecostal groups, but its links there have provided it with new members and leaders.

The other mainline denomination with a significant Latino presence is the **American Baptist Churches**. As stated in chapter 3, the denomination claims the first Latino convert and the first Latino Protestant churches in the United States, established in New Mexico, in the 1850s. But it discontinued this work and did not reestablish Latino ministries until the twentieth century. It continued to grow in Latino membership during the twentieth century, and in the 1990s 40 percent of its church-planting efforts were among Latinas.[35] It is the most diverse of the major mainline denominations with 11 percent of its members being Latina.[36] Because of its denominational structure, Latino churches are tied to Puerto Rico. The denomination reports 377 Latino churches with 40,000 adult church members. Of these congregations, 123 are in Puerto Rico.[37] The links to the island provide Latino churches access to leadership and some potential benefit as the number of people leaving Puerto Rico continues to grow.

The **Church of the Nazarene** has experienced fairly steady growth in the number of new Latino churches and Latino members, such that 7 percent of its members today are Latina.[38] In the early years it focused on putting Latina congregations into Latino districts. But the immigrant waves of the 1980s and 1990s created new interest in Latino ministry that grew beyond the existing Latino districts. In 2001 the denomination established an office to oversee ministry among Latinos in the United States and Canada. Churches have established ministries and districts have planted congregations among Latinos and have created a situation where only 80 of the reported 435 Latino churches are linked to the historic Latino districts. Having started with one model, it now finds that most of the new churches are not a part of it. Yet the historic and symbolic presence of the Latino districts makes it unlikely that they will disappear in the near future. It is yet to be seen how this will

---

34. Juan Vallejo and Andy Butcher, "Foursquare's Hispanic Movement Gains Altitude," *Features*, November 11, 2014, http://www.foursquare.org/news/article/foursquares_hispanic _movement_gains_altitude.

35. Martínez, *Los Protestantes*, 77.

36. Lipka, "The Most and Least Racially Diverse U.S. Religious Groups."

37. Martínez, *Los Protestantes*, 77.

38. Lipka, "The Most and Least Racially Diverse U.S. Religious Groups."

impact growth and the relationship among Latino leaders in the churches that are a part of different structures, or how the denomination will work to develop structures that more closely reflect reality.

The **Concilio Latinoamericano de la Iglesia de Dios Pentecostal de Nueva York** (CLANY) has expanded from its New York City base to twenty-four states and several countries. It reports having 217 churches in the United States, though it does not report membership numbers.[39] Though it is not a large Pentecostal denomination, it is the second-largest Latino-initiated and Latino-led Protestant denomination in the United States. It is not formally linked to the Puerto Rican–based **Iglesia de Dios Pentecostal, Movimiento Internacional**, but it has historical ties and also draws from Puerto Rican migration.

Like its sister denomination, the Church of God, the **Church of God of Prophecy** has had a Latino presence through most of its existence. Though it is a much smaller denomination, it reports 230 Latino churches. Most of these congregations are small, having an average of 50–60 members. Like other denominations its size, it has developed a Bible institute program and prepares materials in Spanish for both its US and Latin American churches.[40]

The **Disciples of Christ** report 200 churches in the United States organized into six Hispanic and bilingual conventions. These churches and conventions form a National Hispanic and Bilingual Fellowship.[41] Latino churches have benefited from strong links to Disciples churches in Puerto Rico. They have drawn members and many leaders from the island throughout the years.

I have limited these short descriptions to denominations or movements that report at least 200 Latino churches or congregations in their statistics. Some denominations would report more than 200 congregations if English-language congregations with some type of Spanish-language ministry were counted. But the ranking of the denominations would remain about the same. There are also a few denominations, like the Lutheran Church–Missouri Synod (LCMS), that are growing and might soon reach the "200 church" threshold.[42] Holland lists the denominations and movements that

---

39. Martínez, *Los Protestantes*, 79.

40. Martínez, *Los Protestantes*, 79.

41. Pablo Jiménez, "Hispanics in the Movement," in *The Encyclopedia of the Stone-Campbell Movement*, ed. Douglas A. Foster et al. (Grand Rapids: Eerdmans, 2004), 396–99.

42. At a conference with Latino LCMS leaders in October 2016, they reported to me that they now have 187 congregations and that they have a plan to establish more churches in the next couple of years.

report at least 10,000 members, even though they might have fewer than 200 churches. Given the growth patterns seen in several denominations and associations, it is likely that some will reach one or the other of those thresholds in the next few years.

Many denominations continue to expand the number of Latina churches and members, so it is likely that other denominations will soon merit mention on one of the lists. Most of those denominations are either Pentecostal or evangelical. But other denominations, mostly mainline, are not only losing members in general but also losing Latino members. So it is possible that some of the mainline denominations mentioned in this survey might end up with fewer than 200 Latino churches or 10,000 members within the next few years.

What this survey makes clear about Latino Protestantism today is the following:

- The denominations with the largest Latino presence are evangelical or Pentecostal; if current trends continue, one can anticipate that most new growth in Latino Protestantism will happen in these types of churches.
- Most of the evangelical growth is happening in Pentecostal churches.
- Both the Southern Baptists and the Seventh-Day Adventists have grown faster among Latinas than they have in several Latin American countries.
- The majority of Latina Protestant churches are concentrated in a relatively small number of denominations.
- Most of the denominations that have at least 200 Latina churches have a significant Latino presence in their overall membership and tend to be more culturally diverse than US denominations in general.
- Those denominations where Latinas are a significant percentage of the membership also have Latinos in denominational leadership positions, though not at the same percentage as the membership.
- Many of the largest Latino Protestant church groups are members of neither the National Association of Evangelicals nor the National Council of Churches. The Southern Baptists, Seventh-Day Adventists, Churches of Christ, Oneness Pentecostals, CLANY, and the Church of God of Prophecy are not members of either group.[43]

43. Holland, "Appendix II," 516–17.

Both the work done by Holland and the surveys in this chapter reflect churches that have a clear Latino identity. The Pew studies do not attempt to differentiate Latinos that attend a clearly identified Latino congregation from those that do not. There is currently no clear way to count the number of Latinas that attend churches not identified as Latino. They are included in the Pew research, but not clearly identified in most denominational records. What percentage of Latino Protestants attend Latina congregations, and what percentage are part of non-Latino churches? Do Latinos have a preference for intercultural churches? Do those who attend non-Latino churches have a lower level of Latina identity than those in Latino churches? How many of them are people of Latino descent for whom a clearly identified Latino church would make little to no sense? Is worshiping in English a sign of assimilation?

Because of the importance of Pentecostalism in the Latino community today, it is helpful to review the varieties of Latina Pentecostal and charismatic churches.[44] One can find theological strains common in Pentecostalism such as Wesleyan-Holiness, Reformed Higher Life, and Oneness. Other types of charismatic doctrines such as word of faith and the prosperity gospel are also found in the community.

But if one looks at the origins of the movements represented in the Latino community, one sees how Pentecostalism is influencing it. The largest group of Latino Pentecostal churches is tied to US-based denominations. Even the historically African American Church of God in Christ (COGIC) has a few Latina congregations. Most Pentecostal denominations have Latino-oriented districts or conferences of churches, though there is also a significant Latino presence in non-Latino churches.

But it is only in the Pentecostal realm where one finds Latino denominations, and clusters or movements of churches started by, and led by, Latinos. These are the closest equivalent to the historically black denominations. Many were started because of racial tensions with white leadership in existing denominations. The most prominent examples are the Apostolic Assembly of the Faith in Christ Jesus, CLADIC, CLANY, and the Asamblea de Iglesias Cristianas (AIC). Though these groups are smaller than most US-based Pentecostal denominations, they are an important part of Latina Pentecostalism.

A variation on the Latino Pentecostal denomination is Victory Outreach. It was not started as a Latino denomination but it was started among Latinas,

---

44. This section draws on work done in Juan Martínez, "Latino Church Next," Center for Religion and Civic Culture, University of Southern California, August 15, 2012, https://crcc.usc.edu/report/the-latino-church-next/; and material published in Martínez, *Los Protestantes*, 81ff.

and a large percentage of its members have historically been Latinos. It continues to have a large presence in the Latina community, though it reaches beyond the community and has ministry in several countries around the world.

There are also a number of Pentecostal/charismatic churches that are linked to movements in Latin America. Iglesia de Dios Pentecostal, Movimiento Internacional (Puerto Rico); Iglesia Pentecostal Unida, International (Colombia); Elim (Guatemala); and Elim (El Salvador) are some of the largest and most well known of these types of churches. The Brazilian-based Iglesia Universal del Reino de Dios is also doing mission work among Spanish-speaking people, though its outreach in the United States goes beyond the Latino community. None of these associations are very large, though all are growing. It is yet to be seen how large of an impact they might have in the future.

A variation on this theme is movements started by Latin American immigrants in the United States. Llamada Final and Iglesia Pentecostal Unida, Inc., are both movements with clear Latin American influences, but were born in the United States. A number of smaller Pentecostal movements have also been established after tensions arose among leaders. Given the free church nature of Pentecostalism, it is likely that these types of churches and associations will continue to grow.

Another group of Latino churches came out of the US charismatic renewal movement, such as Vineyard and Calvary Chapel congregations. Other Latina churches follow movements such as word of faith or the prosperity gospel. Though not many churches clearly identify with these movements, they have had a broad influence in the Latino Protestant community through publications, conferences, and worship styles.

Apart from formal church and denominational structures, there are also many informal links between Pentecostal and neo-Pentecostal churches in the United States and in Latin America. Well-known pastors and evangelists from the south regularly teach and preach in the United States, and US pastors also minister in Latin America. This creates a constant influence and movement between Pentecostal churches in the two places. Occasionally a well-known personality from Latin America establishes a ministry in the United States. One of the most recent high-powered moves was when Dante Gebel became the pastor of the Spanish-language congregation at Crystal Cathedral before it sold its building. The congregation branched out on its own and has grown quickly because of the previously developed popularity of the pastor. River Church anticipates soon reaching ten thousand members.

Developing Latino Protestant Structures

During the last years of the twentieth century and the beginning of the twenty-first, Latino Protestants began to develop a number of regional and national entities to work together and to address issues of common concern. Each of these has served as a platform for Latino and Latina Protestants to speak to Protestant leaders and to a national audience. They have also been places where Latinos could develop their own voices in the social and political arenas.

Probably the most well-known Protestant Latino organization today is the **National Hispanic Christian Leadership Conference** (NHCLC). It was started out of the work of AMEN (mentioned in the previous chapter) and is led by Rev. Samuel Rodríguez, an ordained AG pastor. The NHCLC is linked to the National Association of Evangelicals (NAE) and describes itself as the Hispanic evangelical association. According to its Web site, the NHCLC is "the world's largest Hispanic Christian organization serving as a representative voice for the more than 100 million Hispanic Evangelicals assembled in over 40,118 U.S. churches and over 450,000 churches spread throughout the Spanish-speaking diaspora. . . . We exist to unify, serve and represent the Hispanic Evangelical Community with the divine (vertical) and human (horizontal) elements of the Christian message all while advancing the Lamb's agenda."[45] Rev. Rodríguez is the most prominent spokesperson for Latino Protestants today, and is considered one of the most influential evangelical leaders in the United States today.

A second national organization is the **National Latino Evangelical Coalition** (NaLEC). It "seeks to respond to a real need for Latino and Latina Evangelical voices committed to the common good and justice in the public sphere. . . . [NaLEC seeks to] provide alternative voices to the existing partisan voices and to create national awareness about the growing number of Latino Evangelicals who are not captive to partisan politics. The NaLEC

---

45. "Rev. Samuel Rodriguez," NHCLC, accessed March 22, 2017, https://nhclc.org/about-us/rev-samuel-rodriguez; and "Mission/Vision Statement," NHCLC, accessed March 22, 2017, https://nhclc.org/about-us/mission-vision-statement. It is difficult to ascertain what churches this statement refers to. It is clearly not exclusively Latino churches, since there are only about twenty-five thousand Latino Protestant churches in the United States, and, as observed by Holland, most of the largest denominations with a Latino presence do not have an affiliation with the NAE and others are members of the NCC. The NHCLC site has a legal page where a lawyer certifies the number of member churches (https://nhclc.org/legal). The statement does not give any information about what churches are included in the legal certification.

initiatives can provide a platform for this growing and often unheard demographic." Rev. Gabriel Salguero, also an AG pastor (though he has also served with the Church of the Nazarene), is the founder and president of this organization that seeks to "offer an important leadership voice for the close to 8 million Latino evangelicals in our country."[46] NaLEC is also a member of the NAE, and Rev. Salguero has served on its board. Salguero has also served on the White House's Faith Based Advisory Council and is considered one of the most influential Latino faith leaders in the US.[47]

Esperanza is the oldest of the three national organizations, but it came into national prominence at the beginning of the twenty-first century. Rev. Luis Cortés began Esperanza in 1986 in Philadelphia, in conjunction with other Latino pastors, to address the needs of the local Latina community. Esperanza came into the national spotlight in 2001 when it began to host the National Hispanic Prayer Breakfast and Conference, which is often attended by the president of the United States. It now has "a national network of more than 13,000 Hispanic faith and community-based organizations . . . [and] is one of the leading voices for Latinos in America." It addresses issues "of economic and workforce development, housing, immigration, and education."[48]

Meanwhile, in Latin America

Religious identity is also going through a major shift in Latin America. Though having a Latin American pope has created new interest in Catholicism in the region, the shifts continue. According to the 2014 Pew study of religion in Latin America,[49] there are at least eight localities where the percentage of Protestants is higher than among US Latinos (Brazil, Costa Rica, Dominican Republic, El Salvador, Guatemala, Honduras, Nicaragua, and Puerto Rico). This is a clear indication that conversion from Catholicism to Protestantism is linked to factors far beyond the influence and importance of Protestantism in the United States and the potential role of people becoming Protestant as a way of assimilating into dominant culture.

Several of the places that have a larger percentage of Protestants than the

46. "Who We Are: Our Mission," NaLEC, 2016, http://nalec.org/about-us.

47. See *The Huffington Post*, October 2, 2012.

48. "Rev. Luis Cortés," Esperanza, 2017, http://www.esperanza.us/mission-impact/about-the-agency/luis-cortes-story/.

49. "Religion in Latin America," Pew Research Center, November 13, 2014, http://www.pewforum.org/2014/11/13/religion-in-latin-america/.

US Latina population are sending migrants to the United States in significant numbers. Currently Puerto Rico, El Salvador, and Guatemala are exporting the most migrants from Latin America to the United States. Because they have a growing Protestant population, they are helping fuel the growth of Latino Protestantism in total numbers, but they are also affecting the growth of Protestantism as a percentage of the Latina community.

This growth is having a direct influence on Latina Protestantism. As mentioned earlier, more and more churches among Latinos have a Latin American base. There are also people that migrate north and south bringing songs, religious influences, and practices with them. In particular, neo-Pentecostal churches in Latin America are having a direct influence on US Latinos through satellite television, books, conferences, and pastoral exchanges. Also, a growing number of Latino churches, and Latina-influenced congregations, are involved in mission projects in the countries of origin of their members.[50] As a result, many Latino Protestants are influenced as much by their Latin American counterparts as by US Protestantism. Because of the globalization of communication, this type of influence is likely to continue into the foreseeable future.

From the Margins toward the Center

Historically, Latina Protestants have told their story from the margins. The testimonies of the early converts spoke of the social costs of conversion. Many of them were marginalized, and some suffered direct persecution from the Latino Catholic communities of which they were a part. And becoming Protestant did not provide much of a social benefit. Most found that discrimination by Anglo Protestants kept them from finding a place at the table with their coreligionists. The marginality of Latina Protestants became more pronounced as more of them became Protestants in churches and denominations that had developed on the margins of society and did not see a significant role for Latino churches, or any other churches, in social structures.

Many, if not most, Latina Protestants have historically seen themselves as somewhat marginal to politics. Though they might vote, for the most part they remained outside the political structures of the country. Not all the eth-

---

50. See my study on the issue: Juan Francisco Martínez, "Remittances and Mission: Transnational Latino Pentecostal Ministry in Los Angeles," in *Spirit and Power: The Growth and Global Impact of Pentecostalism*, ed. Donald E. Miller, Kimon H. Sargeant, and Richard Flory (New York: Oxford University Press, 2013), 204–22.

nic subgroups within the Latina community had the same perspective, however. Puerto Rican citizens and Cuban refugees tended toward more participation, while Mexican American and Central American Protestants tended toward less participation. One reason for this is that the latter two communities are more likely to have large numbers of undocumented in their churches, and even pastors and leaders who are undocumented. This tendency was reinforced by the fact that through most of the twentieth century Protestants in Latin America had very little social or political space. When all this was linked to a theology that focused on personal change and questioned the future of a passing world, it is not surprising that Latino Protestants tended not to see themselves as having a role in the social and political order.

That sense of marginality continued well into the twentieth century. As late as the 1980s, one of the favorite hymns in many Latino Protestant churches was "Hay una Senda," which spoke about the social isolation costs of being a (Protestant) believer in Jesus Christ. This hymn framed the issue as one in which following Jesus Christ would always have a cost worth paying. A believer might be isolated in the larger society, but it was worth it because of the benefits gained from becoming a believer.

This sense was reinforced by new migrants from Latin America who not only had a past memory of this type of isolation but were still living it. (To this day there are places in Latin America, mostly in Mexico, where Protestants are not welcome or where they are a very small minority of the population and where they continue to experience the marginalization expressed in the hymn.)

Latino and Latin American Protestant identity, particularly that of the evangelicals and Pentecostals, was forged on the margins. Pentecostal numbers have grown among poor and marginalized peoples. Latin American Protestants were kept out of the social and political structures by law or social pressure. But all this only reinforced the message about believing in a God who saw the people on the margins and gave them hope and a place in his church. The testimonies most often told by converts are of the God who works powerfully in the lives of those who have been broken and gives hope and a future to believe in. The narrative of broken lives made whole by the gospel continues to be compelling. Finding spiritual life in a place of despair and knowing that there is a place at the table in God's banquet have been the ways that we have told our own story.

In Latin America the issue has historically been political and social participation in a predominantly Roman Catholic society where in most countries Catholicism was the official religion. This meant that Protestants could have only a limited role; thus the narrative of marginality was a fairly

accurate story of how Latin American Protestants related to the larger society. As they have grown, some churches still experience corporate life on
the margins, while some of the megachurches find themselves close to the
centers of power.

In the United States the issue has been more complex. Latino Protestants
were on the margins of life in predominantly Catholic Latina communities,
not unlike the situation in Latin America. But they have also been historically marginalized by the larger Protestant society. This is now changing, as
Latinas become an increasingly important part of many churches and denominations. Yet it is still not clear that they will find a clear space, as Latinas,
in denominations where the majority of members are white. And though
Latino Protestant organizations have been able to speak on some political
and social issues, it is not clear that Anglo-majority Protestant organizations
will stand with them when the issue is Latina-specific (such as immigration
reform, education, fair wages, or housing).

Since the traditional narrative of being a Latino Protestant, particularly
a Pentecostal, has been one of God working among the marginalized, it is
difficult to tell our story from a position closer to the center. Many Latina
Protestant leaders still tell our narrative as if we were all still at the margins,
while speaking from the centers of power. It seems like there is a desire to
continue telling the Latino Protestant story from the margins, yet many
leaders desire to be at the center, or at least assume that Latinas cannot have
a clear influence unless they are connected to the center.

As the social location of many Latino Protestants potentially changes,
leaders find that they need to rethink how to address power. Who has a place
at the table in church structures? How does one speak to those in political
and social power? How will Latino Protestant leaders deal with the opportunities of access?

Finding a Voice in Church Structures

The question of how Latino Protestants would fit into Anglo Protestant
churches and denominations, and in US society, has been asked since the
nineteenth century. Emily Harwood wondered about the English-speaking
young Latino Protestants in New Mexico. Presbyterians in Texas tried to
integrate the Tex-Mex Presbytery into Anglo presbyteries and failed. In the
chapter on Latino Protestants in *The Mexican-American People*, the authors
questioned whether Protestant churches would be able to create a space

for Latinos. The assimilationist models and assumptions of the past clearly failed. How would Latinas be a part of the social structures of the United States?

One cannot tell the story of Latina Protestantism without pointing to the racial tensions that have arisen along the way. In many US denominations, Latinos have found themselves marginalized and have had little power to address this issue. The problem has been more pronounced in some Pentecostal denominations, because they have had more significant growth and because the churches have not depended on the denomination for their financial support. During the early years there were several denominational splits, such as CLADIC, CLANY, and AIC, that were directly related to interethnic tensions among leaders. Mexican American or Puerto Rican leaders formed their own denominations because they felt that the white leadership was not giving them the space they had earned (while many majority-culture leaders were convinced that Latinos were not ready for leadership). And leaders from these two Latina communities split among themselves.

To this day, it is the denominations that are growing that have the most challenges, but those denominations have also made the most changes in their efforts to include the largest US ethnic minority in their midst. As Latinas become a core part of the fabric of US society, growing Protestant denominations are also asking what it means to have a growing Latino presence in their midst. For example, what does it mean when two AG districts, the Los Angeles District (traditionally white) and the Southern Pacific District (traditionally Latino), both have Latino churches and both have Latino superintendents? What does it mean when several of the largest churches within the Los Angeles District have large Latina memberships? What about the increasing number of intercultural and predominantly English-language churches in the Southern Pacific District? Clearly the AG is facing this issue more directly because it has the largest number of Latinas and they constitute a significant percentage of its membership. But the AG is merely an example of what can be expected in any other denomination that takes the Latino population seriously.

Internally, Latino churches constantly face the challenges of relationships between immigrants and those born in the United States. This tension is often felt in the larger Latina community, but it also plays out in Protestant churches. The tensions have a clear cultural frame, but are often described in spiritual terms. The immigrants assume that the US-born no longer have the same spiritual fervor as those in Latin America, and the US-born question what they see as the legalism of the immigrants.

Because most Latino pastors have not been formed for ministry in the same ways most Anglo pastors have, the question of competence often comes up when leaders are chosen. One of the issues seldom clearly addressed is how church, parachurch, denominational, and seminary structures reflect a certain ethnic and cultural perspective. Therefore, those formed in that perspective are likely to be most successful in ministry in those structures. Because Latinas developed their leadership skills in very different cultural settings, those skills are not immediately transferable to the new setting. How does one choose leaders in that type of complex reality? So far, the naming of Latinas to leadership positions has been a mixed bag. A few have succeeded, but many have failed for various reasons. In fact, the most nationally recognized Latino Protestant leaders are in charge of Latina organizations, not traditionally Anglo structures.

An example of the difficulties of Latino Protestant leadership in the larger Protestant world can be found in Christian institutions of higher learning. To date, there has been one Latino seminary president, two Latino presidents of Christian universities, and a small number of Latina seminary deans. In most cases their tenures have been short. Though each of the situations has been unique, in the end there are very few examples of successful Latino Protestant leaders in traditionally majority-culture Protestant institutions of higher learning.

Finding a Place at the Political Table

Throughout most of the twentieth century, Latinos in general and Latino Protestants in particular were on the margins of political participation. At first it was because the community was small. The only place Latina voices were heard was where their population concentration made them impossible to ignore.

In both Latin America and the United States, the small size of the Latino Protestant community gave it too little clout to be seen as an important voting bloc. As the size of the community grew in the United States in the latter part of the twentieth century, it faced other challenges. On the one hand, too many Latinos were not citizens and could not vote. Also, Latinas were concentrated in states that are not competitive in national elections, such as California and Texas. This has greatly diluted Latina voting power and has allowed the major political parties to take for granted, ignore, or marginalize the Latina vote. Right after the 2016 presidential election, there was some question as to the percentage of Latinos who voted for Donald Trump, with numbers as low as 18 percent and as high as 28 percent.[51] But, except for Florida, Trump clearly won the election without counting on the Latino vote.

Though immigration reform is not the only national issue that most Latinos care about, it has tended to be a bellwether issue for understanding how the major political parties interact with Latinos, and Latina Protestants in particular. The process during the first part of the twenty-first century has been an example of the complex relationship between white and Latino Protestants and the role and influence of Latina Protestants within larger US society.

During the "heady" years of potential immigration reform, particularly after the massive marches of 2006, Latino Protestants were at the forefront of what the future might hold. National organizations like the NHCLC and Esperanza USA were in the middle of the immigration issue. When various evangelical organizations came together to form the Evangelical Immigration Table, the major Latino Protestant organizations were a part. It seemed like evangelicals would unite around this issue important to Latinos.

Yet, in spite of the growing influence of Latinos and Latino Protestants, there has been no significant movement on the issue of immigration reform. And though most surveys state that a majority of white evangelicals favor immigration reform that provides a way for the undocumented to legalize their status, this has never been a high enough priority for the majority of white evangelicals. Other issues have always taken center stage, and it feels like this issue, very important for most Latino Protestants, will become a point of division with white evangelicals instead of a place where evangelicals of all ethnic, racial, and cultural backgrounds can come together.

The election of Donald Trump as president has raised the specter of an anti-immigrant backlash. His rhetoric has attacked and denigrated immigrants. He has promised to rescind the executive orders of the Obama administration that protected the undocumented minors known as Dreamers. He has also claimed that he will build a wall between the United States and Mexico and have Mexico pay for it. Some Latino evangelical leaders supported him and hoped to have an influence on his policies, particularly on his position related to immigrants. Yet, because he was elected without the support of Latino evangelicals, it is yet to be seen whether they will have any significant impact.

51. "Lies, Damn Lies, and Exit Polls," Latino Decisions, November 10, 2016, http://www.latinodecisions.com/blog/2016/11/10/lies-damn-lies-and-exit-polls/.

Telling the Story of Latina Protestantism

One of the important shifts that occurred in the last part of the twentieth century and the first part of the twenty-first century is that Latino Protestants have found the platforms to tell their story. They began writing about ministry in the community in the 1980s, but it was not until the 1990s that they began to extensively study themselves. The first efforts were reviewed in the previous chapter. But as Latino Protestantism matures, members of the community are increasingly telling the story of Latina Protestantism.

During the first part of the twenty-first century, many Protestant denominations published histories of their Latino ministries. These included a retelling of the major events and people connected to the beginning and development of each denomination. There were also a number of scholarly studies of specific denominations or denominational traditions, such as Daisy Machado's *Of Borders and Margins: Hispanic Disciples in Texas, 1888–1945*, Arlene Sánchez-Walsh's *Latino Pentecostal Identity: Evangelical Faith, Self, and Society*, Paul Barton's *Hispanic Methodists, Presbyterians, and Baptists in Texas*, Johnny Ramírez-Johnson and Edwin Hernández's *Avance: A Vision for a New Mañana*, and Gastón Espinosa's *Latino Pentecostals in America: Faith and Politics in Action*.[52] A number of magazine and journal articles and chapters in books also touched on various aspects of the Latino Protestant story.

But a number of studies have also sought to tell a larger story. The efforts have taken several directions. The AHT and APHILA publications, mentioned in the last chapter, were some of the first efforts in the 1990s. In 1999 there was a collection called *Protestantes/Protestants: Hispanic Christianity within Mainline Traditions*.[53] A few years later CEHILA USA published another collection, the previously mentioned *Iglesias peregrinas en busca de identidad. Los Protestantes*, mentioned in chapter 2, added to this collection of publications by Latino Protestants seeking to tell their own story. The most recent of these is *The Hispanic Evangelical Church in the*

---

52. Daisy L. Machado, *Of Borders and Margins: Hispanic Disciples in Texas, 1888–1945* (Oxford: Oxford University Press, 2003); Arlene M. Sánchez Walsh, *Latino Pentecostal Identity: Evangelical Faith, Self, and Society* (New York: Columbia University Press, 2003); Paul Barton, *Hispanic Methodists, Presbyterians, and Baptists in Texas* (Austin: University of Texas Press, 2006); Ramírez-Johnson and Hernández, *Avance*; Gastón Espinosa, *Latino Pentecostals in America: Faith and Politics in Action* (Cambridge, MA: Harvard University Press, 2014).

53. David Maldonado Jr., ed., *Protestantes/Protestants: Hispanic Christianity within Mainline Traditions* (Nashville: Abingdon, 1999).

United States, published by the NHCLC in 2016. Hjamil Martínez-Vázquez, quoted in chapter 2, was writing to a wider audience, but he has given the Latino Protestant community tools to interpret their own story as they envision the future.

Latina Protestants Today

At the time of writing this book, **Rev. Sammy Rodríguez** is probably the most well-known Latino Protestant leader at a national level. As president of the NHCLC, he has developed a national platform that has given access to national politicians and he has also become a spokesperson for issues related to the Latino Protestant community. He has been named the most important Latino evangelical leader by CNN, Fox, NBC, and *Time* magazine. Rev. Rodríguez is an ordained AG pastor of Puerto Rican descent. He has written several books, including *Be Light: Shining God's Beauty, Truth, and Hope in a Darkened World*, and *The Lamb's Agenda*. Apart from his responsibilities with NHCLC, he is pastor of New Season Worship Center in Sacramento, California.

Minerva Carcaño is one of the most well-known Latina leaders among more liberal Protestant churches. She was the first Latina elected as a bishop of the UMC in 2004. She served as the bishop for the California-Pacific Annual Conference and is currently bishop of the California-Nevada Annual Conference. Carcaño also serves as the official spokesperson for the UMC Council of Bishops on issues of immigration. She is a Mexican American born in south Texas who grew up in humble circumstances. She is a third-generation Methodist known for her advocacy of immigrant, workers', and LGBTQ issues.

Luis Cortés formed Esperanza USA as part of his ministry in Philadelphia in 1987. The organization has worked on issues of community transformation locally and nationally. Cortés gained national prominence when he organized the National Presidential Hispanic Prayer Breakfast in 2002. This annual meeting brings Latino pastors and leaders to Washington, DC, to meet with congressional leaders and to learn how to advocate for political issues. Both President Bush and President Obama have participated in the prayer breakfast on various occasions. His local church is tied to the American Baptist Churches, and he has a Puerto Rican background.

On April 4, 2013, *Time* magazine's cover story was "The Latino Reformation." One of the churches featured in the issue was New Life Covenant

Church in Chicago, pastored by **Wilfredo "Choco" de Jesús**. The church is the largest AG church in the United States, and one of the largest Latino Protestant churches in the country. The church started among Puerto Rican immigrants and has been pastored by de Jesús since 2000. His church reflects one of the key issues faced by Latino churches in that the congregation is predominantly English speaking though clearly focused on the Latina community. The church is one of the fastest growing in the Chicago area and has a national impact.

Gabriel Salguero, another leader of Puerto Rican background, is an ordained pastor of the Church of the Nazarene. In 2015 he accepted the call to Iglesia el Calvario, a large AG church in Orlando, Florida. In 2009 he led the National Latino Evangelical Coalition (NaLEC), which had been a regional entity, to become a national organization. It is not as large as the NHCLC, but has a national platform as an alternative voice to the NHCLC. Salguero was most recently recognized for inviting his church to support the victims, and their families, of the massacre at Pulse, the mostly Latino gay bar in Orlando, in 2016.[54]

One of the most successful in crossing the evangelical, Pentecostal, and mainline borders among Latino Protestants has been **Alexia Salvatierra**. She is an ordained pastor with the Evangelical Lutheran Church in America and has served with Clergy and Laity United for Economic Justice (CLUE) in California. But she has also been a key person helping Latino Pentecostal pastors get involved in immigrant rights in southern California and elsewhere. Her book, written with Peter Heltzel, *Faith-Rooted Organizing: Mobilizing the Church in Service to the World*,[55] has served as a tool for many churches and leaders to work for social change from a Christian perspective. Salvatierra has expanded her impact as an adjunct professor at several seminaries around the United States.

Originally from Argentina, **Dante Gebel** is a well-known preacher, motivational speaker, and author in the Spanish-speaking world. He is known for organizing large youth rallies ("Super Clásicos de la Juventud") in various cities in Latin America. He moved to southern California to pastor the Spanish-language congregation at Crystal Cathedral. When that congregation sold its building, Gebel led the congregation to organize as a separate

54. Kate Shellnutt, "Grieving Together: How Orlando's Hispanic Evangelicals Are Reaching Out," *Christianity Today*, June 15, 2016, http://www.christianitytoday.com/ct/2016/june-web-only/orlando-hispanic-evangelicals-reaching-out-lgbt.html.

55. Alexia Salvatierra and Peter Heltzel, *Faith-Rooted Organizing: Mobilizing the Church in Service to the World* (Downers Grove: InterVarsity, 2014).

church. He is an ordained pastor with the AG and has attracted a large number of people. His congregation, now called River Church, meets in River Arena in Anaheim, and anticipates having ten thousand members in the near future.

El Rey Jesús is one of the largest Latino Protestant churches in the United States, and the largest in Florida. **Rev. Guillermo Maldonado**, originally from Honduras, founded it. The church is an apostolic and prophetic church built on the idea that God's supernatural power needs to be manifested today so that people can see that God is at work in the world. Maldonado has a television program on several satellite networks and has written several books in Spanish, some of which have been translated into several languages. He and his wife Ana colead the ministry.[56]

As Latina Protestants have begun to find their voice, it is mostly a prophetic voice. Somewhere between those bookends of immigration and structural assimilation are developing various types of spaces to evangelize, pastor, serve, and work for justice. Because life between the bookends is always fluid and represents a great deal of diversity, Latino Protestant leaders find themselves in different spaces and at different tables.

56. "Guillermo Maldonado (Pastor)," *Wikipedia*, accessed March 22, 2017, https://en.wiki pedia.org/w/index.php?title=Guillermo_Maldonado_(pastor)&oldid=750041172.

Chapter 9

Futures of Latino Protestantism

Daniel Rodriguez calls his book on Protestant ministry in the Latino community *A Future for the Latino Church*.[1] Clearly that book is not about *the* future of Latino Protestantism, since in its title it implicitly recognizes several probable futures. In many ways this book also points to the future and to the complexities of trying to describe that future. Because of the diversity of the Latino community and the various strains of Protestantism, it is difficult, if not impossible, to describe one broad future.

If it is true that there is not one Latino community but a number of Latina communities, it is also true that there will be more than one type of future for those identified as Latinas in the United States. The same can be said about the futures of Latino Protestantism. There are many variants within Protestantism, and so it is not surprising that these theological and denominational variants also reflect different understandings of what Latino Protestantism is now and should be in the future. Pentecostalism, and all free churches in general, often seem to grow as much by division and splits as by unified and planned evangelistic growth. This combination of growing diversity within the Latina population and the growing variations of Protestantism points toward a future in which there will be many types of Latino Protestantism. In the midst of the changing faces of Latina identity, it is unlikely that the Latino community will completely "assimilate" and disappear as a distinct population, though many Latinas have structurally assimilated and many others will do so in the future.

As stated earlier, Latina identity has developed in the space between

1. Daniel A. Rodriguez, *A Future for the Latino Church: Models for Multilingual, Multigenerational Hispanic Congregations* (Downers Grove: InterVarsity, 2011).

conquest and new migrations on one end and structural assimilation on the other. That space has always been dynamic and multidirectional. That is also part of the genius of free church Protestantism, particularly Pentecostalism. The futures of Latino Protestantism will develop in these spaces, but will likely be linked to a number of major issues.

The Future of Latinas in the United States

Given the history of migratory patterns from Latin America to the United States, it should not surprise us if changes in Latin America create a new migratory flow northward. The flow that has been most prominent in the news in 2015 and 2016 has been that of unaccompanied minors fleeing the violence in Central America. Though migration from Mexico has decreased lately, migration from Central America, Cuba, and Puerto Rico continues at a strong rate.

The continual migration is linked to the unresolved issue of 11–12 million undocumented people. In the 2016 US presidential race, Donald Trump used the subject of the undocumented as a rallying cry against some of what he saw as wrong with the United States. He talked about a significant deportation and about building a wall along the US-Mexico border and making Mexico pay for it.

The debate about the undocumented has many implications for the Latina community. During the presidential campaign, Donald Trump made many disparaging remarks about Mexican immigrants. Since most undocumented migrants in the United States today are Latinos, particularly from Mexico, this has meant that the immigration debate often seems to become about how people view Latinos in the United States. The anti-Latino rhetoric also seems to indicate that "Latino" and "undocumented" are clearly linked in the minds of many people. This, even though two of the Republican primary candidates were Latino. (Interestingly, both Ted Cruz and Marco Rubio are Cuban Americans, a segment of the Latina community that has consistently voted Republican, while most other Latinas tend to vote Democratic.)

Given the current political climate, it is not clear if and when the issue of the undocumented will be resolved in any positive way. The amnesty law of 1986 gave the Latina community new blood and an expanded political base. A solution to the current immigration debate will create new opportunities for the currently undocumented; lack of a solution will keep them in the shadows. And if Trump were to develop the "deportation force" he has proposed to forcibly deport 2–3 million undocumented, the social tensions and impacts would likely be profound.

The majority of people in the United States continue to endorse comprehensive immigration reform that provides a solution for those already here. Those working for immigration reform are still hopeful that one day new legislation will address the issue of the undocumented, of temporary workers, and of future flow. But whatever happens will be sure to impact the vibrancy of the community and the ministry focus of many Latina Protestant churches, particularly those with significant numbers of undocumented people in their ranks.

Because the political, social, and economic situation in Latin America tends to impact migratory flows, it is also crucial to understand what is happening there. If the situation in most of the principal sending countries stabilizes, large flows of new immigrants are less likely. The changing status of each of the countries of the continent creates a potential increase or decrease in migration.

For example, the reestablishment of diplomatic relations between the United States and Cuba has left people unsure about how the undocumented from that island will be treated in the future. Between the election of Donald Trump and the death of Fidel Castro, it is unclear what the relationship between the two countries will be. The current policy of giving immediate legal status to almost any Cuban who makes it to US soil might change in the future. Fearful of that potential change, more Cubans have recently attempted to leave the island and reach US soil. But, on the other hand, diplomatic relations might make it easier for people to leave the island legally, though a new freeze in relations might make life more difficult for people on the island. Also, if the current government were to fall, we would likely see a significant increase in movement from Cuba to the States, at least until the situation stabilized.

Another area where an unstable political and social situation is likely to create new migration is Central America. The United States deported gang members that were in US jails, and those gang members are now creating a great deal of insecurity in the small countries of the region. These small countries have also become portals for the movement of drugs from South America into the United States. The amount of illicit money flowing through these countries and the increase in gang- and drug mafia–related violence have resulted in the flow of unaccompanied minors fleeing that violence. Given the unstable situation of many people in the region, it is unlikely that Central Americans will cease looking to the United States as an escape valve. This situation impacts US Latinos. The violence has affected churches in Central America, which has caused new migration. In particular, unaccompanied minors end up at the US border, and new children are brought into the lives of Latino churches in the United States.

The Obama administration's massive deportation policy repatriated hundreds of thousands of Mexicans, and other Latin Americans, many of whom had lived most of their lives in the United States and often spoke English as their principal language. These people often had family networks in the United States. It is yet to be seen whether this deportation policy will create a new group of people trying to return to the United States. To date, overall undocumented migration from Mexico is down, but legal migration continues through family reunification and other legal means. Over 130,000 Mexicans legally migrated to the United States in 2014, and those numbers seem likely to remain steady, even if the number of undocumented Mexicans does not increase.[2]

At the time of writing this book there was significant discussion about the future of Puerto Rico. The island's government was in default on its loans and its economy was struggling. There seemed to be no clear solution to the problem, in part because there is no clear understanding of what Puerto Rico is as a political entity and what power it has to resolve its own issues. Previous US laws created a model of financial dependency that now cannot be easily addressed. Because of its unique status, it cannot appeal to federal bankruptcy laws to protect itself. Therefore Congress had to intervene. The legislation that was approved took all power from the Puerto Rican people and gave it to a nonelected oversight board. What viable solutions they can propose given the status of the island is yet to be seen.

In 2016 the Supreme Court also ruled, in two different cases, that Puerto Rico is "foreign in a domestic sense" (to borrow a phrase from a previous Supreme Court ruling on Puerto Rico). US law on bankruptcy issues does not protect it, so it cannot default on its debt. But it also does not have the legal authority to enforce its own laws in the same way that US states do. This means that the island is in fact a colony, something that has long been denied by the United States. It is yet to be seen whether the ruling will have an impact on the status of the island going into the future.[3]

2. Jie Zong and Jeanne Batalova, "Frequently Requested Statistics on Immigrants and Immigration in the United States," Migration Policy Institute, last updated May 26, 2016, http://www.migrationpolicy.org/article/frequently-requested-statistics-immigrants-and-immigration-united-states.

3. Noah Feldman, "Supreme Court Affirms That Puerto Rico Is Really a U.S. Colony,"

This situation has created a new outflow of people from Puerto Rico to the mainland, particularly to Florida. Because these people are not immigrants, they can immediately participate in the political process. It is yet to be seen what impact they will have. Their movement is creating a number of important changes on the mainland that are beyond the scope of this book. But, as a side note, there are now more Puerto Ricans living on the mainland than on the island.

Puerto Rico's future affects the future of Latinos in the United States, particularly Latina Protestantism. Will the political relationship between the United States and Puerto Rico change? If so, how? If the economy does not improve, will people continue to leave the island to live and work on the mainland? What happens when Puerto Ricans change the political dynamic of a state like Florida that is already a swing state? If significant numbers of new Puerto Ricans come to the mainland, and if a significant percentage are Protestants, how will that change the face of existing Latino Protestant churches? Since Puerto Ricans are already "overrepresented" in Latino Protestant leadership, will that reality become more pronounced with new migration?

Related to the debate about immigration from Latin America is the fact that the number of legal Asian immigrants has already overtaken the number of legal immigrants from Latin America. This may not impact the Latina community directly, since legal migration from Latin America continues to be significant. But Latina Protestants will likely need to think about intercultural church relationships in a new way, one in which the relationship with other minority and immigrant communities is as important as the relationship with the Anglo majority.

The future of Latinas in the United States will also be affected by the future role of the Spanish language. Constant migration has kept Spanish a vibrant language in this country for many years. The United States is not only a consumer of Spanish; it also produces a great deal of media in Spanish that is exported to other Spanish-speaking countries. The role of Spanish in the United States is also linked to the future of Puerto Rico. The Spanish language has a legal status in the United States, though only on the island of Puerto Rico. What would happen if Puerto Rico became a state of the Union? Would US Latinos translate their emotional attachment to Spanish into actions that support the continuance of the language as a live

Bloomberg View, June 14, 2016, https://www.bloomberg.com/view/articles/2016-06-14/supreme -court-affirms-that-puerto-rico-is-really-a-u-s-colony.

means of communication in the United States? How would that affect the usage of Spanish in Protestant churches?

There are many scenarios for the future of Latinos in the United States. As stated earlier, the US Census Bureau estimates that in 2044 over half of the US population will not be white. And by 2050, Latinas will be about 28 percent of the US population.[4] But the census is having problems defining who is Latino. How will intermarriage, new migration, the pressures of cultural adaptation, and transnational identities affect how we are "counted" and how we choose to identify ourselves?

The problems the census bureau has in identifying Latinos point to another issue that will affect the future. Will "Hispanic" and "Latino" continue to be useful terms to describe us? They have always put people with very different backgrounds under one umbrella. But with existing differences in the community, cultural adaptation, and structural assimilation, and new migration and intermarriage, will the terms still clearly identify a single group of people in 2050?

The 2016 presidential campaign has also pushed the issue of migration and Latino identity to the forefront. To what extent will Latina Protestants identify with the new immigrants, and to what extent will they seek to develop an identity that is not as closely linked to Latin America and to the new immigrants that will continue entering the country? Will Latino Protestants help the United States make peace with the fact that it is a country of the Americas and help it build bridges, or will they join the ranks of those who seek to build walls? How will Latinos see themselves in the United States?

Part of the problem is that Latino Protestants, like most practicing Latino Catholics (and African American Christians), have a political stance that does not easily fit with the positions of the major political parties as currently construed. Most Latino Protestants stand with the more conservative positions on issues like abortion and same-sex marriage. But they stand on the other side of the ledger on issues like immigration, education, and economic policies. Latino Catholics and most African Americans have tended to vote on the second set of issues, even as they are strongly concerned about the first set. Latina Protestants have struggled more with this dichotomy. When a candidate, like George W. Bush, was strong on the first set but also strong on immigration, he was able to draw a strong majority of

4. Jens Manuel Krogstad, "With Fewer New Arrivals, Census Lowers Hispanic Population Projections," Pew Research Center, December 16, 2014, http://www.pewresearch.org/fact-tank/2014/12/16/with-fewer-new-arrivals-census-lowers-hispanic-population-projections-2/.

the Latina Protestant vote. But when these two sets of issues split along party lines, Latino Protestants tend to split their vote, with a significant minority (and sometimes a small majority) voting for the candidate that holds their views on abortion and same-sex marriage. It is yet to be seen whether Latino Protestants will keep this stance and continue to potentially split their vote in this way.

Latinos as Leaders in US Protestantism

At this moment, except for Asian American–based denominations, the few US Protestant denominations (and the Roman Catholic Church) that are growing are growing because of Latinos. It is not clear how long that will continue. But this reality points to an increasing Latina presence in US Protestant churches. The question is whether Latinos will find a place at the leadership table, and what that will mean for Latinas within those denominations.

The denominations where Latinas are a significant percentage of the membership are already addressing the issue of Latino participation and leadership. How much of a role Latinos play in Protestant denominations depends on the percentage of the membership they represent, and not only on their numerical size. For example, Latino participation is already significant in denominations like the Assemblies of God, the Church of God, and the Seventh-Day Adventist Church where Latinas are a significant percentage of the overall membership. And, obviously, Latinos are in complete control of the, mostly Pentecostal, denominations they themselves have started. But their roles are much more limited in church groups where, although large in numbers, they are a much smaller percentage of the overall membership, such as the Southern Baptists, United Methodists, or Presbyterians. If this trend continues, it is likely that some denominations will continue to make significant changes as they become more Latino, while others will continue to "only" minister to Latinos.

Though some Latino Protestants have national platforms, most of them lead Latino organizations such as NHCLC, NaLEC, and Esperanza. There are few Latinas at the forefront of national organizations started by Anglo Protestants. It is yet to be seen whether Anglo Protestant organizations are ready to have Latinos at the helm. Until that happens, Latinas will continue to be on the fringe of US Protestantism.

Latin American Protestantism

Because of the transnational links that exist between Latinas and Latin America, it is clear that Latin American Protestantism will continue to be a key influence in Latina Protestantism, particularly in predominantly Spanish-speaking congregations and those with strong links to Latin American churches. Latin America will continue to serve as a resource for US Latino Protestants, a place from which to draw new members, but also new inspiration and spiritual vitality. Because of the continual flow of people both north and south and the development of transnational peoples, this influence will likely continue into the foreseeable future.

Currently, Latin American Protestantism continues in a growth mode, though not at the rapid rates of the last part of the twentieth century. As long as Protestantism continues to grow, particularly in places that send significant numbers of migrants to the United States, such as Puerto Rico, El Salvador, and Guatemala, natural sources of immigration growth for Latina Protestantism are likely to continue. Unless the United States stops all legal immigration from Latin America, one can anticipate new members for churches and new potential converts.

But with the increasing secularization of the countries of the north and the continual dynamic growth of churches in the south, Latin American Protestants are likely to also increasingly see the United States as a mission field. In a world where Christian mission will likely move in multiple directions and not from one center, Protestant Latinas, particularly those who maintain strong links to Latin America, will likely see themselves as the beachhead of efforts to reevangelize a secularizing United States.

This sense of mission to the world will likely expand as Latino Protestants link up with mission agencies and efforts from Latin America to send missionaries to other parts of the world. US mission agencies that are able to learn from Latin American agencies will likely also recruit those types of bilingual and transnational Latinas who are already successfully doing mission in many parts of the world.

The Formation of Latino Leaders for the Churches

From the time the first Latinos entered Protestant ministry in the nineteenth century, there has tended to be a tension between what Latino churches needed and what Protestant denominational structures expected of them.

That tension was seen most clearly in ordination requirements and in the systems set up to prepare Latinos for pastoral ministry. During the nineteenth and early twentieth centuries, the denomination that most exemplified this tension was the Presbyterian church, particularly the (Northern) PCUSA. During the early years only one *neomejicano* was ordained, José Ynés Perea. He had studied in the United States before the takeover of the Southwest and was able to meet the denomination's educational requirements for ordination. All other *neomejicano* pastors during the early years were only lay or licensed pastors. Even though Perea was not the most successful of the *neomejicano* pastors, he was given a prominent leadership role because he was the only one who was ordained.

The rest of the local pastors could not meet educational requirements for ordination. The Presbyterians attempted to address the problem by setting up the College of the Southwest (see chap. 3). But this institution was short-lived, because it was not financially viable. And it only offered an opportunity to the small number of people who could meet the entrance requirements.

The only other group that set up a seminary that focused on preparing Latinos for ministry was the American Baptists, who established Seminario Bautista Hispano Americano in Los Angeles in 1921. Throughout its years of existence it graduated pastors and leaders who served in the United States, Puerto Rico, Mexico, and Central and South America. It closed in 1964 due to financial problems and an inability to recruit students and place them after completing their studies.[5] There would be no other attempt to establish a seminary geared exclusively toward the Spanish-speaking people in the United States.

Throughout the twentieth century denominations that expected or required seminary education for their ordained pastors found that very few Latinos could meet all the qualifications. And those that did study in US seminaries were often educated away from their communities. Seminaries were preparing them to serve in environments foreign to the lived realities of most Latina communities or creating expectations that those communities could not meet.

Even during the nineteenth century, many denominations responded to this by establishing Bible institutes or programs for lay ministers. This model fit Pentecostal and many evangelical denominations very well, since

5. Eduardo Font, "Iglesias Bautistas Hispanas del suroeste," in *Hacia una historia de la iglesia evangélica Hispana de California del Sur*, ed. Rodelo Wilson (Montebello, CA: AHET, 1993), 105–6.

the goal was to prepare people to evangelize and serve churches, not necessarily to learn to "think theologically." They often were more like tech schools for ministry, providing basic tools for the task. In the first part of the twentieth century the AG created the Latin American Bible Institutes in California and Texas and its various extensions, the Baptists in Texas formed the Mexican Bible Institute, the Seventh-Day Adventists developed several schools, and independent churches developed institutions like Río Grande Bible Institute (Edinburg, Texas), Colegio Bíblico (Eagle Rock, Texas), and Instituto Evangélico (La Puente, California). Other denominations developed internal, short-lived programs. These types of institutions proliferated in the second half of the twentieth century, crossing denominational and theological lines.

Bible institutes have also proliferated in the Latino (and Latin American) Protestant community for many other reasons. On the one hand, these are low-cost institutions that are usually run by Latinas. These schools tend to look like the churches and leaders that start them. Though this may make them weak in some ways, it does tie them to the local community and encourage local funding. Because they are small with a small footprint, they are usually flexible. Bible institutes can be easily started, and courses can be offered anywhere there are teachers, students, and space.

Bible institutes provide access to theological education that has usually not been available in formal Protestant structures. For example, because these programs are not accredited, a lot of admissions prerequisites are not required of the students. Almost all students who want to study the Bible, theology, and ministry can qualify, in part because there are few or no educational requirements for entry into most programs, at least for entry-level programs. Language issues are also not a problem, since most of these programs can be taught in Spanish or in a bilingual format without creating major problems. The informality of the programs also means that Bible institutes can accept students without worrying about legal documentation.

Because of this flexibility and because of the limited, if any, educational requirements for ordination in many denominations, Bible institutes have been the principal place for the formation of the majority of Latino Protestant pastors (including this author). Traditional US seminaries, with their significant educational prerequisites, are not seen as the way forward by the vast majority of those who sensed God's call on their lives. In most Pentecostal and evangelical denominations, the criteria for identifying leaders for Latino churches do not include a high level of formal education; a clear sense of God's call to ministry and demonstrated giftedness for the task are what's important. This fits most Latino Protestants very well, since most of the growing Latina churches require little formal education.

Throughout the years Bible institutes have been the principal formal means used by Latino Protestants to prepare the next generation of leaders for ministry. (Many Latino pastors have no formal preparation and have been formed for ministry through the mentorship of experienced pastors and on-the-job training.) The seminary model, particularly as it now exists in the United States, has not fit the realities of most Latino pastors. Formal accredited seminary education has assumed that students earn a bachelor of arts (BA) degree and then complete a master of divinity degree. Because of historical educational and financial limitations, and linguistic realities, very few Latinos could get into seminary.

The number of Latinas involved in formal seminary education is growing as the number of Latinos with BA degrees also increases. But even today, with the growth of the Latina community and Latino Protestantism, Latinos constitute only 6 percent of the student population of schools in the Association of Theological Schools (ATS).[6] Of the over 270 ATS seminaries, only 8 have more than one hundred Latino students, and 3 of those schools are in Puerto Rico.[7] Among Latinos, 64 percent attend evangelical schools, 20 percent mainline seminaries, and 16 percent Catholic institutions. Nonetheless, it is estimated that the Latino student population in ATS schools will continue to grow. But, given current trends, it is likely that most of that growth will occur in evangelically oriented schools.[8]

Historically, there has been little connection between the seminaries and the Bible institutes. These institutions served different constituencies and had different objectives. But years ago the ATS instituted the "special student" category, which allowed seminaries to accept students who did not have BA degrees. Seminaries could decide whether or not to use this category and under what circumstances. Some used it to enroll Bible institute students, or those who had studied in unaccredited programs; these seminaries tended to increase their Latina student population.

---

6. "2015–2016 Annual Data Tables," Association of Theological Schools, accessed March 23, 2017, http://www.ats.edu/uploads/resources/institutional-data/annual-data-tables/2015 -2016-annual-data-tables.pdf.

7. Based on data obtained by the author directly from the ATS office on enrollment in ATS schools, 2015.

8. "Racial/Ethnic Students Represent Largest Growth Area for Theological Schools," Association of Theological Schools, accessed March 23, 2017, http://www.ats.edu/uploads /resources/publications-presentations/documents/racial-ethnic-growth.pdf.

But many Latino seminary students were not preparing for ministry; they were already in ministry and looking to continue their education. There were also those who realized that an accredited degree would make it easier to interact with other pastors and the local community; it was a form of social accreditation. As Latinas moved from the margins toward the center, many leaders realized that a seminary degree would make it easier for them to find a place among their seminary-educated ministry peers.

Because Bible institutes often have fairly informal structures, and because they usually instruct in Spanish, it has been very difficult for them to consider accreditation, even as a Bible college. A few have gone through the accreditation process, such as Mexican Baptist Bible Institute in San Antonio, which is now the Baptist University of the Américas, and Río Grande Bible Institute in Edinburg, Texas. More recently, the Latin American Bible Institute (LABI) in La Puente, California, has accredited a two-year associate degree. But several of these institutions have kept parts of their programs outside of the accreditation process, such as programs in Spanish or extension programs. It is these latter programs that are often the largest and are preparing the most people for ministry.

Other Bible institutes have developed articulation agreements with seminaries in their regions so that their graduates can enroll in them. Some seminaries have also developed programs to help Bible institute students address academic deficiencies in order to enter them. The seminaries that have been open to these types of options have seen their Latino student population grow.

Another type of effort has been to create a "certification" program for Bible institutes that could not meet accreditation requirements but could demonstrate a solid level of education. One of the first of these was developed by the Asociación Teológica Hispana (ATH) in conjunction with the ATS. To this day, Bible institutes in southern California can go through a certification process with ATH. Those that successfully complete the process are certified as having solid programs and consistent levels of education. Several seminaries in southern California and elsewhere accept graduates from these certified programs into seminary degree programs.

A more recent effort, at a national level, has been developed through the Asociación para la Educación Teológica Hispana (AETH), again in conjunction with the ATS. Bible institutes that meet the institutional and academic standards are certified by AETH as teaching at a baccalaureate level. ATS seminaries are then free to accept students from these programs, knowing that they have met ATS-approved criteria, even though they did not study at an accredited institution. The goal is for this certification process to open the door for more Latina students to study at ATS schools.[9]

These efforts are opening new doors for Latinos, even as they are raising new questions. ATS schools are losing their traditional students, as historic churches and denominations continue to lose members. If the United States becomes a majority minority country during the 2040s, it is likely that US churches will see that shift occur in the 2030s, since it is mostly whites who are becoming secularized and leaving churches. But because ATS schools also accept international students, it is likely that the ATS student body will become majority minority as early as the 2020s. How will seminaries respond to this shift, particularly as it pertains to Latinos, and Latin Americans?

For example, how many seminaries will accept students from schools certified by the AETH (or ATH)? Will seminaries continue to expect students to earn a BA degree as a prerequisite for admission? How many seminaries will offer programs in Spanish, or at least use Spanish as a language of instruction?

Of course, accreditation also raises questions for Latino Bible institutes. If they accredit their programs, do they eliminate the types of people they have trained in the past because of new educational requirements? Since it is easier to accredit programs in English, what happens to Spanish speakers? And if their accredited programs are only in English, can they compete with other English-language programs? Should they try? Does accreditation change the focus to a different set of students? What is the unique contribution of an institution that offers the same programs, in the same language, and in similar formats as other institutions? By drawing toward the center, Latino institutions have to ask themselves about their continuing role, something they did not have to address when they were working on the periphery.

Issues for the Future of Latino Protestantism

The concept "Latino" has always been a fluid one. In *Walk with the People*, this author argues that Latino churches will most likely attract people with a strong Latino identity. So the issues of adaptation, acculturation, and structural assimilation all impact Latino Protestant churches. But because many Latinas maintain a strong Latino identity, it seems likely that "traditional"

---

9. "Certification of Bible Institutes," Asociación para la Educación Teológica Hispana, 2015, http://www.aeth.org/en/certification-bible-institutes/.

Latino churches will continue to grow even as more Latinos attend "non-Latino" churches.

Ethnic identity as defined by a census box and ethnic identity as daily life do not necessarily line up well, particularly on the more assimilated edges of Latina Protestant identity. There is a growing part of the Latino community for whom much of what is being said in this book will seem foreign, at best something for "those people" and not for themselves. The questions of the future of Latino Protestantism will likely not make much sense to those who have not experienced Protestantism as a "Latino" phenomenon, or those who perceive Latino Protestant churches to be part of their past, not their future.

Of course, that gets more complicated because there are Latinos who have a strong sense of ethnic identity but experience Protestant faith outside of their "Latino-ness" or prefer to express their faith in intentionally multicultural environments. And there are also Latinos for whom being in a Latino church is one of the last clear markers of Latino identity. It will be a lot easier to track the future of those parts of Latino Protestantism that clearly self-identify as such. But the community is much more complex than that. This book has been able to track the history of those who have clearly identified themselves as Latina Protestants. Others will have to study those Latinos who are Protestant but who might not see their faith mediated through the lenses of their ethnic identity.

As Latinos inhabit multiple realities, it is clear that Latino Protestantism will also need to "grow" leaders that can minister in that type of intercultural and multicultural environment. Latino Protestantism has strong spiritual vitality, something needed by US Protestantism. But Latino Protestant churches are also spaces that are already intercultural, and often transnational. There are many emerging leaders in Latina churches that have these gifts and experiences that will be crucial for developing intercultural churches. As Latino Protestants see themselves as agents of God's mission in the United States, they will be able to send into the larger society a new generation of young Latinas who bring with them the spiritual vitality of the south linked to the intercultural and transnational skills learned by being polycentric people.

In what ways will Latino Protestantism continue to be clearly Latino and clearly Protestant? Or is that the wrong way to frame the question? In his article on the unification of the Hispanic Baptist Convention of Texas (HBCT) with the Baptist General Convention of Texas (BGCT), former BGCT president Alberto Reyes recognizes that Baptists in Texas will need to have a broad strategy when thinking about how to reach Latinos in their state. He is clearly describing one of the ways that Latino Protestants will need to think about their mission in the next few years.

> To meet the spiritual needs of our changing communities, Texas Baptists will need to continue growing predominantly Spanish-speaking congregations, bilingual/bicultural congregations, English-speaking Hispanic led congregations, and Anglo churches that intentionally make room for Hispanics. HBCT churches serve the needs of those who prefer to worship and function in Spanish, but these churches also have the potential to reach out to bilingual and bicultural Hispanic congregations as well as English-speaking Hispanic congregations.
>
> Hispanics along the continuum of acculturation will find a place at the table in Spanish-speaking congregations, bilingual/bicultural congregations, multi-cultural congregations, and predominantly Anglo congregations in Texas.[10]

The various Protestantisms that have developed among Latinas will likely continue to expand and be the generators of new expressions and developments in the Latino Protestant community. Latino Protestantism is thriving because new people have found new life in new faith encounters and have taken those expressions in new directions. If one thinks of the fluid nature of Latina identity, the dynamic changes in Protestantism, and the new Protestant expressions in Latin America, one will likely find that their intersections will continue to create increasing diversity among Latina Protestantism.

What seems likely from the patterns that have developed both among Latina Protestants and in Latin American Protestantism, is that Latino Protestantism will continue to be more Pentecostal, more charismatic, and more theologically conservative than US Protestantism at large. There is already a Latino presence in all forms of US Protestantism, including historically black denominations and liberal denominations with an overwhelming white membership, but current patterns would seem to indicate that the community will continue to skew strongly toward Pentecostal/charismatic churches and most other growing Latino Protestant churches will tend to be Pentecostalized, at least in worship style. Because of the probable continual dynamic growth of churches in the Global South, one can also anticipate that Latina Protestants will often reflect that same spiritual dynamic.

10. Alberto Reyes, "Unification to Integration: A Brief History of the Hispanic Baptist Convention of Texas," *Baptist History and Heritage* 40, no. 1 (Winter 2005): 52–53.

The umbrella of denominations and movements called Protestantism provides a lot of space for the continuing diversification of Latina Protestantisms. Some forms will look very much like their majority-culture counterparts. The bulk of Latina Protestants will look like culturally specific variations of their majority-culture denominational colleagues. But there will also be a growing number of new expressions that will fit under the Protestant umbrella but will have very clear Latino or Latin American expressions.

The number of clearly identifiable Latino Protestant churches continues to grow, particularly in Pentecostal denominations. Also, new movements among Latinos will likely become recognizable as denominations in the future, and will grow and develop, particularly in areas with a large concentration of Latinos and where there are new immigrants. These clearly identifiable churches will likely continue to be at the core of what we call Latino Protestantism.

Most Latino Protestant churches are already more diverse than most outsiders might assume. They have people of many national backgrounds and often also include non-Latino Spanish speakers and people who have married into the community. They also reflect the racial and ethnic diversity of Latin American reality. They are intercultural, within the framing of the global Latina experience.

But because most of them worship in Spanish or identify themselves as Latina churches, they are not perceived as being multicultural or intercultural. Some churches are more intentional about not identifying as Latino churches, even though their services are in Spanish. More commonly churches change the church name to English and conduct services in both English and Spanish. Others keep the Spanish name but call themselves a church in English. Because most of these churches are either in predominantly Latina communities or have a long history among Latinos, they clearly continue to be predominantly Latino churches. But the lines continue to blur.

Latinas as US Protestants

Clearly Latino Protestants have a larger role in those denominations where their numbers are increasing the most and where they are a significant part of the total membership. But Latinas are also flocking to those churches where they feel most welcome and where the message speaks to them directly. There is a clear relationship between growth in number of Latinos and the role they play in the churches they join. This confirms the earlier-quoted Pew data that says Latinos prefer to go to churches that have Latino clergy, a Latino presence, and services in Spanish (whether or not they attend those services).

But, in spite of the growing presence of Latino Protestants, so far it seems that the most significant role Latinas have played in most US Protestant denominations is providing numerical growth. Latinos have been at the margins of most major denominational discussions, debates, and decisions of recent years. The historic denominations with a long history in the Latino community talk about the importance of ethnic diversity, but they are whiter than the US population at large and have usually not taken ethnic minority voices into account when making major decisions.

In denominations where Latinos have more of a presence in leadership positions, it is yet unclear what impact they will have. They are gaining a platform, but it is unknown how the platform will be used. There is a growing number of Latino leaders, and other Pentecostal and evangelical leaders, who hope that Latinos will serve as the basis for spiritual renewal among US Protestants. Those praying for this impact want the spiritual vitality of the churches in the south to impact churches in the United States. They hope Latinas will keep that spiritual dynamic even as they are impacted by the secularizing influences of life in the United States.

But it is not yet clear that white Protestants are ready to listen to and learn from their Latina sisters and brothers, even in those denominations where Latinos are a significant percentage of the membership. To date, most Protestant denominations still see Latinas primarily as a mission field and not as potential partners in mission. Will Latinos bring their vitality to the churches of the north, or will they adopt the more nominal ways of their majority-culture counterparts?

Latino Protestants also have other experiences to offer the larger US Protestant communities. They have lived on the margins of power; they have lived a Christian faith where God is an active part of their lives; they have lived in intercultural realities; they have learned to do ministry with limited budgets; they have built a sense of family in their congregations; and they can offer US Protestants many other things needed to be faithful in a post-Christendom world. Will these potential contributions be recognized and valued? That is yet to be seen.

Faces of the Future

As Latino Protestants look toward their future, they need to look in multiple directions. On the one hand, migration has been and will continue to be one of the sources of growth for Latino Protestant churches. The eternal "first generation" will continue to be one of the mainstays of Latino Protestantism.

As Latina Protestants continue to express their faith and to walk in the power of the Spirit, they will continue to invite others to faith. Latino Protestantism will likely continue to have a strong conversion testimony. Latina churches will continue to have a large number of people who will give testimony of how God intervened and brought transformative change into their broken lives and how God transformed them and their families and friends.

But Latino Protestant churches will also need to keep many of their young and emerging adults. This raises important questions that have yet to be answered about the faith of Latina youth. The only major study of the religious tendencies of Latino young people was done as part of the National Study of Youth and Religion from 2002 to 2008. *Pathways of Hope and Faith among Hispanic Teens: Pastoral Reflections and Strategies Inspired by the National Study of Youth and Religion*[11] provided a way to use what was learned for ministry among Latino youth. Instituto Fe y Vida,[12] a national Catholic nonprofit institute, participated in the study and has continued to develop materials for ministry among Latina emerging adults. But there is a need for a new extensive study of the faith of this important segment of the US population.

Latino millennials are a crucial part of the Latino communities and of the US population as a whole. They constitute 21 percent of all US millennials and 25 percent of the Latino population.[13] They share many similarities with millennials from majority culture, including a growth in the number of nones.[14] But they are also quite different, particularly those who

11. Ken Johnson-Mondragon, ed., *Pathways of Hope and Faith among Hispanic Teens: Pastoral Reflections and Strategies Inspired by the National Study of Youth and Religion* (Stockton, CA: Instituto Fe y Vida, 2007).

12. See the organization's Web site at http://www.feyvida.org.

13. Eileen Patten, "The Nation's Latino Population Is Defined by Its Youth," Pew Research Center, April 20, 2016, http://www.pewhispanic.org/2016/04/20/the-nations-latino-population -is-defined-by-its-youth/.

14. See "The Shifting Religious Identity of Latinos in the United States," Pew Research Center, May 7, 2014, http://www.pewforum.org/2014/05/07/the-shifting-religious-identity-of -latinos-in-the-united-states/.

are foreign-born. Overall, they have a much more positive view of the future of the United States and of their role in it. Latino millennials believe in the American dream and want to be a part of it. They view education as more important than do their majority-culture counterparts. But, overall, they are also very different in their transition into adulthood. Because of the needs of family and their difficult social location, many Latina youth have to take on the responsibilities of adulthood well before their majority-culture counterparts. Also, issues like immigration directly or indirectly affect many of them. Because they are part of a minority community, they are also in the midst of developing polycentric identities.[15]

It is these young people, both US-born and foreign-born, who will play a key role in the Latino Protestant church of the future, including Latino Protestant millennials. Be they Latin American–born, US Latinos, or millennials of Latino descent, they will be the faces of Latino Protestantism. It will likely be possible to distinguish between them, even as they walk under the same umbrella.

So, what will the next generation of Latina Protestant leaders look like? Given the patterns of the community going into the twenty-first century, it is clear that there will be many types of leaders, representing the ethnic, cultural, and theological diversity that is the Latino Protestant community. But it is likely that those in recognized leadership, with a clear Latina identity, will share a number of characteristics.

- These leaders will possess a strong sense of an encounter with God. Those who will lead a spiritually dynamic community will have a sense of God's working in their lives. Latina Protestant leaders of the future will be people who believe in God's future.
- These leaders will be influenced by the spiritual dynamism of the south, but with a clear desire to learn from the north. They will interact with both and will work to bring both of those influences into their lives and ministries.
- These leaders will tend to have transnational life experiences, either because they were born in the south, because they spent time there, or because they were strongly influenced by people from the south.
- Because they have a clear sense of being part of a minoritized community, these leaders will naturally have developed a polycentric identity.

15. See *Understanding and Relating to Latina/o Youth: A Toolkit for Bilingual and Intergenerational Conversations* (Pasadena: Fuller Youth Institute, 2017).

They will implicitly know how to deal with people of different cultures and will tend to have good intercultural skills, learned through life experience.

- Most of these leaders will have a strong sense of being a part of an extended family or network, but will also be strongly influenced by US individualism. The pull of both will influence how they look at themselves and how they think about life and ministry.
- These leaders will recognize the importance of education, but will also recognize the limitations of a quality education. Many of them will have university degrees, but their ministry preparation will usually have begun with mentorship and on-the-job training. A significant percentage will have gone to a nonaccredited Bible institute, even if they have university and seminary degrees.

And so, Latino Protestantism has a dynamic future. It will look different from the past, even as each stage in Latina experience has changed the face of Protestant churches. Yet these emerging leaders will hear God's call and carry the mission in the power of the Holy Spirit like their spiritual forebears. And so the story continues.

Concluding Thoughts on a Living History

The history of Latina Protestantism is the story of how our past frames our future and how our present experience reinterprets our roots and our memories. At several points in the last 160-plus years, Latino Protestants have not seemed like agents, but like people who have become parts of movements that exist because of the agency of others. To this day a large percentage of Latino Protestants are converts, people who found a new way to express their faith in Jesus Christ because of the evangelistic fervor of others. But they also confess that this encounter has called them into agency. God used this means to help them find this faith expression, and now they seek to live it out and to invite others into that expression and lived-out faith.

This story has been framed by four themes—history, migration, religious faith, and sociocultural identity—and a fifth, the work of the Holy Spirit, that have shaped who Latina Protestants are. They live at the crossroads of various influences and encounters that have made them who they are and continue to shape their dynamic identities. As seen throughout the book, the encounters have not been painless, and this identity reaches across multiple sides of the complex experiences that have shaped it.

The historical events of conquest, expansion, and intervention continue to frame Latino identity and a specifically Latina Protestant identity. Because Latino history puts a lie to the national myth of completely voluntary migration and to the other myth of the United States being a country that (always) welcomes immigrants, this story will likely continue to be contested. It does not fit the national narrative of this country, nor the traditional Protestant narrative, to talk about conquest and about evangelization as Americanization, so it is unlikely that the story of conquest will ever become a part of how the United States describes itself, nor will most US Protestants acknowledge the role of Americanization in their mission work among Latinos.

So Latinos will continue to be perceived as invisible or at least under-represented in society. This is particularly true for those from Puerto Rico, a place whose identity is vague and whose existence is being defined by others. This also belies the national myth, since it is proof that the United States is one of the countries that still has colonies, even as it denies it.

How do Latinas live into a reality in which they have to recognize that they are the *harvest of empire*, having become US *citizens* because of US intervention in the Americas? But most Latinas are also descendants of the Spanish conquerors. This means that Latinos have been oppressed, but, at times, they have also benefited from the oppression of others. And so they continue living in that complexity. Latino Protestant faith was also born in that complex experience.

The ongoing lack of clarity about Puerto Rico creates a continuing pipeline for migration from the island to the mainland. The unclear future of Cuba has kept migration from that island at a high level. The violence in Central America has made life there intolerable for many. The changing economic situation in Mexico is not disconnected from the anti-immigrant rhetoric of the 2016 presidential election. Even though one previous president (Clinton) started building a fence between the United States and Mexico, and another previous president (Obama) practiced a policy of massive deportations, and the current president (Trump) calls for building a more complete fence across the US-Mexico border and a massive deportation program, the United States continues to be linked to Latin America and Latina identity is permanently linked to all the Americas. Though the United States seems to forget its "backyard" except when there is a crisis, the countries of the American continent (North and South) are linked into a common future. The migratory flows north, and south, may ebb at times, but they are not likely to cease.

One cannot tell the story of Latina Protestantism without remembering this painful history. Latino identity was created in the midst of European expansion into the Americas and later US expansion west and south. The first Latinos became US citizens, not because of migration, but because of conquest and territorial expansion. That reality is reflected in the names of the cities and states in the Southwest and embedded into the subconscious of the United States.

But Latinas are also migrants. The Americas have been settled by wave after wave of migrants. The first "Latinos" came from Spain centuries ago, as part of the expanding Spanish empire, into what is now the US Southwest, and many married into the native communities already living there. Most Latinos trace their lineage to some ancestor who moved north with dreams and aspirations, or who wanted to flee the unsettled reality in the home country (a situation often created, directly or indirectly, by US intervention). Being Latina has expanded with each migratory wave throughout the history of the United States and continues to expand with the arrival of those who cross the border as this book is being read.

Because so many Latinos are migrants or descendants of migrants, and because most of those identified as Latina continue to maintain a clearly identifiable minority-culture identity, Latinos have to ask what it means to have a transnational and polycentric identity. Historically, Latinas have been objects of studies that ask about how they "fit" or "assimilate" into majority culture. But Latinos need to continue to ask who they are in a changing world.

As one completes this reflection on the four major themes—history, migration, religious faith, and sociocultural identity—one can name many things that are unique about Latino experience. But one must also recognize that the Latino experience is becoming more "normative" among other minority and migrant peoples. Throughout the world people are moving and finding that they can best thrive if they develop transnational identities that reflect their experience of migration, but also their lived experience in a globalized world. Is the Latina experience something that is best "assimilated" into majority culture in the United States, or might it be a model of how to move forward in a rapidly changing world?

Yet this story is also a testimony to the faith of generations and to a belief that God is at work in the world, through the power of the Holy Spirit. It is a history of the southern churches in the midst of the north. Because these churches exist in the midst of a changing religious environment in the United States, it is yet to be seen whether they will bring religious revitalization to the United States or become more secularized, like their majority-culture counterparts.

But because they are also linked to Latin America, Latina Protestants have to ask about the potential long-term influence of a Latin American pope. Will Catholic faith in Latin America be revitalized? Will this potential revitalization influence the growth of Protestantism in the region? Will revitalized Latina Catholics have an influence on the Catholic Church in the United States?

One cannot tell this story without also telling the story of the changing faith of the United States and of Latin America. At this point Latino Protestants are a growing movement and are having some impact on evangelical and Pentecostal denominations in the United States. Will these trends continue? What impact will they have on the changing religious landscape of the United States?

Clearly, Latina Protestants have much to contribute to Protestantism in the United States. But will US Protestantism recognize the value of those contributions? Will it make room for Latinos, as Latinos, or will it make space only for those who "check their Latino identity at the door" or assimilate into majority culture?

Internally, Latino Protestant churches have to continue to live into the reality that a significant number of Latina Protestants will always be immigrants and that a significant percentage will continue to be undocumented. How does one continue to live on the margins while also wanting to influence the center? What does it mean to be a church that lives into illegality? How does one fit into larger society when a segment of one's community is not allowed into the societal structures?

But as a minoritized people with a significant percentage of immigrants, Latinas need to become subjects of their own experience. It may mean that fitting into US Protestantism includes becoming missionaries to nominal Christian communities and prophets to a Protestantism that has often served as a chaplain to US imperialistic ventures.

Of course, Latino Protestant identity is closely linked to the clarity of Latino identity in the United States. Latinos are in the midst of other peoples, even in places where they are the majority, like southern California, northern New Mexico, and south Texas. Will interaction with other groups and intermarriage mean the eventual end of a clearly identifiable Latino identity? Will they become one more ethnic minority in the United States that only has a symbolic memory of its identity and of its past?

So this book ends where it began. The issues that formed Latino Protestant identity continue to be fluid. Many of the questions raised by that identity in the nineteenth century continue to be raised in the twenty-first. Latino Protestants continue to exist and thrive at the crossroads of the influences that created them and continue to mark them and of the influences that could absorb their unique characteristics into something bigger. The end of a distinctive identity has been foretold many times throughout the history of Latina Protestantism, and yet Latino Protestants continue to exist. Latina Protestant churches today look very different from the congregations of Ambrosio González, Blas Chávez, Alejo Hernández, and my great-great-grandmother Rafaela. Yet Latino Protestantism continues to grow.

Of course, our nineteenth-century forebears could not have foretold the changes described in this book. They might not immediately recognize us, but they would hear the stories of conversion, of personal faith, of reading the Bible, of inviting others to faith, and would recognize that they are the "cloud of witnesses" that rejoice over what we have become. Rafaela made a decision that has had repercussions for generations. It is yet to be seen what impact a new generation will have on this living history.

Works Cited

Note: the author has published under the names Juan Martínez,
Juan Francisco Martínez, and Juan Francisco Martínez Guerra.

American Baptist Publication Society. *Baptist Almanac*. Philadelphia: American Baptist Publication Society, 1851.

Atkins-Vasquez, Jane. *Hispanic Presbyterians in Southern California: One Hundred Years of Ministry*. Los Angeles: Synod of Southern California and Hawaii, 1988.

Barber, Ruth Kerns, and Edith J. Agnew. *Sowers Went Forth: The Story of Presbyterian Missions in New Mexico and Southern Colorado*. Albuquerque: Menaul Historical Library of the Southwest, 1981.

Bardacke, Frank. *Trampling Out the Vintage: Cesar Chavez and the Two Souls of the United Farm Workers*. New York: Verso, 2011.

Barton, Paul. *Hispanic Methodists, Presbyterians, and Baptists in Texas*. Austin: University of Texas Press, 2006.

Bastian, Jean-Pierre. *La mutación religiosa de América Latina para una sociología del cambio social en la modernidad periférica*. Mexico City: Fondo de Cultura Económica, 1997.

Betancourt, Esdras. *En el espíritu y poder de Pentecostés: Historia de la Iglesia de Dios Hispana en Estados Unidos*. Cleveland, TN: Vida Publication and Centro Estudios Latinos Publicaciones, 2016.

"Between Two Worlds: How Young Latinos Come of Age in America." Pew Research Center. December 11, 2009. Updated July 1, 2013. http://www.pewhispanic.org/2009/12/11/between-two-worlds-how-young-latinos-come-of-age-in-america/.

Brackenridge, R. Douglas, and Francisco O. García-Treto. *Iglesia Presbiteriana: A History of Presbyterians and Mexican Americans in the Southwest*. San Antonio: Trinity University Press, 1974.

Brettell, Caroline B., and James F. Hollifield. *Migration Theory: Talking across Disciplines*. New York: Routledge, 2015.

Buffington, Sean T. "Dominican Americans." Countries and Their Cultures. Accessed

March 20, 2017. http://www.everyculture.com/multi/Bu-Dr/Dominican-Americans .html.

Cather, Willa. *Death Comes for the Archbishop*. New York: Knopf, 1927.

Changing Faiths: Latinos and the Transformation of American Religion. Washington, DC: Pew Research Center, 2007. http://www.pewforum.org/files/2007/04/hispanics-reli gion-07-final-mar08.pdf.

"Colombian Diaspora in the United States, The." Migration Policy Institute. Revised May 2015. http://www.migrationpolicy.org/sites/default/files/publications/RAD-Colombia II.pdf.

Cordova, Lou. *Directory of Hispanic Protestant Churches in Southern California*. Pasadena, CA: AHET, 1986.

Costas, Orlando E. *Christ outside the Gate: Mission beyond Christendom*. Maryknoll, NY: Orbis, 1982.

———. *Liberating News: A Theology of Contextual Evangelization*. Grand Rapids: Eerdmans, 1989.

Craig, Robert M. *Our Mexicans*. New York: Board of Home Missions of the Presbyterian Church, USA, 1904.

Darley, Alex M. *Passionists of the Southwest: Or the Holy Brotherhood*. Reprint. Glorieta, NM: Rio Grande Press, 1968.

Davis, Kenneth. "Brevia from the Hispanic Shift: Continuity Rather Than Conversion?" In *An Enduring Flame: Studies on Latino Popular Religiosity*, edited by Antonio M. Stevens Arroyo and Ana Maria Diaz-Stevens, 205–10. PARAL Studies Series, vol. 1. New York: Bildner Center for Western Hemisphere Studies, 1995.

De La Torre, Miguel A., and Edwin David Aponte. *Introducing Latino/a Theologies*. Maryknoll, NY: Orbis, 2001.

Dias, Elizabeth. "¡Evangélicos!" *Time*, April 15, 2013.

———. "The Rise of Evangélicos." *Time*, April 4, 2013. http://nation.time.com/2013/04/04 /the-rise-of-evangelicos/.

Díaz, Benjamín. "Compendio de la historia de la Convención Bautista Mexicana de Texas." Unpublished manuscript, n.d.

Driver, Juan. *La fe en la periferia de la historia: Una historia del pueblo cristiano desde la perspectiva de los movimientos de restauración y reforma radical*. Guatemala City: Ediciones Semilla, 1997.

Duany, Jorge. "The Puerto Rican Diaspora to the United States: A Postcolonial Migration?" Paper presented at the workshop on Postcolonial Immigration and Identity Formation in Europe since 1945: Towards a Comparative Perspective, International Institute of Social History, Amsterdam, November 7–8, 2008. https://centropr.hunter .cuny.edu/sites/default/files/past_events/Jorge_Duany_Puerto_Rican_Diaspora.pdf.

Dussel, Enrique, and Comisión de Estudios de Historia de la Iglesia en Latinoamérica. *Historia general de la iglesia en América latina*. Salamanca, Spain: Sígueme, 1983.

"El español: Una lengua viva: Informe 2016." Instituto Cervantes. 2016. http://cvc.cer vantes.es/lengua/espanol_lengua_viva/pdf/espanol_lengua_viva_2016.pdf.

Ennis, Sharon R., Merarys Rios-Vargas, and Nora G. Albert. "The Hispanic Population: 2010." 2010 Census Brief. United States Census Bureau. May 2011. http://www.census .gov/prod/cen2010/briefs/c2010br-04.pdf.

Espinosa, Gastón. *Latino Pentecostals in America: Faith and Politics in Action.* Cambridge, MA: Harvard University Press, 2014.

Espinosa, Gastón, Virgilio P. Elizondo, and Jesse Miranda. *Hispanic Churches in American Public Life: Summary of Findings.* Notre Dame: Institute for Latino Studies, University of Notre Dame, 2003.

"Fact Sheet: Hispanic Catholics in the U.S." CARA at Georgetown University. Accessed March 29, 2017. http://cara.georgetown.edu/staff/webpages/Hispanic%20Catholic%20 Fact%20Sheet.pdf.

Feldman, Noah. "Supreme Court Affirms That Puerto Rico Is Really a U.S. Colony." *Bloomberg View,* June 14, 2016. https://www.bloomberg.com/view/articles/2016-06-14 /supreme-court-affirms-that-puerto-rico-is-really-a-u-s-colony.

Fernández-Amesto, Felipe. *Our America: A Hispanic History of the United States.* New York: Norton, 2014.

Francis, E. K. "Padre Martinez: A New Mexican Myth." *New Mexico Historical Review* 31 (October 1956).

García Verduzco, Pablo. *Bosquejo histórico del Metodismo Mexicano.* Nashville: Cokesbury Press, 1933.

Gibson, Campbell, and Kay Jung. "Historical Census Statistics on Population Totals by Race, 1790 to 1990, and by Hispanic Origin, 1970 to 1990, for Large Cities and Other Urban Places in the United States." United States Census Bureau. Population Division. Working Paper no. 76. February 2005. https://www.census.gov/population/www/doc umentation/twps0076/twps0076.pdf.

Gonzalez, Juan. *Harvest of Empire: A History of Latinos in America.* New York: Viking Penguin, 2000.

González, Justo L. *Mañana: Christian Theology from a Hispanic Perspective.* Nashville: Abingdon, 1990.

———. *Santa Biblia: The Bible through Hispanic Eyes.* Nashville: Abingdon, 1996.

González, Justo L., ed. *¡Alabadle! Hispanic Christian Worship.* Nashville: Abingdon, 1996.

———, ed. *Each in Our Own Tongue: A History of Hispanics in United Methodism.* Nashville: Abingdon, 1991.

Gonzalez-Barrera, Ana. "More Mexicans Leaving Than Coming to the U.S." Pew Research Center. November 19, 2015. http://www.pewhispanic.org /2015 /11/19 /more-mexicans-leaving-than-coming-to-the-u-s/.

Gonzalez-Barrera, Ana, and Jens Manuel Krogstad. "U.S. Deportations of Immigrants Reach Record High in 2013." Pew Research Center. October 2, 2014. http://www.pewresearch.org /fact-tank/2014/10/02/u-s-deportations-of-immigrants-reach-record-high-in-2013/.

Grebler, Leo, Joan W. Moore, and Ralph C. Guzman. *The Mexican-American People: The Nation's Second Largest Minority.* New York: Free Press, 1970.

Grijalva, Joshua. *A History of Mexican Baptists in Texas, 1881–1981.* Dallas: Baptist General Convention of Texas, 1982.

"Guide to the Home Missions Council of North America Records." Presbyterian Historical Society. Accessed March 29, 2017. http://www.history.pcusa.org/collections /research-tools/guides-archival-collections/ncc-rg-26.

Gutiérrez, David G., ed. *The Columbia History of Latinos in the United States since 1960.* New York: Columbia University Press, 2004.

Hagan, Jacqueline Maria. *Migration Miracle: Faith, Hope, and Meaning on the Undocumented Journey*. Cambridge, MA: Harvard University Press, 2008.

Hamilton Garmany Horton File. Southwest Texas Conference, United Methodist Church Archives. San Antonio, n.d.

Harwood, Thomas. *History of the New Mexico Spanish and English Missions of the Methodist Episcopal Church from 1850–1910*. 2 vols. Albuquerque: El Abogado Press, 1908.

Hodgson, Roberto. "History of the Hispanic Church of the Nazarene in the United States and Canada." Paper presented at the Ibero-American Theological Conference, San José, Costa Rica, October 18, 2004. http://didache.nazarene.org/index.php/region theoconf/ibero-amer-theo-conf/507-iberoamo4-eng-24-usa-canada/file.

Hoffman, Pat. *Ministry of the Dispossessed: Learning from the Farm Worker Movement*. Los Angeles: Wallace Press, 1987.

Holland, Clifton L. "Appendix II: A Statistical Overview of the Hispanic Protestant Church in the USA, 1921–2013." In *The Hispanic Evangelical Church in the United States: History, Ministry, and Challenges*, edited by Samuel Pagan, 495–517. Sacramento: NHCLC, 2016.

———. *The Religious Dimension in Hispanic Los Angeles: A Protestant Case Study*. South Pasadena, CA: William Carey Library, 1974.

———. "Table of 20 Largest Hispanic Denominations in the USA: By Number of Congregations, 1993." PROLADES. 1993. http://www.hispanicchurchesusa.net/hsusa2.htm.

Holland, Clifton L., comp. "A Chronology of Significant Protestant Beginnings in Hispanic Ministry in the USA." PROLADES. Last revised July 31, 2003. http://www.pro lades.com/historical/usa-hisp-chron.pdf.

Holland, Clifton L., ed., comp., producer. "Historical Profiles of Protestant Denominations with Hispanic Ministries in the USA: Listed by Major Traditions and Denominational Families." PROLADES. Last updated August 15, 2012. http://www.hispanic churchesusa.net/denominations/hsusa_historical_profiles_15August2012.pdf.

Home Missions Council. *Eighteenth Annual Report of the Home Missions Council and Council of Women for Home Missions*. New York: Home Missions Council, 1925.

———. *Fifteenth Annual Report of the Home Missions Council and Council of Women for Home Missions*. New York: Home Missions Council, 1922.

———. *Fourteenth Annual Meeting of the Home Missions Council and Council of Women for Home Missions*. New York: Home Missions Council, 1921.

Houston 85: The National Convocation on Evangelizing Ethnic America. April 15–18, 1985. Conference documents.

Hunt, Larry L. "The Spirit of Hispanic Protestantism in the United States: National Survey Comparisons of Catholics and Non-Catholics." *Social Science Quarterly* 79, no. 4 (December 1998): 828–45.

"Iglesia Presbiteriana (E.U.A.)/Presbyterian Church (USA) Directorio Nacional Ministerios Hispano/Latinos Presbiterianos National Hispanic/Latino Presbyterian Ministries Directory: Iglesias, Misiones, Caucuses, Organizaciones, Liderato, Seminarios y Comités." Louisville: Oficina de Apoyo Congregacional Hispana/Latina Ministerios Etnico Raciales, and Agencia Presbiteriana de Mision/Presbyterian Mission Agency, 2015. http://www.presbyterianmission.org/wp-content/uploads/National-Hispanic -Latino-Presbyterian-Min-Directory.pdf.

Jiménez, Pablo. "Hispanics in the Movement." In *The Encyclopedia of the Stone-Campbell*

Movement, edited by Douglas A. Foster, Paul M. Blowers, Anthony L. Dunnavant, and D. Newell Williams, 396–99. Grand Rapids: Eerdmans, 2004.

Johnson-Mondragon, Ken, ed. *Pathways of Hope and Faith among Hispanic Teens: Pastoral Reflections and Strategies Inspired by the National Study of Youth and Religion.* Stockton, CA: Instituto Fe y Vida, 2007.

Kellogg, Harriet S. *Life of Mrs. Emily J. Harwood.* Albuquerque: El Abogado Press, 1903.

Krogstad, Jens Manuel. "With Fewer New Arrivals, Census Lowers Hispanic Population Projections." Pew Research Center. December 16, 2014. http://www.pew research.org/fact-tank/2014/12/16/with-fewer-new-arrivals-census-lowers-hispanic -population-projections-2/.

Krogstad, Jens Manuel, and Mark Hugo Lopez. "Hispanic Nativity Shift." Pew Research Center. April 29, 2014. http://www.pewhispanic.org/2014/04/29/hispanic -nativity-shift/.

———. "Hispanic Population Reaches Record 55 Million, but Growth Has Cooled." Pew Research Center. June 25, 2015. http://www.pewresearch.org /fact-tank/2015/06/25/u-s-hispanic-population-growth-surge-cools/.

Lipka, Michael. "The Most and Least Racially Diverse U.S. Religious Groups." Pew Research Center. July 27, 2015. http://www.pewresearch.org/fact-tank/2015/07/27/the -most-and-least-racially-diverse-u-s-religious-groups/.

Livermore, Abiel Abbot. *The War with Mexico Revisited.* Boston: American Peace Society, 1850.

Lopez, Mark Hugo, and Ana Gonzalez-Barrera. "What Is the Future of Spanish in the United States?" Pew Research Center. September 5, 2013. http://www.pewresearch.org /fact-tank/2013/09/05/what-is-the-future-of-spanish-in-the-united-states/.

Machado, Daisy L. *Of Borders and Margins: Hispanic Disciples in Texas, 1888–1945.* Oxford: Oxford University Press, 2003.

Maldonado, David, Jr., ed. *Protestantes/Protestants: Hispanic Christianity within Mainline Traditions.* Nashville: Abingdon, 1999.

Maldonado, Jorge E., and Juan F. Martinez, eds. *Vivir y servir en el exilio: Lecturas teológicas de la experiencia latina en los Estados Unidos.* Buenos Aires: Kairos Ediciones, 2008.

Martínez, Juan. "Latino Church Next." Center for Religion and Civic Culture. University of Southern California. August 15, 2012. https://crcc.usc.edu/report/the-latino-church -next/.

Martínez, Juan Francisco. *Caminando entre el pueblo: Ministerio latino en los Estados Unidos/Walk with the People: Latino Ministry in the United States.* Nashville: Abingdon, 2008.

———. *Los Protestantes: An Introduction to Latino Protestantism in the United States.* Santa Barbara, CA: ABC-CLIO, 2011.

———. "Ministry among United States Hispanics by an Ethno-Religious Minority: A Mennonite Brethren Case Study." ThM thesis, Fuller Theological Seminary, School of World Mission, 1988.

———. "Origins and Development of Protestantism among Latinos in the Southwestern United States, 1836–1900." PhD diss., Fuller Theological Seminary, School of World Mission, 1996.

———. "Remittances and Mission: Transnational Latino Pentecostal Ministry in Los

Angeles." In *Spirit and Power: The Growth and Global Impact of Pentecostalism*, edited by Donald E. Miller, Kimon H. Sargeant, and Richard Flory, 204–22. New York: Oxford University Press, 2013.

————. *Sea La Luz: The Making of Mexican Protestantism in the American Southwest, 1829–1900*. Denton: University of North Texas, 2006.

————. "What Happens to Church When We Move *Latinamente* beyond Inherited Ecclesiologies?" In *Building Bridges, Doing Justice: Constructing a Latino/a Ecumenical Theology*, edited by Orlando O. Espín, 167–82. Maryknoll, NY: Orbis, 2009.

Martínez Guerra, Juan Francisco. "The Bible in Neomejicano Protestant Folklore during the 19th Century." *Apuntes* 17, no. 1 (1997): 21–26.

Martínez Guerra, Juan F., and Luis Scott, eds. *Iglesias peregrinas en busca de identidad: Cuadros del protestantismo latino en los Estados Unidos*. Buenos Aires: Kairos Ediciones, 2004.

Martínez-Vázquez, Hjamil A. *Made in the Margins: Latina/o Constructions of US Religious History*. Waco: Baylor University Press, 2013.

McLean, Robert N. *The Northern Mexican*. New York: Home Missions Council, 1930.

McNamara, Patrick. "Assumptions, Theories and Methods in the Study of Latino Religion after 25 Years." In *Old Masks, New Faces: Religion and Latino Identities*, edited by Antonio M. Stevens Arroyo and Gilbert Cadena, 23–32. PARAL Studies Series, vol. 2. New York: Bildner Center for Western Hemisphere Studies, 1995.

Methodist Episcopal Church, South. Minutes of the Annual Conference, 1851, 1870–1900.

"Mexicans." El Pueblo de Los Angeles Historical Monument. City of Los Angeles. 2016. http://elpueblo.lacity.org/historyeducation/ElPuebloHistory/Mexicans/index.html.

Mirande, Alfredo. *Gringo Justice*. Notre Dame: University of Notre Dame Press, 1987.

Montoya, Alex. *Hispanic Ministry in North America*. Grand Rapids: Zondervan, 1987.

Morán, Carlos. "Breve Reseña de los Latinos de la Iglesia de Dios en los Estados Unidos." Unpublished paper by the national director of Hispanic Ministries, Church of God, 2011.

Murray, Andrew E. *The Skyline Synod: Presbyterianism in Colorado and Utah*. Denver: Golden Bell Press, 1971.

Náñez, Alfredo. *Historia de La Conferencia Río Grande de La Iglesia Metodista Unida*. Dallas: Bridwell Library, 1980.

Navarro-Rivera, Juhem, Barry A. Kosmin, and Ariela Keysar. "U.S. Latino Religious Identification 1990–2008: Growth, Diversity and Transformation." Hartford, CT: Program on Public Values, Trinity College, 2010. http://commons.trincoll.edu/aris/files/2011/08/latinos2008.pdf.

Nwosu, Chiamaka, and Jeanne Batalova. "Immigrants from the Dominican Republic in the United States." Migration Policy Institute. July 18, 2014. http://www.migrationpolicy.org/article/foreign-born-dominican-republic-united-states.

"On-Line Handbook of Hispanic Protestant Denominations, Institutions and Ministries in the USA, An." PROLADES. August 31, 2012. http://www.hispanicchurchesusa.net/index-new-model.html.

Ordoqui, Agustina. "América Latina, cada vez menos católica y más protestante." *Infobae*. November 23, 2014. http://www.infobae.com/2014/11/23/1610174-america-latina-cada-vez-menos-catolica-y-mas-protestante/.

Orozco, E. C. *Republican Protestantism in Aztlán: The Encounter between Mexicanism and Anglo-Saxon Secular Humanism in the United States Southwest*. Glendale, CA: Petereins Press, 1980.

Ortiz, Manuel. *The Hispanic Challenge: Opportunities Confronting the Church*. Downers Grove: InterVarsity, 1993.

Pagán, Samuel, and the National Hispanic Christian Leadership Conference. *The Hispanic Evangelical Church in the United States: History, Ministry, and Challenges*. Elk Grove, CA: NHCLC, 2016.

Parker, Theodore. "The Mexican War." *Massachusetts Quarterly Review* 1 (December 1847).

Passel, Jeffrey S., D'Vera Cohn, and Mark Hugo Lopez. "Hispanics Account for More Than Half of Nation's Growth in Past Decade." Pew Research Center. March 24, 2011. http://www.pewhispanic.org/2011/03/24/hispanics-account-for-more-than-half-of-nations-growth-in-past-decade/.

Patten, Eileen. "The Nation's Latino Population Is Defined by Its Youth." Pew Research Center. April 20, 2016. http://www.pewhispanic.org/2016/04/20/the-nations-latino-population-is-defined-by-its-youth/.

"Racial/Ethnic Students Represent Largest Growth Area for Theological Schools." Association of Theological Schools. Accessed March 23, 2017. http://www.ats.edu/uploads/resources/publications-presentations/documents/racial-ethnic-growth.pdf.

Ramírez, Daniel. *Migrating Faith: Pentecostalism in the United States and Mexico in the Twentieth Century*. Chapel Hill: University of North Carolina Press, 2015.

Ramírez-Johnson, Johnny, and Edwin I. Hernández. *Avance: A Vision for a New Mañana*. Loma Linda, CA: Loma Linda University Press, 2003.

Rankin, Melinda. *Twenty Years among the Mexicans: A Narrative of Missionary Labor*. Saint Louis: Christian Publishing Co., 1875.

Read, Hollis. *The Hand of God in History; or, Divine Providence Historically Illustrated in the Extension and Establishment of Christianity*. 2 vols. Hartford: H. E. Robins, 1858.

Recinos, Harold J. *Who Comes in the Name of the Lord? Jesus at the Margins*. Nashville: Abingdon, 1997.

"Religion in Latin America." Pew Research Center. November 13, 2014. http://www.pewforum.org/2014/11/13/religion-in-latin-america/.

Rendón, Gabino. "Mientras miro los años pasar." Unpublished manuscript, preached on August 20, 1961, or September 20, 1961, Gabino Rendón file, Menual Historical Library, Albuquerque.

Rendón, Gabino, as told to Edith Agnew. *Hand on My Shoulder*. New York: Board of National Missions PCUSA, 1953.

Reyes, Alberto. "Unification to Integration: A Brief History of the Hispanic Baptist Convention of Texas." *Baptist History and Heritage* 40, no. 1 (Winter 2005): 44–56.

Reyes, José. *Los Hispanos en los Estados Unidos: Un reto y una oportunidad para la iglesia*. Cleveland, TN: White Wing Publishing House, 1985.

Rivera, Raymond. *Liberty to the Captives: Our Call to Minister in a Captive World*. Grand Rapids: Eerdmans, 2012.

Rodgers, Darrin J. "Assemblies of God 2014 Statistics Released, Reveals Ethnic Transformation." Flower Pentecostal Heritage Center. June 18, 2015. https://ifphc.wordpress.com/2015/06/18/assemblies-of-god-2014-statistics-released-reveals-ethnic-transformation/.

Rodriguez, Daniel A. *A Future for the Latino Church: Models for Multilingual, Multigenerational Hispanic Congregations*. Downers Grove: InterVarsity, 2011.

Rodríguez-Díaz, Daniel R., and David Cortés-Fuentes, eds. *Hidden Stories: Unveiling the History of the Latino Church*. Decatur, GA: AETH, 1994.

Rosas, Ana Elizabeth. *Abrazando El Espíritu: Bracero Families Confront the US-Mexico Border*. Oakland: University of California Press, 2014.

Rudolph, Joseph R., Jr. "Border Fence." Immigration to the United States. Accessed March 29, 2017. http://immigrationtounitedstates.org/381-border-fence.html.

Ryan, Camille. "Language Use in the United States: 2011." United States Census Bureau. American Community Survey Reports. August 2013. http://www.census.gov/prod/2013pubs/acs-22.pdf.

Rytina, Nancy. "IRCA Legalization Effects: Lawful Permanent Residence and Naturalization through 2001." Paper presented at conference on the Effects of Immigrant Legalization Programs on the United States, the Cloister, Mary Woodward Lasker Center, NIH Main Campus, Bethesda, MD, October 25, 2002. https://www.dhs.gov/xlibrary/assets/statistics/publications/irca0114int.pdf.

Salvatierra, Alexia, and Peter Heltzel. *Faith-Rooted Organizing: Mobilizing the Church in Service to the World*. Downers Grove: InterVarsity, 2014.

Sánchez Walsh, Arlene M. *Latino Pentecostal Identity: Evangelical Faith, Self, and Society*. New York: Columbia University Press, 2003.

Sandoval, Moisés, ed. *Fronteras: A History of the Latin American Church in the USA Since 1513*. San Antonio: Mexican American Cultural Center, 1983.

Scott, James C., Jr. *Aimee: La gente Hispana estaba en su corazon*. Seattle: Foursquare Media, 2010.

———. "Foursquare Hispana—Part 2." *Features*. Last updated April 30, 2013. http://www.foursquare.org/news/article/foursquare_hispana_part_2.

Serrano, Orlando. "Historia de la Iglesia del Nazareno Hispana." Unpublished manuscript, n.d.

"Shifting Religious Identity of Latinos in the United States, The." Pew Research Center. May 7, 2014. http://www.pewforum.org/2014/05/07/the-shifting-religious-identity-of-latinos-in-the-united-states/.

"Statements and Resolutions." National Farm Worker Ministry. 2017. http://nfwm.org/statements-resolutions/.

Storrs, Richard S. *Discourse in Behalf of the American Home Missionary Society*. New York: American Home Missionary Society, 1855.

Strong, Josiah. *Our Country; Its Possible Future and Its Present Crisis*. New York: Baker and Taylor Co., 1858.

Taylor, Jack. *God's Messengers to Mexico's Masses: A Study of the Religious Significance of the Braceros*. Eugene, OR: Institute of Church Growth, 1962.

Taylor, Paul, Mark Hugo Lopez, Jessica Hamar Martínez, and Gabriel Velasco. "When Labels Don't Fit: Hispanics and Their Views of Identity." Pew Research Center. April 4, 2012. http://www.pewhispanic.org/2012/04/04/when-labels-dont-fit-hispanics-and-their-views-of-identity/.

"2015–2016 Annual Data Tables." Association of Theological Schools. Accessed March 23, 2017. http://www.ats.edu/uploads/resources/institutional-data/annual-data-tables/2015-2016-annual-data-tables.pdf.

Vallejo, Juan, and Andy Butcher. "Foursquare's Hispanic Movement Gains Altitude." *Features.* November 11, 2014. http://www.foursquare.org/news/article/foursquares _hispanic_movement_gains_altitude.

Van Biema, David, et al. "The 25 Most Influential Evangelicals in America." *Time.* February 7, 2005.

Van Marter, Jerry L. "Jorge Lara-Braud, Pastor, Theologian, Fighter for the Poor Dies at 77." *Presbyterian Outlook.* July 2, 2008. https://pres-outlook.org/2008/07/jorge-lara -braud-pastor-theologian-fighter-for-the-poor-dies-at-77/.

Vasquez, Manuel. *La historia aun no contada: 100 años de Adventismo Hispano.* Nampa, ID: Pacific Press Publishing Association, 2000.

Villafañe, Eldin. *The Liberating Spirit: Toward an Hispanic American Pentecostal Social Ethic.* Grand Rapids: Eerdmans, 1993.

Wells, Ronald A. "Cesar Chavez's Protestant Allies: The California Migrant Ministry and the Farm Workers." *Journal of Presbyterian History* (Spring/Summer 2009): 5–16.

Whalen, Carmen Teresa. "Colonialism, Citizenship, and the Making of the Puerto Rican Diaspora: An Introduction." In *Puerto Rican Diaspora: Historical Perspectives*, edited by Carmen Teresa Whalen and Victor Vazquez-Hernandez, 1–42. Philadelphia: Temple University Press, 2005.

Wheatherby, Lela. "A Study of the Early Years of the Presbyterian Work with the Spanish Speaking People of New Mexico and Colorado and Its Development from 1850–1920." Master's thesis, Presbyterian College of Christian Education, 1942.

Whitam, Frederick L. "New York's Spanish Protestants." *Christian Century* 79, no. 6 (February 7, 1962): 162–64.

Wilson, Rodelo, ed. *Hacia una historia de la iglesia evangélica Hispana de California del Sur.* Montebello, CA: AHET, 1993.

Zong, Jie, and Jeanne Batalova. "Asian Immigrants in the United States." Migration Policy Institute. January 6, 2016. http://www.migrationpolicy.org/article/asian-immigrants -united-states.

———. "Frequently Requested Statistics on Immigrants and Immigration in the United States." Migration Policy Institute. Last updated May 26, 2016. http://www.migra tionpolicy.org/article/frequently-requested-statistics-immigrants-and-immigration -united-states.

Index

230